S0-ADD-974

GARVEY

The Story of a Pioneer Black Nationalist

Also by Elton C. Fax

Contemporary Black Leaders

Seventeen Black Artists

GARVEY

THE STORY OF A PIONEER
BLACK NATIONALIST

ELTON C. FAX

Foreword by John Henrik Clarke

Illustrated with photographs

DODD, MEAD & COMPANY
NEW YORK

ISBN: 0-396-06521-X

Library of Congress Catalog Card Number: 77-38520
Printed in the United States of America
by The Cornwall Press, Inc., Cornwall, N.Y.

To Rosina and Leon

ACKNOWLEDGMENTS

Of the many sources from which I obtained material essential to the authenticity of this narrative, the Arthur L. Schomburg Collection of The New York Public Library ranks close to the top. Without the books, papers, and periodicals in the collection I could not have produced this particular account of Marcus Garvey and his work. My gratitude, therefore, goes to Curator Jean Hutson who along with her assistants, particularly Cora Eubanks and Ernest Kaiser, placed those necessary materials at my disposal.

I am grateful also to the Afro-American Institute of Harlem led by Richard B. Moore. During the latter part of 1970 the Institute presented an informative discussion of Garvey in which scholars Moore, Keith Baird, and John Henrik Clarke reviewed the man Garvey and his movement. Their comments aided me in forming the structure this narrative would follow.

Among individuals supplying me with first-hand views of the Garvey movement at its zenith, George A. Weston is a standout. I am especially appreciative of the taped interview granted me by this knowledgeable and personable octogenarian whose activities as an officer of the Universal Negro Improvement Association spanned the peak years of the movement. And Mrs. Marianne Samad is likewise due thanks for sharing with me memorabilia and recollections of her late Garveyite father.

To Florence Bailey who generously lent me valuable out-of-print books from her private collection I am indebted as I am to Jean Bacchus Maynard for the loan of materials from her personal library.

My thanks go also to Reginald McGhee and Jerome Tucker of the James Van Der Zee Institute. Without the remarkable Van Der Zee photographs, this little book would lack a badly needed documentation that only good pictures can give. The portrait of the late Amy Ashwood Garvey comes from the photo library of *The New York Times.*

I must not neglect to thank my faithful partner, Betty, for her excellent typing of the manuscript and my friend John Henrik Clarke for writing the introduction. And to Anne Judge I am indebted for her careful reading and checking of the galleys.

Finally I extend my thanks to my friend, editor Allen Klots, for his guidance and for that very special talent he has for letting this writer tell his story in his own way.

FOREWORD

In the appendix to the second edition of his book, *The Black Jacobins*, (Vintage Books, 1963), the Caribbean scholar, C.L.R. James, observes that two West Indians "using the ink of Negritude wrote their names imperishably on the front pages of the history of our times." Professor James is referring to Aimé Césaire and Marcus Garvey. He places Marcus Garvey at the forefront of the group of twentieth century black radicals whose ideas and programs still reverberate within present day liberation movements. Marcus Garvey was a man of his time, who, in retrospect, was far ahead of his time. This is proved by the fact that his ideas have resurfaced and are being seriously reconsidered as a major factor in the liberation of African people the world over.

Professor James further reminds us that Marcus Garvey, an immigrant from Jamaica, is the only black man who succeeded in building a mass movement among Afro-Americans. He advocated the return of Africa to the Africans and people of African descent. He organized, maybe too hurriedly and with a shortage of competently trained people, the institutions and enterprises that would make this possible. His movement began to develop an international framework around 1921. By 1926 the structure of the movement was shaken by internal strife and power-hungry personalities fighting for control. This in-fighting was part of what led to the arrest, trial, and subsequent deportation of Marcus Garvey. This is the bare essence of the situation. C.L.R. James extends the explanation in this way:

> But Garvey managed to convey to Negroes everywhere (and to the rest of the world) his passionate belief that Africa was the home of a civilization which had once been great and would be great again. When you bear in mind the slenderness of his resources, the vast material forces and the pervading social conceptions which automatically sought to destroy him, his achievement remains one of the propagandistic miracles of this century.

In the midst of what can be called a Marcus Garvey renaissance, Elton Fax has written a book that explores and explains a dimension in the life, mission and legacy of Marcus Garvey that has been neglected by previous writers. This book reflects the fact that there is no way to understand Marcus Garvey without some insight into the history of the West Indies in general and Jamaica in particular. The crucial legacy of slavery and colonialism helped to produce a Marcus Garvey. When he was born in 1887, in Jamaica, West Indies, the so-called "scramble for Africa" was over. All across Africa the warrior nationalists, who had opposed European colonialism throughout the nineteenth century, were either being killed or sent into exile. The Europeans with territorial aspirations in Africa had sat at the Berlin Conference of 1884 and 1885 and decided how to split up the continent among them. In the United States, the black Americans were still suffering from the betrayal of the Reconstruction in 1876. The trouble within the world black community that Marcus Garvey would later grapple with had already been started when he was born. In the years when he was growing to early manhood, his people entered the twentieth century and a new phase of their struggle for freedom and national identity.

In 1907 Marcus Garvey was involved in the Printers' Union strike in Jamaica. After this unsuccessful strike ended in defeat for the printers, he went to work for the Government Printing Office and soon after edited his first publication, *The Watchman.*

In 1909 Garvey made his first trip outside of Jamaica to Costa Rica. In this poor and exploited country he observed the condition of black workers and started an effort to improve their lot. His protest to the British Consul brought only bureaucratic indifference. He was learning his first lesson about the arrogant stubborness of a European colonial power.

In 1912 he was in London working, learning, growing, and seeing new dimensions of the black man's struggle. The ideas that would go into the making of his life's work were being formulated. His close association with Duse Mohammed Ali, an Egyptian scholar and nationalist, helped to sharpen his ideas about African redemption. He worked for a while on the monthly, edited by Duse Mohammed Ali, *The African Times and Orient Review.* Here in London he read a copy of the book *Up From Slavery* by Booker T. Washington. This book and its ideas had a strong influence on his concept of leadership and its responsibility. The theoretical seed of what would later become Garveyism had been planted during his first years in London.

The atmosphere into which he emerged was being prepared long before he was born. In view of this condition it is no accident that Marcus Garvey had his grestest success in the United States. A form of black nationalism began to grow among the "free" blacks early in the nineteenth century. Rumors about the success of the Haitian revolution gave encouragement to the early black abolitionists. In 1829 David Walker published his *An Appeal to the Colored Citizens of the World.* Walker called on the enslaved and colonized Africans everywhere to rise up and break the chains of their oppression. In the troubled years ahead men like Frederick Douglass and John P. Russworm brought the black press in the United States into being. At this time two of the three most massive slave revolts had already occurred. The African Colonization Society was to some extent a "back to Africa movement." During the eighteen fifties a number of black Americans literally went back to Africa. Some of them were searching for areas for resettlement. Martin R. Delany, sometimes referred to as the father of black nationalism, was the most outstanding of these searchers. A hundred years before phrases such as "black is beautiful" and "black power" were heard for the first time, Martin R. Delany was calling attention to his blackness and proving that he was proud of it. Delany is one of the great nineteenth century black nationalists who was temporarily lost from history. In the November 1971 issue of *Tuesday Magazine*, the writer, Philip St. Laurent, calls attention to his importance for today in this manner:

> Martin Robinson Delany crammed a half dozen lifetimes into one, and trying to categorize him is as futile as trying to grasp quick silver between your fingers. He was a dentist, a writer, an editor, a doctor, an explorer, a scientist, a soldier and a politician. Today he would be called a Renaissance man.
>
> Delany was also an articulate advocate of ideas that today, eighty-five years after his death, are topical. Even while the vast majority of his brothers remained in slavery, he was proud

> of his race and his blackness, resented his surname as a hand-me-down from a slave-holder, advocated black people's rights to self-defense, demanded equal employment opportunities, urged a self-governed state for blacks in which they could control their own destinies and, yes, argued for women's liberation. "I thank God for making me simply a man," Frederick Douglass said once, "but Delany always thanks Him for making him a black man."

Delany was one of the forerunners of Marcus Garvey. There were other men and events making his future emergence a necessity.

Late nineteenth century imperialism and the Kipling concept of "taking up the white man's burden," gave support to American racism. The United States had now acquired overseas colonies. The rationale for ruling over these people was not much different from the rationale for denying full citizenship to black Americans. The northern politicians and social reformers who had been the defense of the rights of blacks were now silent. The editor of the *Atlantic Monthly* noted:

> If the stronger and cleverer race is free to impose its will upon the new-caught peoples on the other side of the globe, why not in South Carolina and Mississippi?

The black American had entered the twentieth century searching for new directions politically, culturally, and institutionally. The black woman was very much a part of this search. Booker T. Washington's Atlanta Cotton Exposition Address (1895) had set in motion a great debate among Black people about their direction and their place in the developing American social order. The black woman was very much a part of this debate. New men and movements were emerging. Some men, principally Bishop Henry McNeal

Turner, were questioning whether black people had any future in America. The black woman answered this question in the affirmative by pouring massive energy into the building of new institutions, mainly schools.

In the years following the end of the First World War, when America's promise to us had been betrayed, again we looked once more toward Africa and dreamed of a time and place where our essential manhood was not questioned.

A leader emerged and tried to make this dream into a reality. His name was Marcus Garvey. The personality and the movement founded by Marcus Garvey, together with the writers and artists of the Renaissance period, helped to put the community of Harlem on the map. While the literary aspect of the Renaissance was unfolding, Marcus Garvey and his Universal Negro Improvement Association, using Harlem as his base of operation, built the largest mass movement among black people that this country had ever seen. This movement had international importance and was considered to be a threat to the colonial powers of Europe which were entrenched in Africa.

For about 12 years, Harlem was Marcus Garvey's window on the world. From this vantage point, he became a figure of international importance. This magnetic and compelling personality succeeded in building a mass movement after other men had failed. This may be due to the fact that he was born and reared in an age of conflict that affected the world of African peoples everywhere.

The appearance of the Garvey movement was perfectly timed. The broken promises of the postwar period had produced widespread cynicism in the black population which had lost some of its belief in itself as people. Adam Clayton Powell, Sr. wrote of Garvey: "He is the only man that made

Negroes not feel ashamed of their color." In his book, *Marching Blacks,* Adam Clayton Powell, Jr. wrote:

> Marcus Garvey was one of the greatest mass leaders of all time. He was misunderstood and maligned, but he brought to the Negro people for the first time a sense of pride in being black.

The Garvey movement had a profound effect on the political development of Harlem and on the lives of both the Adam Clayton Powells. The fight to make Harlem a Congressional District began during the Garvey period.

The Garvey movement began to fragment and decline concurrently with the end of the Harlem Renaisaance. This period had a meaning that is generally missed by most people who write about it. This movement had indigenous roots and it could have existed without the concern and interest of white people. This concern often overstated, gave the movement a broader and more colorful base, and may have extended its life span. The movement was the natural and logical result of years of neglect, suppression, and degradation. Black Americans were projecting themselves as human beings and demanding that their profound humaneness be accepted. It was the first time a large number of black writers, artists, and intellectuals took a unified walk into the North American sun.

The black nationalists and freedom fighters before and after Marcus Garvey were saying, no more or less than Garvey had said in word and deed: "Up! Up! You mighty race. You can accomplish what you will."

—John Henrik Clarke

INTRODUCTION

Who a generation ago would have believed that it would soon be considered good manners to call black Americans "black"? Or who could have foreseen the popularity of Africa-oriented styles of dress and grooming in America's black communities? Time and the events of history do indeed alter human habits. You don't, for instance, use the word "Negro" in designating black Americans without running the risk of insulting large numbers of them. "Negro" and "nigger" have become synonymous to many younger blacks.

Rare indeed is the sight of the black American male wearing, even in the privacy of his home, the once-cherished stocking cap. That grease-stained relic, the wearer's insurance against being caught in public with a "nappy head," has passed into limbo. Today most black males, particularly the young, let it all sprout out naturally. And they preen their Afros with special combs of an Africa-inspired design. Such a positive acceptance and flaunting of his natural attributes reflects the black American's view that he no longer regards his blackness as a loathsome stigma.

Actually, this is not a "new view" black Americans are taking of themselves. It is a revival, with present-day modifications, of what took place in the United States a full half century ago when an angry and eloquent black man from the Caribbean Island of Jamaica stormed across this nation thundering a doctrine of black nationalism. That was Marcus

Garvey. As was true in his day there are those now who view the present cult of blackness as a passing phenomenon.

The timid earnestly pray that it will all soon just go away and black Americans will soon return to their normal pattern of life in the American mainstream. The story of Marcus Garvey is a reminder that black Americans have never had a normal pattern of life in America nor have they ever been in the American mainstream. Moreover, the basically human desire to join the rest of the nation in sharing the mainstream goodies will not just go away.

None knew that better than Marcus Garvey. He was convinced, moreover, that the masses of black people here would never get into the mainstream created by whites, and that their only hope lay in creating one of their own. Using that premise as a fulcrum, Garvey sought to lift the black masses to a level of self-esteem from which it was assumed they would rise to group self-sufficiency. His efforts created a national furor.

The opposition branded him a bombastic, self-seeking rabble-rouser who knowingly and selfishly bilked gullible followers out of a fortune. The faithful were as ardent in their worship of their leader as detractors were deprecating. What were the truths about Garvey?

To understand the man thoroughly, his strengths and weaknesses alike, one must be allowed to see him juxtaposed against friends and foes in the *two* environments that molded him. They were the Jamaica of his birth that bred and nurtured Garvey, and the uneven world of black-white relations inside and outside Jamaica that troubled and motivated him. This narrative seeks to show Garvey in relation to *both* settings.

The Caribbean Island of Jamaica that cradled the infant boy, Garvey, also cradled racism. From the instant Europeans set foot, first upon the land, then upon the necks of its indigenous Indians, racism had a home in Jamaica. With the introduction of African slaves those racist attitudes expanded under the heated pressures of master-slave relationships. Then, BOOM! Slave insurrections and rebellions began to erupt throughout the island during the mid-1600's and lasted until the slaves were emancipated in 1838. When Garvey was born a half century later, vestiges of the class-and-color-caste aspects of slavery were still around for him to see and feel.

Class distinction was occasioned by the early influx to Jamaica of poor white indentured servants who preferred life in the Caribbean to death on the gallows and in the jails of Europe. Color caste separated whites, mulattoes, and blacks into upper, middle, and laboring classes respectively. Such was the general Caribbean setting into which the black infant Garvey was thrust.

During his first twenty-nine years of life, Garvey had a chance to see color discrimination at work in Latin America and in England. The scene greeting him when he entered the United States in 1916 was also racist. American color caste within the black group, while not as religiously adhered to as in the West Indies, still made its presence felt. An old racist dictum carried over from the American slave period and declaring any person of Negro ancestry to be a Negro was (and still is) accepted as a biological and social fact of American life. White Americans with their superior numbers were not obliged, as were the British in the West Indies, to create a buffer class of "coloreds" to hold the blacks in check.

Still, as any black American knows, differences have been made between light- and dark-skin blacks. J. C. Furnas, in *Goodbye to Uncle Tom,* points that out. And cynical black pundits in America will quickly remind the forgetful that "high yaller," brown, or black, we are collectively placed in one bag by racist whites who then matter-of-factly label the bag "nigger."

Because of his own bitter experience as a jet-black Jamaican, the touchy, perceptive Garvey understood and was responsive to what he found in the United States. The black masses here who gravitated to Garvey reciprocated by eagerly responding to his angry and eloquent rhetorical outbursts. Examination of the Garvey orations reveals that they are applicable to the problems of today's black peoples. Indeed one finds in *The Philosophy and Opinions of Marcus Garvey* the source of many of the statements of the late Malcolm X and current black nationalist spokesmen.

One reviews the discontent to which Garvey's appeal was so electric and discovers that the fabric binding Garvey to his followers was not woven on the evil loom of a troublemaker from Jamaica. It had been woven generations before when the first shiploads of black slaves were dumped in the colonial Caribbean and along the shores of the colonial Americas.

What Garvey did in his revivalist orations was to rouse black masses out of their colonialist-induced torpor. He told poor, obscure people something they had seldom been told before—that they were a comely race with a proud history. "BLACK," Garvey thundered, "IS BEAUTIFUL!" He then organized the rank and file members of his Universal Negro Improvement Association (U.N.I.A.) with consummate skill. Conferring titles upon them and decking them out in colorful ceremonial regalia, he hammered away at the lessons of self-help, moral and physical strength and cleanliness, and *complete* economic independence of whites.

And Garvey, no less human than the rest of us, made mistakes. The most blatant of them were as spectacular as his dazzling coups. His stubborn and egotistical excursions into realms thoroughly alien to him involved expenditures of huge sums of money for ridiculously useless junk along with some useful investments. That his investments, for instance, in several steamships and real-estate holdings were ill advised made little difference to noncritical Garvey disciples.

Nor did their leader's unrealistic assessment of how far vested white interests would *permit* him to colonize in Liberia diminish their image of his greatness. Even when the opportunistic thieves, thugs, and yes-men, both inside and outside the U.N.I.A., revealed the true nature of their interest in the Garveyan philosophy, the organization's masses rallied to Garvey's support. Their fanatical loyalty, seen in the light of their previous deprivation, was not difficult to understand.

Conversely, the Garvey presence alternately amused, puzzled, and frightened most whites, while it roused the suspicions, contempt, and fear of established black leadership. The latter, appealing to white liberalism and the black middle class, leaned heavily upon both for support. Certainly they were not reaching, or being supported by, the black peasant class, and Garvey's success with that hitherto untouched group projected him as a threat to the black intellectuals. Garvey's suspicions of the latter as tools and lackeys of white racists were confirmed in his mind by their conduct toward him and the U.N.I.A.

The black press at large joined established black leadership in ridiculing the Garvey mold and manner. They made no pretense at concealing pleasure upon discovering structural weaknesses in the Jamaican's program. Some of its spokesmen became publicly ecstatic when Garvey, after plunging disastrously into a series of financial debacles, was finally charged and jailed for allegedly using the mails to defraud.

Then a curious thing happened. Many of the same black critics, sensing the flimsiness of the United States Government's case against Garvey, began to seek clemency for the fallen leader. Editorials in the black press scored the manner in which their government was treating the cocky and uncompromising little Jamaican. It was as if they suddenly realized that black Jamaican, black Chicagoan, Mississippian, New Yorker, Virginian, or whatnot, they were indeed all scrambling around together in that common bag labeled "nigger."

The following narrative, while zooming in on Garvey, never fails to see him woven within the fabric of the environment. The man, certainly far from perfect, reveals in his human flaws a flamboyant quality quite as memorable and revealing as were his not inconsiderable virtues. His environmental stage likewise teems with human souls no less revealing than he. Some are noble; others far less than noble. None, however, ever succeeds in upstaging the star performer.

Marcus Garvey still stands as one of modern history's great personalities and dynamic visionaries. The charges he leveled in his day at this nation are equally valid in this day. Make no mistake about it. Whenever and wherever the dark slums and their angry tenants bubble and fester in hopeless squalor, the ghost of Marcus Garvey haunts the premises. In the haunting, one hears the echoing exhortations answered by the cry mingled with the terrible snarl. And that is the collective voice of those convinced that the *only* thing they have to lose is the misery of their obscurity.

CHAPTER ONE

Although it pushed off to a quiet start, it turned out, before it was over, to be a rousing New York spectacular. Beginning on Sunday, the first of August, 1920, it got right into the guts of Harlem. Never before had that black community whirled with such excitement as, on the following day, it played host to a parade to end all parades. Marcus Mosiah Garvey, President of the Provisional Republic of Africa and President-General of the Universal Negro Improvement Association, had called his organization's first International Convention.

Fifty thousand black delegates strutted along sun-drenched Lenox Avenue to the syncopated rhythms of twelve bands. Representing twenty-five lands, the marchers hailed from every state in the Union, from the West Indies, Central and South America, and Africa. The solemnity of the previous day's religious services and silent march through Harlem gave way to the brand of full-blown pageantry the community loved but seldom had the chance to enjoy. Men, women, children stood deep along the sidewalks to watch and to cheer. They were not disappointed.

The Universal African Legion headed the column of march. Draped in dark blue uniforms with narrow, red, trouser stripes, spit-and-polished shoes, and snappy military caps, the Legion stepped briskly up the avenue. The only arms they carried were the gleaming dress swords worn by their officers. Still, the robust bodies suggested a disciplined dedication to top-notch physical conditioning. Behind them came the others.

These were the white-uniformed Universal Black Cross Nurses, the children's contingent, and the general membership representing every conceivable facet of the world's black community. And they marched beneath the newly designed U.N.I.A. banners of red, black, and green, as well as the more familiar Stars and Stripes. The bands played like hell. It was *some* parade.

That evening between 20,000 and 25,000 U.N.I.A. delegates jammed old Madison Square Garden. They were there to hear their President-General tell them and the world what U.N.I.A. members wanted and how they intended to get it. First, however, there was entertainment furnished by several expert musical groups. Marcus Garvey always hired first-rate black talent for such occasions, considering that an essential part of his program for reaching the people.

Then the man of the hour, resplendent in an academic cap and gown of purple, green, and gold, rose to speak. A thunderclap of applause and a roar of approval filled the garden, and it was fully five minutes before he could begin to talk. At last the hush, mingled with quick, muffled coughs, was broken by Garvey's announcement that he had just sent a cablegram to Eamon De Valera of Ireland. In dramatic fashion he then read a copy of that message.

> Twenty-five thousand Negro delegates assembled in Madison Square Garden in mass meeting representing 400,000,000 Negroes of the world send you greetings as President of The Irish Republic. Please accept sympathy of Negroes of the world for your cause. We believe Ireland should be free even as Africa shall be free for the Negroes of the world. Keep up the fight for a free Ireland.

Again prolonged applause rose and fell and Garvey came quickly to the core of his address.

> We are the descendants of a suffering people. We are the descendants of a people determined to suffer no longer. Our forefathers suffered many years on both hemispheres, many years of abuse from an alien race . . . We shall now organize the 400,000,000 Negroes of the world into a vast organization to plant the banner of freedom on the great continent of Africa. . . . We new Negroes, we men who have returned from this war . . . we will dispute every inch of the way until we win.

The throng's pulse beat accelerated with every phrase as the electrifying Jamaican delivered a scalding denunciation of racism. Not only did he score racism in the Americas, but European colonialism in Africa as well, particularly that of Belgium in the Congo. Garvey then lifted the crowd out of its seats as he thundered his conclusion.

> Wherever I go, whether it be in France, Germany, England, or Spain, I find that I am told that this is a white man's country, and that there is no room for a nigger. The other races have countries of their own and it is time for the 400,000,000 Negroes to claim Africa for themselves!

That was the spirit with which the U.N.I.A. opened its first convention. It lasted one week. America read about it in the columns of the prestigious *New York Times.* Garvey's own newspaper, the *Negro World,* reported in great detail and with partisan enthusiasm on the success of the event. Interestingly enough, however, neither the dignified little *New York Age* nor the larger *Chicago Defender,* both respected black weeklies with national circulations, as much as mentioned it.

Adopting the attitude of the black intellectual community, those two newspapers took the view that there was little in that New York gathering worth reporting to their readers. Garvey, they held, was just another crackpot and a charlatan who would soon be exposed and forgotten. But they were wrong. They had misread the man. With all their collective scholarship and worldly wisdom, they had, in the preoccupation of their own participation in the national struggle for equality and justice, overlooked the things that constituted the very essence of Garvey.

They had permitted the pompous and gaudy Garvey *exterior* to offend them. And they had put the man down without first taking careful note of the depth and character of the mold from which he had been so faithfully cast. It was a mold clearly stamped, "Made in Jamaica, B.W.I." Moreover, it bore the stamp of an intelligent young man who had seen the struggles of black men elsewhere in the world, and had unhesitatingly equated them with his own. The Garvey concepts were farther reaching than those of many of his American detractors.

JAMAICA! That exotic island, called Xaymaca (Isle of Springs) by its aboriginial Arawak inhabitants, was discovered by Columbus on the fourth of May, 1494. It is the largest of the Caribbean islands, and three years after Columbus's death in 1506, his son, Diego, as Governor General, named Don Juan de Esquivel governor of the territory. For the next 146 years Jamaica remained under Spanish domination. During that period the mild and inoffensive Arawaks, a people of the Indian race, were oppressed and exterminated.

The Spaniards were not alone in seeking occupation of this newly found and seductive land. Several unsuccessful attempts to possess it had previously been made by the British. However, Oliver Cromwell, with support from Admiral William Penn and General Robert Venables, seized Jamaica from Spain in 1655. Three years later the Spaniards were completely driven from the island.

British rule became absolute, undisputed, ruthless, and corrupt. White men of all descriptions held positions of power. Even the notorious Welsh pirate, Henry Morgan, had been named lieutenant governor of Jamaica and was later made commander in chief of all the island's ships of war. From his positions of prominence it was easy under the system for ex-buccaneer Morgan to become *Sir* Henry Morgan.

In the interim, African slaves belonging to the Spaniards took advantage of the latter's conflict with the British. Coming from the proud Gold Coast and Nigerian tribes, and eager for freedom, they fled westward to a mountainous area of the island. There they ensconced themselves in the deep and formidable mountain fissures and canyons known popularly as "The Cockpits." Those daring and resourceful fugitives came to be known as *Maroons.*

Their very name spelled terror to those who tried to capture or conquer them. Corrupted from the Spanish *Cimarron,* it means "wild and unruly." So between 1655 and 1795 the Maroons gave white men no rest as they bloodily and successfully maintained a guerrilla advantage from their lofty battleground in The Cockpits. If the British boasted of their colonels—Walpole, Sandford, Gallimore, and their Captain Craskell—the Maroons had their captains—Cudjoe, Accompang, and Old Montagu. They felt they could also count upon a white ally, Major James.

An island superintendent, like his father before him, James had been brought up among the Maroons. He knew them and their ways as few white men ever did, and a brotherhood existed between the white maverick and the black renegades. As much as the British wished they could have elicited Major James's help, they dared not trust him. The Maroons were truly occupying the proverbial "catbird seat" high in their mountain fortress. Historian W. J. Gardner, certainly no Maroonophile, has this to say of them in his *A History of Jamaica.*

> But for one hundred and forty years these people, afterward known as Maroons . . . with numbers continually augmented by runaway slaves, were a plague to the colony. To sketch the history of Maroon depredations would be impossible. They became less ferocious in after years, but in the earlier days of colonial history they rarely gave quarter to any who fell into their hands. Soon after Sedgewicke died a party of forty soldiers were cut off by these people as they straggled carelessly from their barracks. Detachments sent in pursuit only killed some seven or eight, for the Maroons readily retired into mountain fastness where they could exist in comfort without any of those appliances which are indispensable to white men.

The Maroons were never conquered in battle. When, finally, a considerable force of British militiamen, aided by hounds imported from Cuba, waged all-out war on them in the late 1700's, the Maroons shrewdly negotiated a settlement. On the sixth of August, 1795, six hundred Maroons (by no means their entire number) were placed aboard a vessel at Port Royal and exiled to Halifax, Nova Scotia. A short time later those who survived the climate were sent to Sierra Leone. And with that crippling thorn removed from its great paw, the British lion groaned its relief.

The dehumanizing experiences that were happening meanwhile to that slave majority who did not find sanctuary with the Maroons explain why the mountain fugitives were so stubbornly fierce. After all, they, too, had known the horrors of enslavement.

The average colonial Jamaican slavemaster was inordinately cruel. In addition to providing the barest sustenance for his slaves, he administered tortuous punishments for even the slightest infractions of his rules. For "negligence," culprits received bloody beatings with lancewood switches and with straps made from the hide of the sea cow. The latter had to be discarded, however, because they left scars identifying the victims as "troublesome" and hence difficult to unload on the market. Unsuccessful escape efforts were rewarded by the chopping off of half of the slave's foot. Rebellion, however, was *the* capital offense. Here again we quote from Gardner's *History of Jamaica.*

> The poor wretch was fastened down on the ground with crooked sticks on every limb; they then applied the fire by degrees, from the feet and hands, burning them gradually up to the head whereby their pains are extravagant.

Still rebellions continued, actually increasing in ferocity. The first serious outbreak occurred in 1690, starting on the

Sutton estate about a mile from the village of Chapelton. Sutton, one of the first to establish a sugar estate in Jamaica's interior, was absent when the lone white man left in charge was swooped upon by a band of three or four hundred enraged slaves. They trampled his lifeless body as they made for the arms and ammunition kept to defend against Maroon attacks. The armed band then rushed the next plantation, and failing to get the terrified slaves there to join them, returned to Sutton's. A pitched battle between the slaves and quickly organized whites ensued, during which the former were routed and their ringleaders summarily executed.

Seventy years later, a more successful rebellion by the Coromantyns from West Africa's Gold Coast swept across Jamaica. With a man named Taki as their leader, a band of a hundred slaves charged Port Maria early on Easter Monday. Seizing four barrels of powder, forty muskets, and bullets from the fort's magazine, they gathered numbers as they proceeded toward the interior. Slaughtered whites, their properties in flames, lay in the wake of the insurrectionists. Taki was cornered and killed. His closest followers committed suicide rather than be taken by the enemy. Of that episode Gardner makes an arresting revelation.

> The governor lost no time in sending by different routes two parties of soldiers, each accompanied by a troop of the mounted militia. Orders were also sent to the Scotts Hall Maroons to advance from the east and thus it was hoped to surround the rebels. The Maroons behaved badly; they marched to the rendez-vous appointed, but refused to act unless certain arrears they claimed were paid.

A similar comment is made by Higginson in his study *Black Rebellion.* In commenting on Maroon action in that foray he writes:

> When left to go on their own way they did something towards suppressing it; but when placed under the guns of the troops, and ordered to fire on those of their own color, they threw themselves on the ground without discharging a shot.

Gardner further takes note of Jamaica's rebellious slaves who, though not Maroons, had originated from the same areas of West Africa as had the mountain guerrillas.

> The negroes from the Gold Coast were known generally as Coromantyns. The Ashantees and Fans, described by Chaillu, were included in this term. They were strong and active and on this account valued by the planters. The Spanish and French colonists shunned them on account of their ferocious tendencies; but attempts to prohibit their importation into Jamaica failed, though they were the instigators and leaders of every rebellion.

Slave rebellions were a natural response to the naked brutality of slavery itself. And as has been noted, slavery in the West Indies and the United States was even more brutal than it was in Latin America. In the latter area the dominant Roman Catholic Church publicly condemned the slave trade. From the papacy of Pius II in 1462 through that of Gregory XVI in 1839, the Church made no secret of its opposition to slavery. Moreover the Spanish Slave Code of 1789 imposed restraints upon Latin American slaveholders. Not so in territories controlled by the British, Americans, Dutch, and Danish.

Indeed the British and Americans placed obstacles in the way of manumission. In the Protestant setting all *presumptions* of slavery favored it. There was, for instance, the presumption of equating all black people with slavery and that extened to mulattoes and others of mixed blood in both the West Indies and the United States. In both places blacks and mulattoes were pitted against each other. And in both places, statutes supporting the presumption of slavery placed upon all blacks and mulattoes alike the onus of *proving* that they were free. Attempts at enlightening slaves, even under the guise of soul-saving, were roundly discouraged.

In Jamaica the Moravians established a settlement in 1732, bringing their message of liberty and brotherhood to the slaves. Slaveholders were outraged. Only after the abolition of the slave trade in 1807, when slavery itself was in its death throes, did legal action favoring the teaching of West Indians come into being.

It was 1831 when Jamaica's slaves, believing they had been freed but that word of their freedom was being deliberately withheld from them, went on a rampage. Before they could be calmed they took many landholders' lives and destroyed property valued at £657,000.

Dr. Eric Williams in his book *Capitalism and Slavery* reports:

> The climax came with a revolt in Jamaica during the Christmas holidays. Jamaica was the largest and most important British West Indian colony, and had more than half the slaves in the entire British West Indies. With Jamaica on fire, nothing could stop the flames from spreading.

After three agonizing years, slavery in Jamaica came to an end. Settlement with the Maroons had been in effect for nearly forty years; and the birth of a man, one of whose sons would later make his name famous, was imminent. The man's name was Garvey—Marcus Garvey.

Some have reported that his father was a Maroon. Certainly in the spirit and tradition of that unvanquished group of mountain renegades, Marcus Garvey, senior, was taciturn, aloof, and solitary. The only stone-and-brick mason in Saint Ann's Bay, he was master not only of his trade but of his home as well. No one joked or engaged in light banter with "Mister Garvey," for that was how he was addressed, even by his family. A man of pure African blood and obvious physical power, he commanded a kind of awesome respect by the distant manner in which he conducted himself and his affairs.

Though he had little formal education, Mister Garvey's natural intelligence was enhanced by the fact that he was exceedingly well read. He collected and read good books and was the owner of the town's only private library. Both the white schoolmaster and the Anglican priest borrowed books from Mister Garvey. And as Saunders Redding reports in his *Lonesome Road,* "Though he lent he scorned the borrowers." For his fellow black men who had no interest in reading, Mister Garvey held nothing but scornful pity.

Sarah, his charming and gregarious wife, was also of undiluted African blood. But she was her husband's antithesis. Where he was cold, noncommunicative, and unforgiving, she was warm, talkative, and charitable. Neighbors recalled her as a beautiful woman with large soft eyes and the irridescent black skin and delicately modeled features characteristic of the West African women of Guinea and Senegal. Sarah Garvey was well known, especially to fellow members of the Wesleyan Methodist Church which she attended regularly.

She was an excellent pastrymaker whose culinary skill, combined with her outgoing public manner, enabled her to bake and sell cakes to their neighbors whenever Mister Garvey chose not to work at his skill. He was neither a needy nor a lazy man, but one given to withdrawing to solitary reading and meditating, a tendency that became especially pronounced in his later years. During those periods Sarah was able to take up the slack in a manner allowing her to function as a self-employed entrepreneur rather than as one who hired herself out to others. Pride, fierce and unyielding, governed the public behavior of the Garveys.

Because Mister Garvey's mason's skill kept him in constant demand, his earnings were well above average. At several periods in his life he had amassed small fortunes and would probably have left a respectable inheritance to his heirs. But his intractable nature involved him in costly litigations, and the family fortunes dwindled away. As his troubles multiplied and his suspicions of others increased, Mister Garvey withdrew more and more into his private world of solitary study and morose silence.

This strangely sustained union of Marcus and Sarah Garvey produced eleven children. Only two, however, lived to reach maturity. They were a girl, Indiana, and the youngest, a boy born in the little town of Saint Ann's Bay. The infant boy uttered the first of his many protesting cries on the seventeenth of August, 1887. His parents named him Marcus Mosiah Garvey.

CHAPTER TWO

BECAUSE HE was her last child, Sarah Garvey considered "Little Mose" her baby. And because of his father's distant and moody ways the child grew up quite close to his mother. To her he was a source of warmth and comfort. His skin was black like hers, though he lacked her graceful good looks, leaning more toward a chunkiness of build. In a setting such as Jamaica, where blackness of skin automatically relegated one to a low niche in the social pattern, little Mose received his earliest lesson in racism.

Writing later of his life in *Current History Magazine* for September 1923, Garvey had this to say of his youth:

> I grew up with other black and white boys. I was never whipped by any, but made them all respect the strength of my arms. I got my education from many sources—through private tutors, two public schools, two grammar or high schools, and two colleges. My teachers were men and women of varied experiences and abilities; four of them were eminent preachers. They studied me and I studied them. With some I became friendly in after years; others and I drifted apart, because as a

boy they wanted to whip me, and I simply refused to be whipped. I was not made to be whipped. It annoys me to be defeated; . . .

To me, at home in my early days there was no difference between black and white. One of my father's properties, the place where I lived most of the time, was adjoining that of a white man. He had three girls and two boys. The Wesleyan minister, another white man, whose church my parents attended, also had property adjoining ours. He had three girls and one boy. All of us were playmates. We romped and were happy children, playmates together. The little white girl whom I liked most knew no better than I did, myself. We were two innocent fools who never dreamed of a race feeling and problem.

At fourteen my little white playmate and I parted. Her parents thought the time had come to separate us and draw the colour line. They sent her and another sister to Edinburgh, Scotland, and told her she was never to write or try to get in touch with me for a I was a "nigger."

That first experience cut deep into the boy, and because he hated defeat in any form, he never forgot it. Never again would he be caught so defenseless. And it was at that moment that he began to understand and appreciate the cold reserve and aloofness of his father. The son was "Little Mose" no longer.

Along with her brother, Sarah Garvey owned a plot of land that yielded citrus and pimento crops. As part of his growing up young Marcus took great pride in helping his mother at harvest time. For his aid in the reaping and selling he could always count upon some special treat. Young Garvey and his mother were still close, but the warmth of that mother-son relationship did not obscure the truth that son was hurtling into manhood.

The twentieth century was barely a year old when young Marcus, now fourteen years old, was obliged to leave public school. Mr. Garvey's resources had been all but depleted by the legal judgments he had brought upon himself, and his young son was forced out on his own. Luckily the latter had a godfather who could help him. It is traditional in the West Indies that the young person with a godfather looks to him for aid in such instances. Godfather Burrowes was a printer, and the youth entered his shop as an apprentice.

Burrowes, like Mister Garvey, was a man who loved to read good books and discuss their content with others of similar bent. So there in the printer's shop the boy learned more than the rudiments of a good trade. From the discussions he heard as the older ones talked, Marcus learned much of what was happening in the world, and more important, *why* it was happening.

He began, for instance, to hear talk of the Berlin Conference that was held between 1884 and 1885 just a couple of years before his birth. With great attentiveness he listened to stories of how during the last quarter of the preceding century the map of Africa had undergone great revisions.

Formerly only Britain, Portugal, and France had shown any marked interest in Africa. But when in September 1876 Leopold II of Belgium took the initiative in the modern partitioning of Africa, significant alterations were made. Other European powers, Germany, Austria-Hungary, Italy, and Russia, sat in with Belgium, England, and France on a completely unofficial meeting. For three days they planned and deliberated. How best could they explore and open up the African interior to commerce and trade from which they would be the beneficiaries?

Eight years later, with the calling of the official Berlin

Conference, all the aforementioned powers of Europe were joined by others. Denmark, Sweden, Norway, Holland, Spain, Turkey, and the United States completed the group. Together they decided who should have what parts of Africa—North, South, East, West, and Central!

Back in Jamaica, meanwhile, vital changes in the government had taken place. The governorship of Edward John Eyre, with its new taxes, administrative blunders, and blatant abuses of justice, bred dangerous discontent. The smouldering fires leaped into flames when, on October 11, 1865, the rage of black insurgents erupted at Morant Bay. There the chief magistrate and eighteen other whites met violent deaths. Eyre's harsh handling of those accused, particularly the hanging of George William Gordon, a leading black dissenter and spokesman, resulted in Eyre's removal and replacement by Sir John Peter Grant.

With Sir John's appointment came the establishment of the Crown Colony in 1866. And the constructive program of Sir John continued for the six years of his regime. Under Grant black peasants were fairly treated and Jamaica was tranquil. But Grant's successors were not as skillful, and a new Legislative Council had to initiate major reforms.

The Council was made up of the governor, five officials, five nominated members, and nine members elected on a limited basis. Any six of the latter could block passage of bills dealing with finances, though the Governor could override them in certain cases. In 1895 the Council's elected members were increased to fourteen, one for each parish. The nominated members rose to ten. There was only one necessary ingredient missing from the Legislative Council. A black face. As Peter Abrahams observes in his study, *Jamaica, an Island Mosaic,* "Not all the whites were *pure* white, but nobody very dark entered the Council chamber." And blacks comprized three fourths of Jamaica's population!

So Garvey, the young printer's apprentice, was made well aware of the slicing of the rich African pie many miles away, as well as of the character of domestic political upheavals. But that was not all. He also learned the amazing truths about the banana and how its exploitation had completely altered the economy of his native land. As he performed his chores, young Garvey heard the intellectuals who frequented his godfather's shop discuss what the development of the banana trade had done to Jamaica and its people.

That succulent yellow fruit had been introduced to the new world in 1516 by the Portuguese, who had brought it from Africa. It then made its debut in Spanish Jamaica shortly thereafter. It was 1835, however, when the variety, Gros Michel, that formed the basis of the Jamaican banana industry, was introduced into Jamaica from Martinique. While it became immensely popular in a short time, no one dreamed that the banana would ever challenge sugar as an export crop. But someone had taken a small shipment of the fruit from Cuba to New York, starting the banana trade with the United States.

A little later, 1866 to be exact, Jamaica was approached for bananas for the American market. That did it. Within two decades Jamaica's neglected sugar-cane estates were bought up by Americans and converted to banana plantations. And the island's revenue from the fruit alone amounted to 32.27 percent. King banana replaced sugar as Jamaica's chief export.

The old British sugar planters of Jamaica, who had formerly regarded the banana trade as a small time "nigger enterprise" well beneath their notice, began to have second thoughts. They wanted "in" as marketeers. But the big American outfits said "no," limiting the old planters to the role of growers. The big holding companies then raised the prices they paid for the crop and they cut its selling price. Caught in that squeeze, the would-be Jamaican competitors, as well as smaller American companies, were completely shut out. The inevitable trade, or "Banana," war ensued, out of which on March 20, 1899, a monopoly was born. It came to be known as *The United Fruit Company*.

Young Marcus Garvey was twelve years old in 1899. As he listened, a couple of years later, to the men discussing the United Fruit Company, he knew what they were talking about. And as an alert country lad he was conscious that his island was producing a commodity from which someone other than his people were getting rich.

Then came disaster. Nature unleashed one of her terrible forces, this one a hurricane. The storm struck the Jamaica countryside in 1903, bringing devastation as the gale-swept rains ruined all vegetation. And weary of all the emotional battles he had engaged in throughout his life, Mister Garvey died.

Not only had Sarah Garvey lost her husband but her precious little plot of land as well. Completely inundated as it was, all of Sarah's hopes of reaping a harvest swirled away in the raging muddy waters of the storm. Young Marcus allayed the fears of his distraught mother by sharing with her his plan to go to Kingston, where he would find work as a printer. He would send for her as soon as he was settled. Marcus kept his word.

But Sarah Garvey never made a happy adjustment to life in Kingston. The good life, from her viewpoint, was having lots of grass and trees around. It was having one's own plot on which one raised one's own food, one's chickens, and fruit. It was being able to sit and gossip with a neighbor, to share in the domestic joys and sorrows of those immediately around. She found none of these in busy, impersonal Kingston. For Sarah Garvey the city symbolized decay and death. Within a year she followed her husband to the grave.

Though his roots were rural, Marcus Garvey had discovered great excitement in Kingston. He had found gainful employment as a printer, which gave him a sense of being quite able to take care of himself. At the end of a day's work he did not have to look about for interesting things to do, see, or hear, as was true in Saint Ann's Parish. Kingston vibrated with activity. A port city, it attracted ships and humanity from all areas of the world, and there were lures of all sorts to make Kingston attractive to both its permanent and its transient residents.

So in addition to the places and things of frivolous and passing pleasure, there were also other places and things. There were, for instance, those serious street-corner, barroom, and barber-shop debates over serious issues. Marcus, having been exposed to his father's scholarship and to the atmosphere of godfather Burrowes's printing shop, was attracted to the latter.

He stood on the edge of the knots of black men who listened and responded to the preachments of sweating black street-corner exhorters. At first Garvey listened without interrupting. But as some speakers frequently revealed their lack of familiarity with their subject, the youth from Saint Ann's, who had heard much of it from the older experts of his village, would speak out in disagreement. Hostile eyes zoomed in upon Garvey. How dare he, a country bumpkin—and a jet-black one at that—dispute his city betters? They called him "country boy" and they told him to "shut up." The searing acid of their remarks ate deep into Garvey's proud consciousness. But never mind them and their stupid remarks. He, Marcus Mosiah Garvey, knew a few things himself, and he'd show them yet!

Garvey busied himself with acquiring more knowledge and a more adequate preparation for debating. He increased his reading. Satisfied that he was on the right course, he then sought to improve his delivery—to speak in a manner that did not betray his rural background. The churches were excellent places to hear oratory that swayed audiences, and Garvey attended their services. Moreover he read aloud, listening to his tone and intonations for flaws that might draw ridicule.

He had meanwhile found work at the printing firm of the P. A. Benjamin Company, and Garvey, a master printer at age twenty, had become foreman of the shop. The young man from Saint Ann's Parish was rising swiftly. In the interim a man who was to have a profound influence upon Marcus Garvey came to Jamaica in 1889. A native of Nassau in the Bahamas, his name was Robert Love. Love was a well-educated man.

Peter Abrahams reports in *Jamaica, an Island Mosaic* that "Love had been educated in the United States where he had been ordained as an Episcopalian priest." Abrahams further states that Love had worked in the United States prior to going to Haiti. In Haiti, it is said that Love became friendly with President Salomon, who had been in exile in Jamaica at the time of the Morant Bay uprising. President Salomon had known and admired George William Gordon, who, as has been stated, was executed by Governor Eyre. Abrahams deduces that it was Salomon who inspired Love to settle in

Jamaica. But Amy Jacques Garvey describes Love as a medical doctor, and the question of his specific training is moot. That the man was very well trained and able is undeniable.

It was in the areas of journalism and politics, however, that his powers were most strongly felt in Jamaica. There he published a weekly paper, *The Jamaica Advocate*, in which he presented the Island's social and political problems from the *black* point of view. One of his constant themes was that blacks should have political representation on the Legislative Council. Whites were aghast. What ailed this man—this black overeducated foreign intruder? In scorn and derision the British openly sneered at "Loveism," declaring that it was the brainstorm of a confused mentality.

Dr. Love was unperturbed. He had many believers and followers, among whom was young Marcus Garvey. The ambitious printer thrilled to the Love exhortations. "Educate your black *girls!*" Love insisted. "A people cannot rise above the standards of its womanhood." And Dr. Love cajoled and scolded the timid. "Our people shrink from a clash which gives promise of unpleasant accompaniments." Nor did Love ever cease to urge black Jamaicans to run for public office. In the elections of 1896 Love succeeded in putting up two black candidates. The island's people numbered 600,000, with the blacks outnumbering the coloreds and whites six to one. Not more than one percent of the population was registered, however. Both black candidates lost.

Dr. Love tried again at the turn of the century, offering himself as the candidate for the seat at Saint Andrews. Simultaneously Alexander Dixon, whom Love had supported previously, was running in the parish of Saint Elizabeth. Realizing fully that he, himself, would scarcely win in a predominantly white and colored (mulatto) Saint Andrew's Parish, Dr. Love threw his support to Dixon. The campaigning was bitter, racist, and personal. The following brief exchange from a debate between Love and John V. Calder, who supported Dixon's rival, is a sample.

Said Calder:

> Dr. Love must remember that his ancestors were my ancestors' slaves, and as such could never be my equal. He is aggrieved because my forefathers rescued him from the bonds of thraldom and deprived him of being King of The Congo, enjoying the epicurean and conjugal orgies and the sacrificial pleasures of his ancestral home in Africa.

And Dr. Love retorted:

> The men who enslaved my ancestors were not the men who released them. The men who enslaved my ancestors were the Blackbeards and the Morgans, a type of Calder; the men who released them were the Wilberforces and the Granville Sharpes, a different type altogether. After all, slavery is but a preying of the strong upon the weak, and all nations have undergone the ordeal in their time, including Calder's nation.

Dr. Love lost in Saint Andrews Parish, but Alexander Dixon became the first black man to sit in the Jamaica Legislative Council. A short time later Love himself ran again in Saint Andrews and won. The year was 1906. A new political day was dawning in Jamaica. Studious young Marcus Garvey, completely enamoured of the style and manner of Dr. Love, was thoroughly attentive to what the older man had accomplished.

Then it happened again. On the afternoon of January 14, 1907, another natural disaster, a major earthquake, hurled itself upon Jamaica. The tremors practically leveled the port city of Kingston, while huge fires created by the upheaval added to the destruction and confusion. Eight hundred people lost their lives and property loss was estimated at $10 million.

So complete was the destruction and so impoverished was the city that the British Government had to supply the money for its rebuilding. And because food and other human necessities were in short supply, that money lost much of its original buying power. The low wages most workers received were not sufficient to meet the demands of the emergency and the financial squeeze became more and more painful to the working class.

Along with the rest of Kingston's citizens, skilled artisans and craftsmen such as Garvey felt the negative economic effects of the great quake. They immediately demanded more wages to fill in the gaps. The printer's union, Jamaica's first, was not remiss. Indeed, the printers' demands not only for higher pay but for better working conditions as well were loud and clear. When they were ignored, the men struck. Benjamin's printery, Kingston's largest, quickly offered foreman Garvey an increase in pay in the hope that he would keep the plant operating. Garvey instead walked out with his men.

Moreover, Garvey was chosen by the men to organize their strike strategy, which he did, much to the chagrin of his company's management. Like all other monies in stricken Kingston, union funds were short. The situation of the striking printers grew desperate and the workers sent out a call for aid. Substantial help from the United States did finally reach the beleaguered Jamaica printers. But a thief in the union seized and fled with the money before it could be distributed. With their morale smashed the Jamaica printers watched as linotype machines were brought into Kingston along with men who could operate them. That was it. Their strike was broken. Although most of the men eventually went back to work, Garvey, because of his stand against management, was blacklisted by all private printers. He took a job at the government printing office.

That strike experience sharpened and strengthened young Marcus Garvey's desire to press for an *organized* program for improving the condition of black working people. What he needed most was an organ through which he could communicate his ideas, so he founded a periodical called *Garvey's Watchman*. Realizing that what he sought to do required full-time attention, Garvey gave up his job at the government printing office. *Garvey's Watchman* did not do too well. Its founder, with the assistance and encouragement of his friend, Dr. Love, then formed a political group, The National Club. Then, encouraged by Dr. Love, Garvey founded another publication which he titled *Our Own*.

Love was, himself, devoting a great deal of his time and money to stimulating learning and a feeling of self-pride among Jamaica's majority *black* peasants. And in view of Caribbean attitudes about color, Dr. Love's aims were most meaningful to Garvey and other black Jamaicans. The British had divided the island peoples into three general classes, white, colored, and black. The whites formed the numerical minority. Then came the coloreds, and the blacks, the latter greatly outnumbering the first two. The coloreds were described as any mixture of European and nonwhite ancestry and that included mixtures of Europeans with Africans, Orientals, or Indians. British strategy was easy to understand. Since whites were the minority and blacks the overwhelming majority, the ruling British, to retain their ruling position, created a buffer group as a cushion against the surging black mass. The coloreds formed that cushion.

In addition to color distinctions, class distinctions also exist in the Caribbean. Upper, middle, and lower classes are to be found in Jamaica. Fernando Hendriques in his book *Jamaica, Land of Wood and Water* makes the following comments on class and color.

> There is an upper class, a middle class and a working class. These are to a great extent identifiable with colour but not universally. Thus practically all whites are in the upper class, even if they are poor. Most black people are workers or peasants. The coloured of all shades are generally in the middle group. But there are exceptions in all classes due to the particular background and activity of an individual.
>
> One's place in the scheme of things in Jamaica is thus largely determined by how you look in relation to the European. But that is not the whole story. The respectability of your family name, your profession, the type of marriage you make, and perhaps most important of all how much money you have, all help to advance or hinder your 'colour.' Thus it is not at all easy to decide to which particular category a person belongs, unless observation is made over a considerable period.

Hendriques, a little further in his discourse, does however make the point:

> A coloured man in one of the professions will not be handicapped. For example, the brilliant barrister has little to fear, even if he is a full-blooded Negro, but he must not expect to be a social success outside his own particular group.

Such snobbery cut deep into the consciousness of Marcus Garvey. He saw it as a divisive tactic used with deadly effectiveness to keep the nonwhite majority under white minority control. That Dr. Love, whom he profoundly respected, shared the same view, encouraged him to seek wider experiences and through them to enlighten himself and the poor and despised among his people. Besides, he needed to go where he could earn more money than Jamaica offered. So in 1910, at the age of twenty-three, Marcus Garvey left Kingston for Central America.

CHAPTER THREE

MARCUS GARVEY had by now become a more confident and poised young man. So improved was his public oratory that he was able to help others with theirs. Young men and women desirous of learning elocution would seek his advice. And he began to organize local oratorical contests. How quickly the climate for Garvey was changing. Just a few years before he was laughed at when he tried to express himself verbally in public. Not only had they snickered at his country speech but at his clothes as well, especially the trousers hiked high over the country brogues. "High waters and low quarters," they had called them.

Garvey met their taunts with a resignation edged with bitterness. Let them laugh. Let the poor fools laugh themselves into a delirium if that was all they had to contribute. They would be doing far better, though, to rivet the scorn of their frustration upon the white man who encouraged them to laugh at their brothers' efforts to advance the race. Couldn't they see it was the reactionary British Government and not Marcus Garvey who benefited from the lack of political unity among black West Indians? The white man, and only the white man, benefited when Jamaican coloreds and blacks "put each other in the dirty dozens" by referring unflatteringly to one another's ancestry. Such was Garvey's thinking as he brushed the scoffers aside and moved ahead with his studying and planning.

Through reading and conversation Garvey knew that African slaves had been imported into Central and South America. He knew, moreover, that bad as their condition had been, certain safeguards to their human dignity had not been wholly violated. Roman Catholic vigilance had seen to that. Now Garvey would see, firsthand, how the descendants of those slaves were faring. He would go first to Costa Rica. Conditions there could scarcely be worse for blacks than were those in Jamaica. Indeed Garvey hoped to find gainful employment there.

Numerous black Jamaicans had settled in Costa Rica, among them a maternal uncle of Marcus Garvey. With the formation of the United Fruit Company only a decade earlier, and the subsequent growth of the banana industry, black laborers had followed the new crop. Jamaica took the lead in cultivating the fruit for export, and Costa Rica was not far behind.

The strips of land, originally called Nueva Cartago, was later named Costa Rica (The Rich Shore) by Columbus on his last voyage to America. Because they had observed the Indians along its Caribbean coast wearing gold earrings, the Spanish explorers assumed that Costa Rica was virtually smothered in gold. They proceeded, therefore, to enslave and to massacre the Indians so they could take over the treasure for themselves. In the anxiety of their greed, however, they overlooked something. Although the precious metal was there, the Spaniards did not know where to find it. And the Indians weren't talking. So with the indigenous inhabitants dead or dying off, the early Spanish settlers, unfamiliar with the land, failed to prosper.

Costa Rica's independence from Spain came in 1821. And with the exception of border disputes with her neighbors, Nicaragua and Panama, she has had a relatively peaceful history. Still, Costa Rica is no veritable Garden of Eden. Attempts accurately to ascribe to it such idyllic qualities as "Land of Eternal Spring" and "Central American Switzerland" are not based upon the total truth.

For instance, while the plateau is delightfully temperate, the tropical lowlands are hellishly hot and steamy. Politically the island is relatively calm. Compared to other Central American countries Costa Rica has been less plagued by, though not completely free of, the violence incurred by dictatorships. Its rate of literacy is the highest in Central America, and it does have more school teachers than soldiers. But its police and coastguardsmen more than make up for its lack of an army. The former, in particular, have been kept busy in recent years, having to deal with bands of marauders, particularly in the northern province of Guanacaste.

Upon Marcus Garvey's arrival in Costa Rica he was assisted by his uncle, who saw that he secured work. As a timekeeper on a tract of land being cleared for banana planting, Garvey soon saw the conditions under which black men toiled. The sight was familiar. Low wages for backbreaking work in areas infested with poisonous snakes, insects, and jungle animals constituted the norm. In addition, workers were constantly waylaid by local bandits who robbed and murdered their victims with alarming frequency. The scene angered Marcus Garvey. Losing no time, he went to the port city of Limón to protest the gross mistreatment of the black Jamaican workers to the British consul. He may as well not have made the trip.

But if the indifference of British officialdom was shocking, the apathy of the victims themselves was more so. Garvey discovered that when he tried, through the founding of yet another paper, *La Nacionale,* to overcome that apathy, many for whom the paper was written could not read. Those who could, didn't bother. Their lack of organization, plus the chilly disregard whites held of their rights, revealed to young Garvey the powerful grip of those two forces upon the masses of the working poor.

There is little doubt that, blood ties notwithstanding, Garvey's uncle was becoming uncomfortable as his nephew continued to push. After all, Garvey was bucking forces to which black Costa Rican laborers looked for their daily existence. The older man lost no time, therefore, in getting enough money into Marcus's pocket to move him away from Costa Rica. Bocas del Toro in the Republic of Panama came next.

The great canal was well under construction when Garvey reached Panama. And he found that most of the laborers had come from the West Indies. Their arrival in 1904 was not, however, the first migration of West Indians to reach there. As early as the 1850's black workers from the Caribbean had come along with laborers from other parts of the world to build the Trans-Isthmian Railroad. The task consumed all of four and a half years.

Then in the early 1880's, when the French began the construction of the Panama Canal under Ferdinand Marie de Lesseps, other West Indians arrived. Indeed, in 1883 more than half of the French canal laborers were black Jamaicans.

Five years later 18,000 of the 20,000 canal workers were West Indians, some of them clerks averaging as much as $125 per month.

But the French effort to complete the great waterway failed during the late 1800's, leaving the black recruits from the Caribbean stranded in Panama. Those, along with others who had remained on the Isthmus following the building of the railroad, joined the workers brought in by the United States when it took over from France.

What a massive and dangerous task they faced in that hot, filthy, disease-ridden area! The eminent Panamanian historian, journalist, and diplomat, George Westerman, comments on it in his study, *The West Indian Worker on the Canal Zone.*

> From the outset of the Panama Canal enterprise it was recognized by the North American authorities that a program of sanitation was the essential prerequisite to actual construction operations. At the time there were no systems of water works, of sewerage, or of drainage on the Isthmus. The filth of ages had accumulated around the dwellings and in the streets; pools of stagnant water had existed for years in proximity to buildings, and insect-breeding swamps lay undrained adjacent to the cities and many of the towns.

The initial job, therefore, was that of cleaning up the filth, exterminating the fever-bearing mosquito, and establishing sewerage, roads, and public utilities necessary to basic health. The next job was that of handling the equipment as it landed at the docks. Since, in the early stages of the canal project, machinery for such work was nonexistent in Panama, West Indian laborers furnished the muscle that kept the cargo from the United States moving in. And much of it was deadly material. In the decade between 1904 and 1914 Westerman estimates that "hundreds of West Indians died violent deaths or sustained permanent physical or mental injuries by premature or delayed explosions of dynamite, asphyxiation in pits, falling from high places, train wrecks, landslides, and falling rocks in the Canal cut, and other hazards of their work."

Along with such spectacular occupational perils were other obnoxious features occasioned by racist attitudes introduced to the Canal Zone by the American presence. First there were the white southern supervisors who prided themselves on their superior "understanding" and "handling" of black laborers. First they relegated the blackest workers to the lowest social and economic levels. Then they placed any others having the slightest African ancestry, or showing any disposition to associate with the low-level blacks, in the same category. That cleavage, separating the West Indian Panamanians from their Latin brothers and sisters, has not yet been fully closed.

Finally came the American establishment of the "gold" and "silver" standards governing employment, pay, and every other conceivable area of economic and social life. Gold employees were those in executive, supervisory, professional, and highly skilled positions. They were invariably white. Their pay equalled that which they would have earned in the United States, plus an extra 25 percent for working in a "hardship post" outside their country. Silver workers were described as "natives of the tropics," mostly West Indians. Theirs were the ranks of the unskilled and semiskilled laborers.

A significant postscript is that thirty-three years after the completion of the canal the terms "gold" and "silver" were replaced by "United States Rates" and "Local Rates." And the discriminatory practices became more despicable. Black laborers, by then in command of skills, still received less for their labors than whites. A black senior mechanic, for instance, received the maximum pay of $1.28. The maximum pay for United States employees was $2.31.

But the Panama seen by Marcus Garvey in 1910 is what is germane here, since that left its indelible mark upon him. He could never forget the place where black men from the West Indies sought a better life than they had left in Barbados, Martinique, Guadaloupe, Trinidad, St. Kitts, St. Vincent, British Guiana, Grenada, St. Lucia, and Jamaica. What they and Garvey found was a steamy Isthmian hellhole dominated by malaria, yellow fever, and white racism.

The "great ditch" conceived and designed by French minds, financed by American dollars, and built by black labor, was nearing completion. And those whose sweat was making a reality of a drawing-board dream were no better off than their brothers back in the islands. Troubled, but by no means defeated, by the sights on the Zone, Garvey went to Colón, Panama's second city. There he established another newspaper, *La Prensa.* But that failed to catch on and he left Panama to travel in Ecuador, Nicaragua, Honduras, Colombia, and Venezuela.

Colombia and Venezuela, as colonies of Spain, had held African slaves, and their descendants were there to greet Marcus Garvey in 1910. Only seven years previously Colombia had lost Panama through a secession, aided by the United States. At the same time, Venezuela, under military President-General Cipriano Castro, was in trouble. Her ports were blockaded by warships from England, Germany, and Italy, because Castro had been double-dealing with investors from those countries.

Meanwhile, Colombia, Nicaragua, and Honduras had sold or leased vast tracts of jungle land to American fruit companies for the cultivation of bananas. And black workers from the Caribbean had gravitated to each of those countries in search of an existence. Garvey noted that their general condition differed little from that he had observed in Panama. Actually it all began to fall into a pattern quite consistent with the monopolistic growth of the United Fruit Company and the military intervention of the United States itself in Latin American disputes. With reference to the latter it was claimed to be "for the protection of American lives and property" that United States marines were dispatched to Nicaragua as an occupying force in 1912 and later in 1927.

Marcus Garvey concluded, after observing West Indian workers in Nicaragua, that what had been happening to them politically and economically was not to their advantage. It was but a repetition of the same conditions he had seen elsewhere and it made him sick at heart. He had been traveling for a year now and he resolved to return to Jamaica and report what he had seen to his fellow islanders. However, on behalf of the Jamaican laborers in Latin America, he would first lodge a strong complaint with the British authorities in Kingston. Perhaps this time they would be ready to listen to him.

Garvey could have spared himself the trouble. The British authorities back home tersely suggested to him that if conditions among Jamaicans and other black British subjects were so appalling they could always return to the West Indies. Garvey was furious. "Return *here*—to WHAT?" he expostulated. The officials blandly shrugged. Garvey turned then to his own people.

Reflecting upon that period of his development, Garvey later wrote the following challenge in his *Philosophy and Opinions:*

> I asked, "Where is the black man's government? Where is his King and his Kingdom? Where is his President, his country, and his ambassador, his army, his navy, his men of big affairs?" I could not find them; and then I declared, "I will help to make them."

The response of those among the people who were sympathetic to Garvey was a call for the establishment of a group. It was to be a group dedicated to the improvement of black West Indians at home and abroad. And it could be called the Universal Negro Improvement Association. Amy Jacques Garvey reports in her account of her husband's life and work, *Garvey and Garveyism,* that there were objections among some to the word "Negro" in the title. "Negro" had strong and unpleasant connotations to, and prevented help from, middle-class colored people, who equated the term with those of low and inferior status. So formation of the Universal Negro Improvement Association was delayed. Jamaicans were entangled in economic problems and in the snare of their caste and color prejudices.

Though it is a subject that many otherwise objectively frank Jamaicans are loath to discuss, the truth of its intragroup color discrimination is all too well known. Earlier references made to it in this narrative are given full airing in Fernando Hendriques' book, *Jamaica, Land of Wood and Water.* Writing in 1957 on the question of "Colour," Hendriques makes the following observation:

> There is a magic in the possession of a white skin in Jamaica, but it is a magic which can work only if everyone believes in it, white and non-white alike. Generations of slavery, when to be white was to be free and possessed of all the virtues, have left this legacy of paradox.

The author then proceeds to detail the various ways in which pigmentation or lack of it has affected the behavior and governed the lives of Jamaicans. Kinky hair is "bad" and straight hair "good." Women of fair skin are often preferred mates of dark men. Of the three classes, upper, middle, and lower, most black Jamaicans belong to the lower or peasant class. Well-trained dark girls will find employment in private business firms and banks more difficult to attain than will their lighter sisters; though since 1944 a constitutional order has made the government hiring of dark women more commonplace.

A pitch-black and successful barrister, however, will become professionally and materially successful without attaining unqualified social esteem within fairer-skin circles. Lighter members of a family will shun open association with darker relatives, and color distinctions are found in fraternal orders, social clubs, and churches.

Hendriques suggests, however, that as of the time of his 1957 report, changes were in the making.

> The old argument that only whites and near whites could do certain things is almost dead. Appeal has to be made to the blacks by the brown and the coloured if they are going to be successful in politics. This is bound to lead to a belated recognition of their equality with the fair and the whites.
>
> The University College of the West Indies in Jamaica has also helped to dispel, to some extent, the ideas of the alleged

inferiority of the black and dark people. In the future its role will be much more compelling in this direction.

Such were the general mores of Jamaica as recently as the mid-1950's. Forty years prior to that, when Garvey was seeking to unify his people, the lines of color and class were even more tightly drawn. And one of the great ironies of that period was that the 1913 Jamaica census listed 630,181 out of a total of 831,383 as black! None was more painfully aware of the color lines with their self-defeating inconsistencies than black Marcus Garvey.

Indeed the cruel and colossal stupidity of it was to leave its indelible mark upon Garvey—a mark that he would carry for the remainder of his life. It was a mark that would prevent this turbulently intelligent man from dealing naturally and easily with certain black leaders in the United States who happened to have light skin. And though there have been attempts here to separate the dark and light members of the black race, those attempts could never be wholly successful. In a climate where to racist whites "all coons look alike," intragroup color divisions become laughable. They were, however, far from laughable in Garvey's Jamaica.

Garvey knew well that the majority of Jamaicans were, like himself, black and that they were peasants. He also knew that the color distinctions were most closely observed by the middle class. They, fearful of losing caste by associating too closely with peasants, were drawing back. And the penniless peasants to whom Garvey would have greater appeal could not support his organization. Jamaica's financial problems, incurred by continued hurricanes, were mounting. But Marcus Garvey was convinced there had to be black people somewhere who would see what was so obvious to him. If nothing more, mere contact with them could sustain him until he was able to project his plan, namely, the founding of the Universal Negro Improvement Association.

He thought of London. There he would surely find African scholars and even West Indian seamen who had traveled and seen what he had seen. Yes, that was it. A sojourn in that famed city on the Thames would be far more of a gain than a loss. So, arriving in 1912, Garvey, a young man in a hurry, lost little time. A massive job lay ahead, and there he was certain he would get a head start on it.

CHAPTER

FOUR

GARVEY'S ARRIVAL in London in 1912, could hardly have been more opportunely timed. The city was alive with the kinds of forces his defiant and inquisitive personality demanded for its survival. And the young man lost little time seeking and finding those forces. Cosmopolitan London was host not only to scholars from all areas of the world, but it was also the center where scholarly writings were published.

Like his father before him, Marcus Garvey was an omnivorous reader. He ferreted out and devoured everything he could find written about (and especially by) black men. Authors Joseph Casley Hayford, the Reverend Attoh Ahuma, John Sarbah, and Duse Mohamed Ali were particular targets. And because the latter, a magazine publisher and editor, was living in London at the time of Garvey's arrival, the two became closely associated. Indeed it was not long before Duse Mohamed Ali had become a moving force in Garvey's career. Meanwhile, the young Jamaican, while learning from direct contact with Duse, read everything he could find that Hayford, Sarbah, and Ahuma had written. The libraries of London offered him a rich selection of their works.

Joseph Casley Hayford was a black Gold Coast barrister of the privileged middle class. A man of brilliant intellect who never ceased to harrass the British Crown in behalf of Gold Coast self-determination, he was as able an author as he was a speaker. Casley Hayford became the founder of the West African National Congress. His group promoted the political aims of the black middle-class intellectuals of Gambia, Sierra Leone, Gold Coast, and Nigeria.

At the time Garvey came to London, Hayford's excellent study, *Gold Coast Native Institutions,* had been in circulation for nine years. And young Marcus Garvey, thumbing its pages, pondered long over such passages as the following:

> It is desirable, at the outset, to clear our minds of certain impressions which recent writers upon the Gold Coast have sought to create. It has been assiduously inculcated that the only object of Great Britain on the Gold Coast is trade—legitimate trade, if you please . . .
>
> There is a keen pleasure in the sense of possession, *My* land, *my* house, as contradistinguished from *your* land, *your* house, will remain, till the end of time, worthy objects of ambition. As with the individual man, so with the individual nation. That being so, when you come across professions on the part of writers upon the Gold Coast and others that Great Britain is on the Gold Coast for trade and no more, do not take them seriously.
>
> Primitive man in primitive society says: "I will have your land, or your hut, if you will give it to me. If not I will take it. When I have taken it, and you cannot retake it, of course, I will keep it." The civilized nations of the world are today like unto primitive man, else international courts of arbitration would more frequently be sitting in one European capitol or

another, and the weak nations of the earth would have a little peace, if not a little justice.

Ha! So Africans, too, were having their troubles with Great Britain, and on their own soil! Garvey soon discovered that Casley Hayford was not alone in his condemnation of European aggression in Africa. Another brilliant Gold Coast lawyer was equally and actively concerned. He was the Honorable John Mensah Sarbah, a member of the Legislative Council. Here, referring to Fanti Customary Laws, is a portion of Sarbah's finding.

> The King, by the law of England, is the supreme lord of the whole soil. Whoever, therefore, holds lands must hold them mediately or immediately of him; and while the subject enjoys the usufructuary possession, the absolute and ultimate dominion remains in the King.
>
> As far as the Gold Coast is concerned, this portion of the English law does not apply, for it is a group of territories under native rulers taken under British protection. It is British territory, but not so by conquest or cession.
>
> According to native ideas, there is no land without owners. What is now a forest or unused land will, as years go on, come under cultivation by the subjects of the stool or members of the village community, or other members of the community.

And John Sarbah's interpretation was supported by wise and sensitive British administrators. Sir William MacGregor, a physician who served as governor of Lagos, was most emphatic in this pronouncement. "One must never touch the rights of natives in lands, or compromise the authority of the chiefs." Sir William, like all informed West Africa observers, knew that the surest way to stir up trouble in that area was even to *suggest* that the African's land was in danger of being taken from him. Marcus Garvey was especially attentive to such information.

As he continued his browsing, a relatively new book reached Garvey's hands. It was *The Gold Coast Nation and National Consciousness* and its author was the Reverend Attoh Ahuma. Mr. Ahuma's real surname was Solomon, and his book, published in 1911, was a compilation of columns that had appeared in *The Gold Coast Leader.*

More strident than the formal and aloof Casley Hayford, Ahuma's appeal to Garvey was founded as much in his vituperative style as in the content of his message. Hayford spoke to white men as he would to errant children, and his was the tone and manner of the wiser black upper-class moderator. It was in the Olympian eloquence of his logic that Garvey, the hungry reader, found so much substance.

Ahuma was quite different. He often addressed himself directly to black readers in the columns he wrote. His style, somewhat florid but sharp and hard-hitting, was designed to rouse the sleepy giant he envisioned Gold Coast Africans to be. For instance, in defining the Gold Coast as a nation, Ahuma used the following phraseology.

> It is strenuously asserted by rash and irresponsible literalists that the Gold Coast, with its multiform composition of congeries of States or Provinces, independent of each other, divided by complex political institutions, laws and customs, and speaking a great variety of languages—could not be described as a nation in the eminent sense of the word. . . .
>
> In spite therefore of the dogmas and *ipse dixits* of those wiseacres who would fain deny to us, us a people, the inalienable heritage of nationality, we dare affirm, with sanctity of reason and with the emphasis of conviction that—WE ARE A NATION, It may be "a miserable, mangled, tortured, twisted

tertium quid," or to quote a higher authority, a Nation "scattered and peeled . . . a Nation meted out and trodden down," but still a Nation.

Then Ahuma proceeded to charge his countrymen to "stand before other races and peoples with heads erect and with a free independent spirit." Upon another occasion he commented upon the difficulty of thinking.

> As a people we have ceased to be a THINKING NATION. Our forebears, with all their limitations and disadvantages, had occasion to originate ideas and to contrive in their own order. They sowed incorruptible thought seeds, and we are reaping a rich havest to-day, though we are scarcely conscious of the debt we owe them. Western education or civilization undiluted, unsifted, has more or less enervated our minds and made them passive and catholic. Our national life is semi-paralyzed; our mental machinery dislocated, the inevitable consequence being, speaking generally, the resultant production of a Race of men and women *who think too little and talk too much.* But neither garrulity nor loquacity forms an indispensable element in the constitution of a state or nation.

Ahuma exhorted his people to be more helpful to one another. Being negatively critical of each other's efforts to attain a kind of perfection was not, he averred, the way to national strength. Nor was it to the advantage of his countrymen indiscriminately to ascribe selfish motives to those within the group who sought change that promised a better life for all. As a columnist, Ahuma was particularly adamant in his resolve to follow a line of impartial reporting of the Gold Coast news. He held that the projection and amplification of pleasant events and the ignoring of unpleasant and unflattering ones was not in the best interests of the nation. With a chiding acidity he exposed the folly of the black clerk earning a mere fifty pounds annually and who, in a show of conspicuous consumption, tried to outdo his boss. "It is time enough," Ahuma wrote, "for such monstrosities to learn that the *mind is the standard of the man* and that Righteousness exalteth a nation."

From such writings young Garvey was learning that responsible leadership never shrinks from its obligation to lead intelligently and honestly, often at the expense of its own personal popularity. The young pupil was getting his initial instruction from veteran practitioners whose ideas coincided with his own. What he received from Ahuma's writings alone undoubtedly nourished the seed from which sprang the famous Garvey exhortation that would later rouse black consciousness in America and elsewhere. "UP YOU MIGHTY RACE. YOU CAN ACCOMPLISH WHAT YOU WILL!"

But more than anything else in London it was contact with Duse Mohamed Ali that was so personally meaningful to the young new arrival from Jamaica. Edmund D. Cronon in his Garvey biography, *Black Moses*, describes the meeting of Garvey with Duse Mohamed in the following words:

> Here he became associated with the half-Negro, half-Egyptian author, Duse Mohamed Ali. Duse Mohamed was greatly interested in Africa and published a monthly magazine, the *African Times and Orient Review*. One of his chief interests was the campaign for home rule in Egypt, but his part-Negro ancestry made him quick to notice the presence of an insidious color bar in England, and his writing also reflected his bitterness at this insult to colored people.

Right here we come to one of those instances in which being black, that is, knowing the black experience for what it is, brings one to a fuller understanding of a black man's feeling. Had author Cronon, splendid researcher and scholar though he is, been black, he would have seen something significant to all blacks as he looked at Duse Mohamed's photograph. Indeed it is the *first* thing any black person would have noticed. And seeing it would never allow a black person to allude clinically and matter-of-factly as Cronon did to Duse's "part-Negro ancestry."

A mere glance at the face and features of Duse Mohamed Ali that frequently adorned his magazine would have set all kinds of bells ringing in the mind of the black viewer. To him the plainly obvious dark skin tone, broad nose with flaring nostrils, broad cheekbones, and full lips of Duse suggest far more than "part-Negro" ancestry. Egyptians do indeed range in color from black to white with hair texture running the gamut from kinky to straight. Black or near-black Egyptians with the features and hair texture generally described as "Negroid" are commonplace in Egypt, as anyone who has been there has seen.

But how "black" or "Negroid" an Egyptian may or may not be is important in this context for one reason only. Young Marcus Garvey, fully aware of and sensitive to what it was to be black in color-conscious Jamaica, would be naturally and understandably reluctant to intrude himself upon a lighter-skin stranger, Egyptian or not. If he happened also to be an intellectual, the reluctance would be even more pronounced. Here, however, was a man to whom the sensitive Garvey could easily relate. In Duse Mohamed, Garvey first saw another suffering *black* comrade-in-arms.

But Garvey's attraction to Duse did not end there. Surely there had to be more than a mere physical affinity present to sustain a meaningful relationship for either man. And there was. Duse had a broad concept of the affairs and difficulties of majority nonwhite men in a world dominated by minority white men. That concept arrested and held the young Jamaican. His own travels in Latin America had begun to expand his view of the black man's problems. They expanded even more as Garvey read Duse's monthly magazine, *The African Times and Orient Review.*

The magazine's very title gave evidence of Duse's acceptance of the common experiences binding the world's nonwhite peoples. Its first issue went on sale in July 1912 at the price of fourpence. It included essays on such subjects as: Hindu Treatment By The Borden Government; The Race Problems Of Hawaii; A Mosque In London; The Negro Conference At Tuskegee Institute.

In his editorial foreword Mohamed stated that there was extensive Anglo-Saxon press coverage of those items of interest to Anglo-Saxons and very little coverage of African and Oriental conditions. He further declared that it was that non-appreciation of the African and Oriental that "has unleashed the hydra-headed monster of derision, contempt, and repression." The editorial concluded with a call to those who would "be well-advised to study the pages of *The African Times and Orient Review.*"

From the point of view of Garvey's subsequent activities, the most significant article in that first issue was "The Negro in Conference at Tuskegee Institute." For three days, beginning April 17, 1912, representative black men from Africa, the United States, the West Indies, and South America met at the famed Alabama school. Some who were invited but found it impossible to attend sent messages. Among them was Joseph Casley Hayford of the African Gold Coast. Hayford's message read as follows:

We feel that the great work that is being done at Tuskegee is a mighty uplifting force for the race. It may be possible, however, to be influenced by the great national tendency which is the basis of our educational system here.

There is an African nationality, and when the Aborigines of the Gold Coast and other parts of West Africa have joined forces with our brethren in America in arriving at a national aim, purpose and aspiration, then indeed will it be possible for our brethren over the sea to bring home metaphorically to their nation and people a great spoil.

You have a great influence for good, under God, and I venture to hope that some of the thoughts which are moving West Africa as one body will appeal through you and other leaders of our race to our people on the other side of the Atlantic.

Delegates from the West Indies were especially interested in developing some form of industrial education for the masses of their people. That, they believed, would provide a better solution to the problem of employment at home than the exodus of West Indian workers to other places had been achieving. The labor void created in Jamaica by those who left the island plantations for work elsewhere was quickly filled by coolies imported from India. Had not Garvey, himself, seen how badly his fellow Jamaicans were faring in Panama and other areas of Latin America?

Small wonder then that the Jamaican representative at Tuskegee, who happened also to be Jamaica's director of education, was keenly attentive to what transpired at that international conference. During the final day's session students and teachers from the Caribbean presented a series of resolutions to the West Indian delegation. They asked those delegates to pledge that they would do their utmost to establish a school like Tuskegee back home in the islands. Moreover, they urged that an invitation be quickly extended to Tuskegee's President, Booker T. Washington, to visit the West Indies and share with its leaders the benefit of his experience.

Young Marcus Garvey read about that convention in the pages of *The African Times and Orient Review.* Those who today believe that Garvey's only knowledge of Tuskegee and its founder came through his reading Washington's *Up from Slavery* fail to do full justice to the international character of *The African Times and Orient Review.* Needless to say, they also miss the profound influence of Mohamed's internationalism upon Garvey, his young protégé. Who knows but that Garvey was directly inspired by his reading of that Tuskegee conference to call his own first International Convention eight years later in New York City? No one person, thank heaven, ever holds the monopoly upon a human idea.

Although *The African Times and Orient Review* was a new-born publication, it feared no man. Its second issue, published August 1912, carried a copy of a letter to Theodore Roosevelt from Duse Mohamed Ali. The letter asked Mr. Roosevelt, four years retired from the Presidency, if he would make a statement to *The African Times and Orient Review* regarding his "intentions touching the political and social amelioration of the ten or eleven million Negroes of the United States of America." Mr. Roosevelt's secretary, Frank Harper, replied that aside from what his employer had already said and written in the past "Mr. Roosevelt has nothing to say on the subject."

In the same issue, a more positive note was struck by Booker T. Washington in a six-and-a-quarter-page article with photographs, titled simply "Tuskegee Institute." If white American officialdom had nothing it cared to say in the pages of *African Times and Orient Review* about its largest single minority, America's most honored black man of his era did. And no reader was more attentive to Dr. Washington's story than Marcus Mosiah Garvey.

A little more than two-thirds the way through his article, Dr. Washington explained why he made Tuskegee an *industrial* school:

> Tuskegee Institute was started in a small way in the summer of 1881. At that time the Negro had lost practically all political control in the South. As early as 1885 there were scarcely any members of my race in the National Congress or state legislatures and long before this date they had ceased to hold state offices.
>
> It was at this period of the Negro's development, when the distance between the races was greatest and the spirit and ambition of the coloured people most depressed, that the idea of industrial or business development was introduced and began to be made prominent. . . .
>
> It did not take the more level-headed members of the race long to see that while the Negro in the South was surrounded by many difficulties, there was practically no line drawn, and little discrimination in the world of commerce, banking, storekeeping, manufacturing, and skilled trades, and in agriculture; and in this lay his great opportunity.

The words began to seep deeper and deeper into Garvey's consciousness. Finally came a light. It was a light that was never extinguished, even during the stormiest and least hopeful hours of his eventful life. Garvey made a resolve. He, himself, would have to establish contact with this great black American educator. Indeed, he would have to get to Tuskegee to see and talk with him. There was much for the two of them to talk about in the land where the black man's opportunity seemed so promising.

CHAPTER FIVE

TWENTY-FIVE-year-old Marcus Garvey supported himself in London as he continued to read and study. And with the encouragement of his mentor, Duse Mohamed Ali, he became a contributor during 1913 to *The African Times and Orient Review.* Most of all, he contemplated the future. The more Garvey thought of the future the greater became his desire to visit America. He had expanded his reading of Booker T. Washington to include the latter's autobiography, *Up from Slavery.* Garvey's admiration from afar of the Washington philosophy of Negro self-help was increasing daily. All was not going too well, however, with Dr. Washington at home.

While he was ardently admired by powerful white American businessmen, by politicians, (President Roosevelt had invited him to dinner at the White House) and by many black Americans, opposition to him was steadily growing. Indeed the year 1913 marked the point at which the tide of Washington's political power began quickly to ebb away. Ironically one of the black men of America whose name would forever more become synonymous with opposition to

Booker T. Washington would also become an antagonist of Marcus Garvey. That man was William E. Burghardt Du Bois. But even before Du Bois and Washington clashed head-on, and before Du Bois and Garvey ever met, Washington had encountered able black opponents. William Monroe Trotter was one of them. Robert H. Brisbane in *The Black Vanguard,* presents a clear picture of the period and the principals involved in the Trotter-Washington feud.

Born in Ohio, fifteen years earlier than Garvey, Trotter was taken to Boston as a child by his progressive parents. Young Trotter attended the best schools, including Harvard College from which he was graduated *magna cum laude,* and became a successful real estate broker. In today's parlance he "had it made." But Trotter, a thinker, bridled at the indignity of being relegated to the banal existence of making money in a black ghetto.

He bridled even more as he contemplated the techniques of compromising accommodation Booker Washington used to gain favor among the whites. More galling yet to Trotter was the total acceptance of Washington by whites, who, with no feeling for blacks, endowed Washington with his power. *That,* Trotter decided, was no solution to the problem of racism in America. In 1901 he and George Forbes, a black Amherst graduate, decided that someone would have to challenge the Washington mechanism, and if possible, destroy it. Together they founded in Boston a weekly newspaper they called, *The Guardian.* Its purpose was to bring Booker T. Washington's kingdom tumbling down.

So effective an organ was *The Guardian* as to cause Washington to file two lawsuits against it in the hope of forcing it out of business. Both attempts failed. Then mimicking the tycoons who supported him, Washington tried to subsidize a local rival of *The Guardian,* but that too failed.

In July of 1903 Trotter and his associate, Forbes, attended the National Convention of the Afro-American Council held in Louisville, Kentucky. It was an important gathering inasmuch as the Council was the largest such group in the nation. Booker T. Washington was the featured speaker of the convention. Trotter and Forbes had planned to engage Washington in open-floor debate. They were thwarted, however, by T. Thomas Fortune, a friend of Washington, who happened to be chairman of the meeting. Trotter's frustration was immense as he and Forbes returned, unsated, to Boston.

Later that year, however, when Dr. Washington was engaged by the Negro Business League to address Boston's black citizens, Trotter organized a group of hecklers to question him. The police, obviously alerted in advance, were waiting for such an event. As Trotter rose to speak they promptly arrested and jailed him. In the ensuing publicity Trotter emerged as a martyr in the nation's black press. Down at Atlanta University, William E. Burghardt Du Bois, a young teacher of sociology and a great admirer of Trotter, rushed to his defense. Du Bois, while critical of Trotter's tactics, was sympathetic to his case against Washington.

Like Trotter, Du Bois was northern born and bred in middle-class New England surroundings. The genteel atmosphere of his Great Barrington, Massachusetts, home gave the boy Du Bois but a hint of the realities of American racism outside. That hint came to him, however, in high school. There he heard parents of some of his schoolmates referring to his dark skin as a thing of misfortune. The effect of such an expression of benign bigotry left its mark upon young Du Bois. Upon graduation from high school with a college scholarship, Du Bois envisioned matriculating at Harvard or Amherst. He was advised by school authorities to "go south among your people." Du Bois did just that. He spent three years at Fisk University in Nashville, Tenessee, before returning north to Harvard, where he took the A.B. degree in 1890.

Study in Berlin followed and Du Bois returned to Harvard to complete his doctoral thesis in history. His unusual preparation and obvious brilliance notwithstanding, Dr. Du Bois received no offers to teach in any of the leading white institutions. So in 1897 he gladly accepted a position as professor of sociology at black Atlanta University. It was while there that he read of Monroe Trotter's imprisonment.

On the surface Du Bois was aloof and cool. Of African and French Huguenot lineage, Du Bois was a handsome young man of medium build with a mocha complexion and finely chiseled features. The Vandyke beard he wore added to his general resemblance to men of the Near East. His bearing was patrician and chilly. No stranger ever came away from a first meeting with Du Bois accusing him of being a "regular Joe." When he was displeased his chilly mien took on the proportions of a giant deep freeze.

Du Bois' disagreement with Washington started with his rejection of the latter's program of industrial education, placation of the South, and the soft pedaling of the black man's civil and political rights. The Du Bois disapproval reached its outraged climax with what the latter described in 1903 in *The Souls of Black Folk* as Washington's "Atlanta Compromise."

Du Bois was referring to a speech by Washington delivered at the Atlanta Exposition in 1895. It was a speech that drew the plaudits of southern politicians and northern industrialists even as it roused the ire of a large segment of the black community. The Alabama educator urged blacks to remain in the South and to concentrate upon acquiring material wealth where, he asserted, such activity would be to the mutual advantage of both blacks and whites.

He was critical of black participation in politics and of black grievances that overshadowed black opportunities. He was poetic in his praise of the patience, loyalty, and good nature of the black masses. And he was particularly disdainful of any suggestion that social equality was sought by blacks. On that issue Washington dramatically proclaimed, "In all things that are purely social we can be as separate as the five fingers, yet one as the hand in all things essential to material progress."

Du Bois was furious. In his essay, "Of Mr. Washington and Others," published in *The Souls of Black Folk* in 1903, he excoriated the educator and his "Tuskegee machine." That *The Souls of Black Folk*, Du Bois' biggest seller, was published the same year its author came to the aid of the imprisoned Monroe Trotter was a fortunate coincidence for the anti-Washington forces.

Actually Trotter's jailing caused Du Bois to alter completely the character of his fight against racism in America. Whereas he had heretofore leaned heavily upon the use of scientific study in tackling the problem, Du Bois now moved into the area of direct political and social action. Within three weeks after Trotter's arrest, he contacted black intellectuals in seventeen states. Would they prepare to meet in Niagara, Canada, from July 11 to 13? The year was 1905. The eleven objectives of the meeting included pushing for civil and political rights for blacks; promoting mutual understanding between blacks and labor unions; and the promotion of a free and unsubsidized black press.

Such was the beginning of the Niagara Movement. Twenty-nine men attended that first meeting, and lying close to the surface of their aims was the hope of bringing an end to the power of Booker T. Washington. But Washington was strongly entrenched. He was even able to suppress news of the Niagara Movement in the black press. So savagely was Du Bois attacked by Washington and his supporters that the Niagara Movement, already weakened by internal dissent for the five years of its existence, finally lost whatever effectiveness it had.

A shocking mob action, however, brought unexpected support to the principles of the Niagara Movement. Out in Springfield, Illinois, a barbaric attack by a white majority on its black citizens during August of 1908 stung the nation's conscience. Among those outraged was southern, white journalist, William E. Walling. Recalling how quick the North was to flay Southerners for similar acts, Walling wrote a scalding exposé of the violence for the magazine *Independent.* He titled it, "Race War in the North." Reaction to Walling's piece was instantaneous. Six prominent white Americans, Jane Addams, Mary White Ovington. William Dean Howells, John Dewey, Joel Spingarn, and Morefield Story, called a meeting. They invited the members of the Niagara Movement to join them. And at that gathering the National Association for the Advancement of Colored People was conceived. The year was 1909.

The organization officially adopted its name the following year and its platform was practically the same as that of the passing Niagara Movement. W. E. B. Du Bois, who had been obliged to struggle along in the shadow of Booker T. Washington, was installed as the N.A.A.C.P.'s director of publicity and research. He quickly founded the organization's official organ, *The Crisis,* a popular magazine that many regarded as Du Bois' special domain. And as the Du Bois star began its ascent, that of Washington and his Tuskegee machine began to sink and fade. Just how well known Booker T. Washington's feuds with Du Bois, Trotter, and other "more radical" black American scholars were to young Marcus Garvey is not certain. Neither is it certain, even if Garvey had possession of the details of the feuds, how clearly he grasped the full import to black Americans. Black-white relations in the United States at the turn of the twentieth century were everything but frank and direct.

The wily byplay inherent in nearly everything the accepted black leader said to the whites to whom he looked for support was always a consideration to be reckoned with. Booker T. Washington was the acknowledged expert at saying those things white folks wanted most to hear. His batting average was not flawless, however. Even so severe a critic of the Washington technique of handling racist whites as black historian Robert Brisbane admits that Washington now and then forgot to be conciliatory. How much of the older, southern, black Americans' soft-soaping operations upon untractable whites was fully understood by the proud and arrogant young West Indian is not clear.

One thing does emerge clearly, however, as one reviews the manners and methods of both men. However enthusiastic Garvey was about Dr. Washington's program of self-help through agricultural and industrial education, the two men operated on opposing wavelengths in other related matters.

Washington fully supported the doctrine of rugged individualist capitalism. Moreover he was an unabashed admirer of the methods white America employed in reaching and maintaining its pinnacle of industrial power in the world. It did not seem to worry Washington, an ex-slave, that his own enslavement and that of his mother had been a contributor to the success he constantly extolled. Indeed, Dr. Washington was given to blaming his people for their deficiencies created by the slave system. And we have author R. H. Brisbane's assurance of Washington's admiration for monopolistic power, as the following quote from *The Black Vanguard* shows:

> By 1905 Washington had achieved something of a press lord's domination over Negro publications. Where he could, he simply bought out already established newspapers. The *New York Age* was a case in point. His control was secured by loans, advertising, printing orders, and political subsidies. His fief included at least one, and probably both, of the then existing Negro press associations.

We learn, moreover, from the same source that the great Alabama educator was not disposed to recommending labor unionism to black workers. Here Washington again took the identical view of his industrialist supporters, that the philosophy and tactics of organized labor were harmful to industry's best interests. Such willing support of unbridled free enterprise was the Washington stance. Along with it he made still another thing crystal clear. He sought black admittance to the white, industrial, inner sanctum through the establishment of a black subsidiary of the system working within the larger white body.

How different indeed was the Garvey approach. Never in his public utterances did Garvey have anything good to say about the methods Europeans and Americans used to attain and hold their power over nonwhites. Nor did Garvey publicly unleash blame upon blacks for their miserable condition. The Jamaican had demonstrated his opposition to monopolistic antilabor practices when he eschewed the foreman's status to join his workers in the Jamaica printers' strike. And Garvey, above all else, constantly preached complete and absolute separation of black men and their interests from all forms of white domination. With such differences marking each man's approach to black liberation, any coalition that Garvey might later seek with Washington would have to be limited, not to mention tenuous.

Actually Garvey later said as much. A study of his *Philosophy and Opinions* reveals the following statement:

> If Washington had lived he would have had to change his program. No leader can successfully lead this race of ours without giving an interpretation of the awakened spirit of the New Negro, who does not seek industrial opportunity alone, but a political voice. The world is amazed at the desire of the New Negro, for with his strong voice he is demanding a place in the affairs of men.

In 1914, two years after he had arrived in London, Marcus Garvey returned to Jamaica, his brain awhirl with ideas. He was ready now to form his own organization and to that end assembled a few faithful followers. On August first the Universal Negro Improvement Association was born in Kingston, Jamaica. Then expansively contemplating its broadening possibilities, Garvey appended the phrase, "and African Communities League." The association's aims, as Amy Jacques Garvey lists them in *Garvey and Garveyism*, did not suffer the encumbrances of modesty. They were as follows:

> To establish a Universal Confraternity among the race; to promote the spirit of race pride and love; to reclaim the fallen;

to administer to and assist the needy; to assist in civilizing the backward tribes of Africa; to assist in the development of independent Negro nations and communities; to establish a central nation for the race, where they will be given the opportunity to develop themselves; to establish Commissaries and Agencies in the principal countries and cities of the world for the representation of all Negroes; to promote a conscientious Spiritual worship among the native tribes of Africa; to establish Universities, Colleges, Academies, and Schools for racial education and culture of the people; to improve the general conditions of Negroes everywhere.

In writing the preamble to the association's constitution, Garvey ventured beyond the boundaries of nationalism in calling for a respect for the "rights of all mankind, believing always in the Brotherhood of Man and the Fatherhood of God." Garvey also made clear his organization's stand against the discontent and confusion emanating from the oppression of the weak by the strong. But the phrase of his preamble to get the most frequent public airing was its rhythmically terse and ringing motto: "One God! One Aim! One Destiny!"

However, the conviction that inspired such noble words found a stiff challenge in the caprices and vagaries of human conduct. Class and skin-tone barriers made successful recruitment into the association a near impossible job. The few blacks who were "making it" were too insecure to look beyond their own personal salvation. Besides, most of that group preferred to move ahead by "improving the appearance of the race." Marrying whites and near-whites and producing "high yaller" and "high brown" progeny was far more fun than the drudgery proposed in the aims and constitution of Marcus Garvey's U.N.I.A.

The black laboring masses who would have been the direct

beneficiaries of Garvey's program were hobbled by fear. They had for so long been conditioned to their position at the bottom of the heap as to be unable to believe things could ever be different for them. With their minds so confined within the cocoon of uncertainty, cleverly spun by the plantations for whom they toiled, their chances of emerging free seemed nil. Two years of struggling to overcome such handicaps were as much as the impatient twenty-nine-year-old Garvey could bear. Again his thoughts turned to America.

As has been mentioned, the second period between 1910 and 1915 marked the waxing and the waning of the powers of W. E. B. Du Bois and Booker T. Washington respectively. The years 1912–1913 in particular saw the *Crisis* under Du Bois' editorship growing immensely popular. Du Bois' determination to make it a black magazine for black readers was paying dividends. Even the powerful white chairman of the N.A.A.C.P.'s board of directors, Oswald Garrison Villard, was unable successfully to dominate Du Bois in that regard. Nor did Villard's resignation from the board following tiffs with Du Bois budge the latter from his position.

If Dr. Du Bois was sitting pretty in his new role in New York, Dr. Washington occupied a seat of nettles in Alabama. The year 1912 saw changes in the structure of the Republican party from whence the Washington strength had come. So desperate were the efforts of Theodore Roosevelt and William Howard Taft to gain white southern support in the coming elections that they found no time to waste on their favorite Negro down in Alabama. And when Woodrow Wilson was elected to the Presidency the following year, Booker T. Washington and his once famous "Tuskegee Machine" began to sink rapidly in the surging flood of the Democratic tidal wave.

Meanwhile a significant mass movement was in progress. Hundreds of tattered, anxious-eyed black migrants were beginning to move northward. From the weevil-infested cotton patches and peanut hills of Dixie they came. Old Black Joe and his fellow tribesmen were no longer heeding the call of drawling plantation voices. The red clay of the South would absorb the padding tread of certain weary black feet for the last time. Slim pickings in Dixie and the bolting of the gates to European immigrants at the outbreak of World War I were to blame for the black movement north. Someone had to do the hard work in the northern centers where materials for war were being manufactured. Black labor was crying for the chance.

Marcus Garvey in Jamaica wrote Booker T. Washington suggesting what a wonderful thing it would be to meet him and see what marvels he had wrought at Tuskegee. Perhaps, Garvey hinted, they could get together on something. Washington's reply was polite and noncommittal. It would be nice to have the young man from Jamaica visit and he would see that he was made comfortable during his stay. Beyond that the fading monarch of Tuskegee promised nothing. Garvey and Washington never met. The celebrated Alabaman died in 1915. And Marcus Garvey, still determined to make it to America, prepared to do it strictly on his own.

CHAPTER SIX

MARCUS GARVEY must have presented a memorable spectacle as he strode into Harlem during March of 1916. Even that cosmopolitan black community, accustomed in those days to the sight of refugees from the Deep South as well as from other blighted areas of the world, must have found him amusing to the eye. For, let's be honest about it, Garvey was never a beauty by any standard. His were the face and figure that could plunge a group of imaginative caricaturists into an orgy of creative malevolence.

The squat pudgy body with its oversized head mounted on a short neck offered an amusing overall silhouette. Encased in the close-fitting garb of the British West Indian immigrant, nature's caprices became cruelly exaggerated flaws. But once the observer got past those comic superficials and focused upon the head and face of Garvey, he was in for a unique experience—one that did not truly lend itself to mirth.

The fleshiness of Garvey's dark brown face was offset by a high, broad forehead and massive jaw. The full, well-modeled mouth, crowned by a carefully groomed moustache, thrust itself defiantly forward. And the nose, flat but not unusually large, vaulted upward to piercing, deep-set eyes strongly suggestive of the Akan lineage from whom his father had sprung. Though there was no surface beauty in Marcus Garvey's face, the perceptive observer would look at him a bit more than casually before turning aside.

But Harlemites at large, like people everywhere, saw only those surface things and they often evoked nothing more than their good humored scorn.

> Humph! Here comes another monkey-chaser fresh from de boat, mon! Hee Hee! Man, getta look at them *togs*, willya! An just look at 'im *strut*. Britannia rules de waves today, mon. Lawd, lawd, lawd! What's gonna come in here, next?

The banter carried a hollow ring, however, for the scoffers were in no position to look down upon the little man from Jamaica. Only recently had they, themselves, arrived in Harlem. And their battle for land—not land to own, but land just to *occupy*—had been an intensive struggle lasting from 1910 until 1915. Prior to 1900 Harlem, the black community, was nonexistent. All Harlem residents were white. Then a twenty-four-year-old black man from Westfield, Massachusetts, made a move that began to change Harlem's complexion. He was Philip A. Payton, Jr., son of a North Carolina-born merchant and barber.

Following graduation from North Carolina's Livingstone College, young Payton married and settled in New York City. There he supported himself by working at the kinds of odd jobs black men, even black college graduates, were permitted to do. He was, in turn, a handyman, barber, and later, janitor in a real-estate office. It was while on the latter job that he began to develop a knowledge of and interest in the real-estate boom that occurred at the turn of the century.

Young Payton went into the real-estate business in 1900, advertising himself as a specialist in the management of colored tenements. Gilbert Osofsky in *Harlem: the Making of a Ghetto,* reports that it was nearly a year before the young man found himself a colored tenement to manage. Then came an unexpected break.

A feud between two white Harlem landlords culminated when one, spiting the other, turned his house over to Payton to fill with "colored tenants." No professional football line ever put a fiercer rush upon a quarterback than that put on Phil Payton by house-hungry black tenants. And white real-estate dealers, far more alert to dollar signs than to color signs, came to bolt upright attention as they contemplated potential profits. They immediately urged Payton to advertise in their journals, and by 1904 the ex-janitor had become New York City's first and most successful black realtor.

In 1906, four of the apartment houses he rented to black tenants bore the names of four black historical figures: Booker T. Washington, John M. Langston, Frederick Douglass, and Paul Lawrence Dunbar. The Afro-American Realty Company which he founded was then two years old. Then followed four years of ups and downs; and the company, after setting a significant trend in opening homes for black residents in Harlem, was no longer doing business. At the zenith of his career Payton owned and managed apartment houses and brownstone residences from 119th to 147th streets. Never before had black residents occupied that area.

By 1914 Harlem's black population numbered 50,000, and many white property owners began to talk about a "black invasion." With apprehension bordering on hysteria, the landlords began to organize drives to keep their neighborhood white. They formed restrictive covenants, swearing sacredly not to rent to blacks until the "danger" they envisioned had been given "time to run its course." Not only did they agree to keep out pitch-black tenants but all others running the gamut from brown to white who could be identified as having African ancestry. This latter move served as a reminder to the forgetful that even in New York City "all niggers look alike" to the frightened white racist.

A particularly vociferous landlord, John G. Taylor, organized The Harlem Property Owners' Improvement Corporation. His group operated between 1910 and 1915 with the blessing and support of the local press, particularly the *Home News* of Harlem. That paper's intemperate descriptions of what it saw as "the black menace" omitted none of the popular abusive epithets in its lurid and alarmist reporting. One of its editorials of 1911 flung this question at its readers:

> When will the people of Harlem wake up to the fact that they must organize and maintain a powerful anti-invasion movement if they want to check the progress of the black hordes that are gradually eating through the very heart of Harlem?

Black realtors, white churchmen, and white theatre owners were courted by the H.P.O.I.C. in its attempt to restrict the movement of blacks into the predominantly white uptown area. Other similar groups born in the frenzy of fear backed the H.P.O.I.C. None, however succeeded in stopping the flow of black humanity into Harlem. Those settling there between 1910 and 1914 found the surroundings pleasant and somewhat elegant. Proof of that is found in an Urban League report of 1914 stating, "Those of the race who desire to live in grand style with elevator, telephone, and hallboy services, can now realize their cherished ambition."

With the run-down San Juan Hill section of the West Sixties losing its more fortunate tenants to Harlem, other downtown black ghetto areas followed suit. Their churches went with them. The biggest churches, Bethel A.M.E., Saint Marks M.E., Mother A.M.E. Zion, and Saint Philips Episcopal acquired Harlem real estate prior to 1915. Saint Philips owned a row of ten apartment houses on West 135th Street near Seventh Avenue, for which it paid $640,000. So by its acquisition of property the affluent black church had much to do with transforming the face of Harlem from white to black.

Marcus Garvey's arrival in Harlem in the winter of 1916 coincided with the change as well as with the beginnings of the aforementioned exodus of southern black laborers seeking work in the north. As James Weldon Johnson states in *Black Manhattan,* preparations of the United States not only to supply munitions to the warring nations, but to enter the conflict along with them, were well under way in 1916. The need for a labor force increased with the departure of European immigrant men and the enlistment of American white men in the United States Army and Navy. Labor had to be drawn from somewhere, and the rural black American South supplied that need.

Much of the brawn hailed from Mississippi, Arkansas, Alabama, Louisiana, Texas, Tennessee, Georgia, the Carolinas, and Virginia. Most of those who settled in New York City and surrounding industrial areas came from the eastern seaboard states. And many came also from the West Indies.

Compared to many of the black southern migrants the Caribbean immigrants were of high intelligence and were generally trained in specific skills. Thrift and a penchant for business pursuits marked the personalities of the West Indian immigrants. Because of their conditioning in the tradition of the British, from whose possessions the bulk of them came, they exuded an air of British aplomb often disconcerting to Americans.

A strange mixture of admiration coupled with envy characterized the attitude of many black Americans toward their West Indian blood brothers. That is why the mere sight of Garvey and other West Indians was a cause for adult laughter. The children, of course, imitated their elders. Rhyming ditties intended as good-natured insults to the new arrivals from the Caribbean were sung in the streets and in the schools. Typical was this:

> When you eat split peas and rice
> You tink you eatin' somethin',
> But mon—you aint taste nuthin yet
> Like monkey hips and dumplin'.

And this:

> When I get ready to leave this world
> Won't need no undertaker
> Just put my body on the river, mon,
> An' I'll float back to Jamaica.

Downright hostile beliefs held by Afro-Americans about West Indians were that, with few exceptions, they were cheap, grasping, pushy, and overbearing. And for many years one of the most hilarious vaudeville skits performed in Harlem was a loud-mouthed quarrel between a southern-born black woman and her West Indian neighbor. Carried off by two male comedians who were masters of dialects, the sequence literally laid Harlem audiences in the aisles. Such were the early relations between American-born blacks and those from the Caribbean. Such was what greeted Marcus

Garvey in the teeming, rapidly expanding Harlem of 1916.

Because he had long ago learned the value of travel and observation, Garvey did not confine himself to Harlem in seeking a first-hand view of the United States. During his first year his travels about the country covered thirty-eight states, enabling him to get a picture of true conditions among Afro-Americans. In addition to their opportunities Garvey also saw their handicaps occasioned by the various patterns of discrimination depriving them of the rights of full citizens.

The year 1916 was marked by incidents reflective of the national discontent born of racism. Not the least responsible reasons for racist feelings was an immensely popular motion picture. Based upon a play, *The Clansman,* by Thomas Dixon, the film, titled *The Birth of a Nation,* was made in 1915 by David War R Griffith. Dixon, a Protestant clergyman, wrote his play as an apology for the outrageous conduct of the Ku Klux Klan. The Klansmen of Dixon's play and of Griffith's film were a far cry from the reality.

Robert Brisbane in *The Black Vanguard* presents a far more convincing picture of the typical Ku Kluxer. Brisbane sees him as a white man of the lower middle class with minimal education and minimal skills. Add to that the Klansman's narrow religionist views and you have a man with but one asset. His whiteness. So with his conviction that the black man exists only to defile whiteness through his defilement of white women, the typical Klansman emerges as an unhappy and insecure half-man. *The Birth of a Nation,* however, glorified him.

Its portrayal of Northern carpetbaggers and newly freed slaves as villains prevented from destroying a defenseless white South only by the gallantry of white knights covered with bed sheets was a shameless distortion of history. Worse still, *The Birth of a Nation* was swallowed whole without question by large segments of the country's population.

That it was the first movie to be requested by an American president for showing at the White House did much to increase its popularity. But even with such an assist by Woodrow Wilson, *The Birth of a Nation* roused the liberals of the country as no other film had ever done.

Carlton Moss in his essay, "The Negro in American Films," included in Lindsay Patterson's, *Anthology of the American Negro in the Theatre,* notes that many blacks and whites united in attacking so biased a distortion of history. Oswald Garrison Villard, Rabbi Stephen Wise, and Eugene V. Debs were vehement in their condemnation of it. And the *Chicago Defender* for February 2, 1916, flayed local black leaders who sat quietly by as Chicago's mayor did nothing to prevent its showing.

Why such a hue and cry over a motion picture? Well, its impact upon the emotions of white viewers, North and South, gave rise to a new wave of national violence. Acts of aggression by whites against blacks took a decided upswing. The following are typical examples.

Early in 1916 President Wilson issued a pardon to two white Oklahoma farmers, Frank Guinn and J. J. Beal. Both men, when serving as election officials, had been convicted in the Federal courts of intimidating and preventing blacks from voting. Further east in Albany, Georgia, Sheriff Potts handed five black prisoners over to a mob of fifty white lynchers. No one was ever punished for the crime.

The February 12 issue of the *Chicago Defender* carried a story datelined Jacksonville, Florida, protesting the treatment of black women railroad passengers traveling alone in the South. Object of the protest was a white baggagemaster who indulged in amorous familiarities with the women in defiance of the presence of black men in the same coach.

When wealthy Mrs. James H. Rees of Memphis, Tennessee's Madison Avenue, opened her palatial home to a formal spring dance honoring her butler and maid, she and her guests became suddenly aware of a disturbance outside. Across the street, in front of the YMCA building, police had to quell a mob of Ku Klux Klan rioters bent upon storming the Rees mansion. Four months later, in August 1916, thirteen black soldiers of the Twenty-Fifth United States Infantry were forcibly removed from a pullman car at West Berkeley and ordered to ride in a car unfit for human travel. The thirteen reneged, choosing instead to walk to their destination. They promptly filed a complaint against the Pullman Company with the United States War Department.

Alert Marcus Garvey, getting about in the various cities and towns of America, paid strict attention to all that was happening. Back in New York he began to speak on the street corners of Harlem. Recalling what he had seen and heard not only in America but in his native Jamaica, Latin America, and London, as well, his words were impressive indeed. Still his black street audiences were skeptical. Garvey did not ride around in a fine limousine, as was the style for accepted leaders. Not only did he have no car, but quite often his shoes were a trifle more than threadbare uppers.

And as Garvey shouted his belief in "Africa for Africans" he, unwittingly, exorcised the spectre of an imposter who between 1913 and 1914 had shouted the same words. The imposter was Alfred C. Sam, who began his fraudulent scheme in Oklahoma.

"King Sam" was still fresh in the memories of many black

Americans. They were reminded of him as they simultaneously heard Garvey and read a news story in the *Chicago Defender* for December 29, 1916. The story, datelined Brooklyn, New York, December 22, and headlined, "The Liberia Returns," read in part:

> Moored to pier in Erie Basin is a huge old rustpot of a steamship, barnacle-encrusted, sticky with mildew and rotten. But three short years ago a thousand persons builded upon her dreams of an empire, of a huge and wealthy country where they would be better than the best in this country.
>
> Some of them have died in their attempt to make their dreams a reality; others, after passing safely through compound dangers of drowning and disease, are now scattered along the west coast of Africa, picking up their living as they can, scorned and mistreated in the land where their empire was to be.
>
> So ends their faith in King Sam, the magic tongued African who had woven the scheme that made happy their sleep with soft dreams. For months now they have been awake and aware that it was all a nightmare.

The story then went on to say that King Sam sold stock at twenty-five dollars a share, with the promise that the holder was entitled to a free voyage to Africa. Once there, land, it was declared, would be given him. King Sam raked in a fortune as the black press labeled him a fraud and the British authorities also sounded warnings against him. But King Sam prospered. He was able to buy a ship for $200,000 cash. Meanwhile, his program, filled with the kind of mysticism that appealed to his followers, moved swiftly forward.

Picking up its first load of passengers at Galveston, Texas, the *Liberia,* with an inexperienced all-black crew, started out for Africa. Although disease and storms reduced his crew, Sam did make it to the West Africa coast. The promised kingdom was not forthcoming, however, and King Sam abandoned the others who were then obliged to shift for themselves. The *Defender* news story concluded with these two lines:

> Sam drifted to a West Coast village and soon put such a spell on the natives that they elected him chief. The *Liberia* had to be *towed* back to America at the end of an 800-foot eight-inch hawser!

That grim reminder of a grim episode in black American history helped put a damper on those who listened to the preachments of Marcus Garvey. But they cooled Garvey's zeal not one bit. And as he continued with his work, the United States of America was drawn deeper and deeper into World War I.

CHAPTER SEVEN

EVEN BEFORE Woodrow Wilson formally declared war on Germany in early April 1917, black Americans were in it. Those who were in the National Guard of the District of Columbia had been called out to protect the national capitol. Then there were black civilians employed in industries producing armaments and related materials in the large urban centers. Most had migrated from the South. Chicago, for example, had seen an increase of 270 percent in its black population, while Gary, Indiana, saw its black residents grow by 1200 percent.

Elsewhere across the nation young black men, eager for excitement and adventure, joined their white counterparts at the recruiting stations for service volunteers. The whites were accepted and the blacks told to go home and forget about it. But the young black men would not be put off. Some even resolved to become enlisted officers. With the passage of the Selective Service Act a month after America's formal entry into the war, the way was opened to black enlistees.

Those who aspired to the rank of officer, however, learned a chilling lesson in army bigotry from the case of Colonel Charles Young. A graduate of West Point, Colonel Young was forced into retirement to forestall his promotion to the rank of general. "High blood pressure" was the official reason given for his retirement. Outraged by the army's act, Colonel Young responded by riding horseback in full field equipment from his Ohio home to Washington, D.C., to prove his physical fitness. And the embarrassed War Department recalled him to a post as military attaché in Haiti. Safely tucked away for the duration, Colonel Charles Young never became a general.

As the tempo of American participation in the war quickened, so also did the heat of war fever grow among the American rank and file. Rumblings began to swell in America's black communities as white-dominated draft boards snatched away young black men in greater numbers than whites. John Hope Franklin's *From Slavery to Freedom* reports that approximately 31 percent of registered blacks were accepted as against 26 percent of registered whites. And a black pundit recalls the remark of the Harlemite who, when asked by his friends when he was going to enlist, replied, "Them Germans ain't done *nuthin'* to me, and if they have I forgive 'em!"

But the real protests, those that ceaselessly harped upon the injustices perpetrated at home by a nation declaring itself determined to "make the world safe for democracy," emanated from the black press. And few were more interested in the rumblings of the black press in 1917 than official white America and Marcus Mosiah Garvey. Because of their sharp and uncompromising stands, the *Crisis*, edited by W.

E. B. Du Bois, and the *Chicago Defender*, edited and published by Robert S. Abbott, were especially effective.

Abbott, like Garvey, was a man of black skin. If anything, he was blacker then Garvey. He was also older, having arrived the same year as Du Bois, 1868. Born in a miserable cabin on a Georgia plantation, Robert Abbott, because of intense blackness, was subjected to the ridicule of his lighter-skin schoolmates at Beach Institute. Such nicknames as "Tar Baby," "Blue Juice," and "Midnight" are commonplace in the black community and Abbott was known by all of them.

Saunders Redding, in *The Lonesome Road*, reports that so deeply hurt was Abbott by his adolescent experience that he shunned the color black as much as possible in his successful adult life as a millionaire publisher. Doubtless the only reason he was able to abide the black ink of his profession was that it was used on white paper. Such self-abnegation was the outgrowth of Abbott's inability to accept his blackness as a perfectly respectable condition. It could very well have been a basic contributing element in his later opposition to the program of Marcus Garvey.

Robert Abbott entered Hampton Institute at the age of twenty. It took him seven years to complete the four-year course in printing. Following graduation he went to Chicago, where he tried desperately and without success to break into that city's black social circle. Not only was he too black but his southern speech was against him. Those with whom he sought social contact studiously shunned him out of fear that association with the bumbling Abbott would cause them to lose the positions they had struggled so hard to attain. Their rejection of him made Abbott all the more determined than ever to "make it big."

He attended and completed law school, but failed to pass

the Illinois bar. Then, looking about among his closest associates, hard-working, emerging middle-class blacks, he noted something. They, the plain, simple, good people with no airs and pretensions had no local periodical that spoke to, and specifically for, *them.* They, too, were interested in fighting racial injustice. But the three existing local black newspapers functioned only to serve the political ends of their publishers.

Abbott had an idea. He would found a newspaper for that particular group of rough-hewn, emerging, middle-class blacks with whom he was so closely identified. On May 5, 1905, the first issue of the *Chicago Defender* was on the streets of Chicago. Now, nationally distributed, it has been appearing ever since. And, as has been said, both the *Chicago Defender* and the *Crisis* began to upset white America in 1917.

Indeed, only a few months previously Abbott had exhorted readers with his uniquely worded editorial approval of the northward-bound black migration.

> We'd like to oblige these unselfish(?) souls and remain slaves in the South, but to their section of the country we have said, as the song goes, "I hear you calling me," and have boarded the train singing "Good-bye, Dixie Land."

Whatever Editor Abbott may have lacked in the area of syntax he more than made up for in spirit and common sense. His readers were legion, and judging from the way they began to swarm into northern cities they were certainly heeding the advice of their favorite writer.

Abbott's editorial drew instant fire. Early in that same year the mayor of Pine Bluff, Arkansas, Mack Hollis, had an injunction issued barring the circulation of the *Defender* in Pine Bluff or Jefferson County. One Dixie sheriff went so far as to journey to Chicago to arrest the *Defender*'s publisher. But Abbott's acquaintance with the law, faulty as the State of Illinois had found it, was sufficient, along with the aid of a few evil-looking assistants, to enable him to stand his ground.

In Washington, meanwhile, South Carolina's James F. Byrnes rose in the Congress to proclaim that he was ready to see to it that A. Philip Randolph went to prison for two and a half years. Randolph had been guilty of defying the Pullman Company by organizing the Brotherhood of Sleeping Car Porters. Byrnes also declared his intention to call upon the United States Attorney General to institute sedition proceedings against W. E. B. Du Bois and Robert S. Abbott. South Carolina, by the way, had joined Georgia and Mississippi in making the reading of the *Defender* a state crime. And being caught in Dixie with the *Crisis* in 1917 was like it would be to go goose-stepping under a swastika banner in Tel Aviv in the 1970's.

Harlem, where Garvey was still plugging away at his street-corner oratory, was beginning to do fairly well. Jobs were plentiful and good paying in 1917, and Harlem residents were being caught up in the fervor of patriotism that pervaded most American communities. A few years previously some effort had been made to form there a regiment of the state militia. There was hemming and hawing, however, until legislation finally passed, authorizing the Fifteenth Regiment as a unit of the New York National Guard. With the formal declaration of war, the regiment received federal recognition. It was called to duty that following summer.

In the interim, word of how black laborers seeking to leave the rural South for the promised opportunities of the North were being detained and terrorized, appeared in black news weeklies. Such news aroused the emotions of Harlemites. Many of them had relatives trying to get North. And as the heat of their passions responded to the impassioned oratory of Marcus Garvey, a new hero was in the making.

On June 12, 1917, an inspired Garvey addressed a throng at Harlem's Bethel A.M.E. Church. It was indeed a memorable occasion for it marked Garvey's first solid impact upon an audience in the world's largest single black community. Nor was it destined to be his last.

Hubert H. Harrison, well known in Harlem for his writings and his lectures, had assembled a large audience at Bethel Church for the purpose of organizing the Liberty League. Harrison was a native of the Virgin Islands. He had worked in New York City as a postal clerk at the turn of the century. A Socialist scholar who studied assiduously, Harrison was a lecturer, who, when he was not addressing street corner crowds, spoke at his own "Harlem School of Social Science." As could be expected, Socialist Harrison was critical of established social, political, and economic patterns and practices.

Upon several occasions Booker T. Washington had been the target of some rather sharp Harrison criticism, at least two of which appeared in the form of letters written to the *New York Sun.* Dr. Washington, as has been said, maintained a national network of "friends" and supporters throughout the nation's black communities. His most faithful supporter in New York was the city's leading black Republican, Charles W. Anderson.

Mr. Anderson was a suave, cultured, and able politician. Through his work as a loyal Republican among blacks, and through the intervention of Dr. Washington with President Theodore Roosevelt, Charley Anderson reached his political peak in 1905. He was named Collector of Internal Revenue for the Second New York (Wall Street) District. When Anderson read Hubert Harrison's sharp criticism of his friend and benefactor in Alabama he went into action. In a very short time Harrison received notice of dismissal from his clerkship in the New York City Post Office.

Hubert Harrison, as James Weldon Johnson says in *Black Manhattan,* never knew whose influence brought about his firing. But, Socialist that he was, he knew that sinister forces opposed to his militant political stance had been at work against him. Instead of being intimidated into silence, Hubert Harrison became more set in his militancy. So, as he planned the meeting at Bethel A.M.E. Church and the formation of his Liberty League, he sought the most forceful personalities he could find as speakers. That is why Marcus Garvey was one of those whom Harrison invited to address that important mass meeting.

During the progress of the meeting the diminutive street speaker from Jamaica was called upon to "say a few words." Marcus Garvey was never a man of few words. Moreover, here, at long last, was his chance to share the platform with Harlem's most respected militant spokesman. The prestige that alone implied would surely not be lost upon the audience.

So Garvey pulled out all the stops. He was eloquence, fire, and massive black persuasion, all rolled into one, as he played the emotions and the intellect of the assemblage. He used all his magnetic selling powers in extolling the advantages of Hubert Harrison's proposal. For days afterward his performance was the talk of Harlem. He knew he had struck a sensitive community nerve and he did not delay in following up with an idea of his own. Here indeed was the place for Garvey to establish his own organization!

First, however, he would call a meeting. Having been reared in the Roman Catholic faith, Garvey, with letters of introduction from church officials in Jamaica, was able to secure Saint Mark's Roman Catholic Church in Harlem for his initial try. As a West Indian he counted upon fellow Caribbean Islanders for his earliest support.

But the first Garvey meeting was an inauspicious affair. Though the audience was sympathetic to his plans for industrial education for blacks, he was not cheered for his proposal to involve them in a global plan for redeeming Africa. Still, the doughty leader pushed forward with his idea and formed the New York Chapter of the Universal Negro Improvement Association. Robert H. Brisbane gives an apt description of the new mood created by Garvey among blacks as he began his work as head of the U.N.I.A. Says Brisbane:

> Garvey now decided that the time was ripe for him to try the Universal Negro Improvement Association on the American Negro. His stature as a race leader had risen swiftly in New York City. His doctrines were hailed in America, whereas they had been laughed at and rejected in Jamaica. Hence, he began to highlight the aims and ideals of the Association. The word "black," long used as an epithet even by jet-black Negroes themselves, was to be dignified. Garvey insisted that all men of African blood must refer to themselves as black men rather than as Negroes or colored men. The Negro's past in Africa, as little as was then known or thought of it, was to be glorified.

War activity was now slipping into high gear all over America. As has been mentioned, the demand for black army officers was increasing among leaders in black communities.

Joel A. Spingarn, head of the N.A.A.C.P., led a citizens' committee to Washington in the spring of 1917 to confer with army authorities on the possibilities. They returned home, as others before them had, thoroughly discouraged. Then a group of college students at Fisk, Atlanta, Howard, and Tuskegee began to agitate for officers' training facilities. Again Spingarn took up the matter with Washington.

This time General Leonard Wood promised that if the agitators could muster two hundred black candidates with college training, he would establish a training program for them. In May 1917 seven times two hundred black college men signed up to be trained as officers in the army of the United States. The ice was broken. Senate and House representatives numbering three hundred approved the idea, as did the N.A.A.C.P. And on October 15, 1917, 639 black army officers—106 captains, 204 second lieutenants, and 329 first lieutenants—received their commissions at Fort Des Moines, Iowa.

Liberal whites and establishment-oriented blacks were delighted. For them an important breakthrough had been accomplished, one that established a sizable number of black fighting men on a level not heretofore opened to them. That victory notwithstanding, things were a long way from racially peaceful on the civilian front. The commissioning of a few black officers was of little import to the masses of nondescript black working people occupying unpublicized jobs throughout the country. And in the turbulent intervening weeks the long night of the 1917 summer settled ominously over a nation at war overseas and prone to violence at home.

CHAPTER EIGHT

As MARCUS GARVEY proceeded to build the U.N.I.A., he encountered opposition that disrupted his initial plan. He had originally wanted to get the New York group moving sufficiently well in the direction of its goals to permit him to return to Jamaica and carry on the U.N.I.A. program there. But according to Amy Jacques Garvey's account, two of the New York officers were attempting to use the association for their own aggrandizement. By delivering large numbers of U.N.I.A. votes to the political parties of their respective choices, they hoped to reap a financial harvest.

Such tactics were, of course, contrary to the Garvey insistence that black people break from the old political patterns that had kept them subservient to whites. A schism quickly formed within the U.N.I.A. The Garvey opposition made full use of any and everything it could find to discredit the leader. They even managed to resurrect Garvey's difficulties in London with his mentor and former employer, Duse Mohamed Ali. But within several weeks Garvey had recreated a new group and was again on the way to forming a strong organization. When local politicians again tried to take over by creating another rift, a small group loyal to Garvey offered him a sound suggestion.

Why, they asked, should Garvey's powers over the New York group be limited? As it stood, Garvey, while president of the parent body of the U.N.I.A. in Jamaica, was no more than an organizer of the New York group. Why shouldn't he become the *official* head of the U.N.I.A. in New York? Never hampered by modesty, Garvey quickly seized the suggestion and had himself elected President-General of the New York body. Then the Association was swiftly incorporated, in accordance with New York State law, as a membership corporation. E. D. Cronon in *Black Moses* reports that under the new arrangement, Garvey claimed a membership increase of more than two thousand in three weeks. The rival group, meanwhile, had fallen prey to the rapacious politicos who stripped it of its money, and subsequently, of any potential force it might have had. With its position now more stable, the U.N.I.A., along with the rest of black America, turned attention to a series of disturbing events, occurring around the nation.

Attention riveted upon East Saint Louis, which had overnight become a symbol of racist mob rule. White workers in that little southwestern Illinois city, frightened and angered by the hiring of blacks in factories handling government contracts, went on a rampage. On July 2, 1917, East Saint Louis's black men, women, and children were set upon by enraged whites. For practically the entire day the black section was under the attack of arsonists whose purpose was to destroy completely the area with everyone and everything in it.

The grisly plan nearly succeeded. Militiamen sent in to

quell the massacre did little more than stand by and watch. Close observers believe that the pillage and death far exceeded the official findings of the attorney general that "eight whites were killed. . . . Many—over 100—Negroes were shot or beaten up, or both. . . . Over 250 buildings were burned." Saunders Redding asserts in *The Lonesome Road* that at least one hundred black persons died (some cooked alive in their burning buildings), six thousand left homeless, and property damage amounted to half a million dollars.

A little later in the month of July, Harlem leaders joined with the N.A.A.C.P. in staging a parade of silent protest. Ten thousand persons marched in silent and orderly fashion down New York's Fifth Avenue in what James Weldon Johnson later described in *Black Manhattan* as "one of the strangest and most impressive sights New York has witnessed." And as they marched, black boy scouts passed out leaflets to spectators captioned: "Why We March." Said the message:

> We march because by the Grace of God and the force of truth, the dangerous, hampering walls of prejudice and inhuman justices must fall.
>
> We march because we want to make impossible a repetition of Waco, Memphis, and East Saint Louis, by rousing the conscience of the country and bringing the murderers of our brothers, sisters and innocent children to justice.
>
> We march because we deem it a crime to be silent in the face of such barbaric acts.
>
> We march because we are thoroughly opposed to Jim-Crow Cars, Segregation, Discrimination, Disfranchisement, LYNCHING, and the host of evils that are forced on us. It is time that the spirit of Christ should be manifested in the making and execution of laws.
>
> We march because we want our children to live in a better land and enjoy fairer conditions than have fallen our lot.

> We march in memory of our butchered dead, the massacre of the honest toilers who were removing the reproach of laziness and thriftlessness hurled at the entire race. They died to prove our worthiness to live. We live in spite of death shadowing us and ours. We prosper in the face of the most unwarranted and illegal oppression.

Marcus Garvey knew all about the grievances and the atrocities. He no doubt witnessed the "Silent Protest Parade." And while he was in full accord with the desire of black leadership to put an end to all racist-inspired injustices, he did not believe the most effective ways of doing it were being used. Indeed he made his feelings on that quite clear when, in his *Philosophy and Opinions* he defined power.

Said Garvey:

> Power is the only argument that satisfies man . . . It is the commercial and financial powers of the United States of America that make her the greatest banker in the world. Hence it is advisable for the Negro to get power of every kind. POWER in education, science, industry, politics, and higher government. That kind of power that will stand out signally, so that other races and nations can see, and if they will not see, then FEEL.
>
> Man is not satisfied or moved by prayers or petitions, but every man is moved by that power of authority which forces him to do even against his will.

Those words of the man from Jamaica were recalled to memory as yet another shockingly sensational outbreak in Houston, Texas, again rocked the country. It was September 1917. The men of the black Twenty-fourth Infantry had become embroiled in a fight with a group of white citizen hecklers. Because the latter would settle for nothing less than complete victory and mastery over the black soldiers, they kept the pot of discontent brewing with harassment and invective. Meanwhile, army authorities disarmed the black soldiers, leaving them vulnerable to continued civilian attacks.

Finally, maddened with frustration and rage, the black soldiers turned upon their tormentors. Breaking into the army arsenal, they seized arms and killed seventeen whites. Their trial was extraordinarily swift. Thirteen were hanged for murder and mutiny; forty-one imprisoned for life, and forty held, pending further investigation. Black America was dismayed and outraged. Whatever faith it might have had in white American justice hit an all-time low. And the angry black press hailed the thirteen executed men of the Twenty-fourth Regiment as national martyrs.

The end of summer surely had brought no end to race hatred. None was more conscious of that grim fact than the nation's leaders in Washington, D.C. Some dramatic official move, they decided, would have to be made. And it was.

On October 5, 1917, Newton D. Baker, America's Secretary of War, announced a startling appointment. Emmett J. Scott, who for eighteen years had served the late Booker T. Washington as confidential secretary, was named a Special Assistant to the Secretary of War. Scott, a man who would be regarded today by most whites as a moderate black leader, was to be Baker's "confidential advisor in matters affecting the interests of ten million Negroes in the United States and the part they are to play in connection with the present war."

Most black leaders of the day hailed the appointment. Dean Kelly Miller of Howard University regarded it "as the most significant appointment that has yet come to the colored race." He and others were pleased that Scott, a man much like themselves, was selected to be the "Negro expert" of the day. They accepted the fact that Scott's opinions on every conceivable area affecting life in America's black communities were eagerly solicited (and often quoted) by whites. And along with many other blacks they approved of the scope of Scott's duties.

The new black appointee was to urge equal and fair treatment of blacks in the Selective Service System. He was to investigate the scores of cases of discrimination against blacks in war industries and in all branches of the armed services where blacks were permitted to serve. And his was the responsibility of supplying the Committee on Public Information with news of black soldiers and civilians for the duration of the war.

In short, Emmett J. Scott was hired to do the job white authority could not do, or, more accurately, *did not want to have done thoroughly*. Not that Scott was incapable. He was as capable as any other intelligent black American who knew the pros and cons of white racism and how it operates. But Dr. Scott, protégé and confidant of Booker T. Washington, was thoroughly "safe" and "dependable." His appointment, indeed unique for its time, lent a cloak of respectable concern for black Americans to Uncle Sam. And Uncle Sam, under heavy criticism from within and without the nation, was in need of such a mantle.

Even the normally defiant W. E. B. Du Bois waxed patriotic. He wrote:

> Close ranks! Let us, while this war lasts, forget our own special grievances and close our ranks shoulder to shoulder with our own white fellow citizens. . . . We make no ordinary sacrifice, but we make it gladly and willingly with our eyes lifted to the hills.

Marcus Garvey read and snorted with contempt. He had long been at odds with such a point of view.

Before the month of October had passed another incident involving black servicemen exploded in the pages of the press. And Special Assistant Emmett J. Scott was sent scurrying to Dixie to see what could be done to patch up the trouble. This time, a member of the aforementioned black Fifteenth Regiment of New York City was involved. That unit had been stationed in Spartanburg, South Carolina under the command of Colonel William Hayward.

A select group of servicemen, the Fifteenth was more than ordinarily proud of the general caliber of its personnel. One of them was a talented and highly regarded musician who served as the Regiment's debonair drum major. His name was Noble Sissle and he held the rank of sergeant. One day Sergeant Sissle entered the lobby of a local Spartanburg hotel in quest of New York newspapers for himself and other members of his unit. The clerk and lobby hangers-on, annoyed at the sight of the handsome young black man in the uniform of the United States Army, grew edgy. Edginess exploded into belligerence as they heard the soldier speak in clear, crisp, Yankee English.

"Take-your-hat-off-in-here NIGGER!" The clerk's command was a deliberate and menacing drawl. Sissle's rejoinder that he was not obliged to remove his hat, barely had a chance to pass his lips. When the battered Sergeant Sissle finally picked himself off the pavement outside the hotel lobby he located his hat in the gutter nearby. Both he and word of what had happened quickly got back to camp. There it took the intervention of officers to prevent the men from returning to town to lay waste to the hotel.

Shortly thereafter the Fifteenth Regiment was moved to

Long Island, New York, where further altercations with southern white troops ensued. Within a matter of weeks the black unit, its training for war far from complete, was shipped to the fighting front in France.

(It should be noted parenthetically here that U.S. Army authorities, stumped as to what to do with its first black fighting unit, found a strange solution to the dilemma. It attached the Fifteenth Regiment as a combat unit to the Eighth Corps of the Fourth *French* army. And thus, under French command, the first American soldier to receive the Croix de Guerre was Sergeant Henry Johnson of the famous "Fifteenth.")

But news of the attack on Sissle did not go begging for national publicity. And again the black community was outraged. Nor did Emmett Scott's plea to black servicemen to be careful not to disgrace the army or the race by repeating the Houston tragedy diminish black anger among simple, hard-working, folk. They had few illusions. Nothing in their experience had led them to believe there were good things in store for them in the humdrum, segregated world of their daily existence. These were the people from whose numbers Marcus Garvey was drawing his following. And the roulette wheel of daily human events was spinning more and more in favor of the President-General of the U.N.I.A.

That Garvey's movement was gaining rapidly was due in no small measure to his having established an organ through which the U.N.I.A. could reach many people. As a former printer and a contributor to Duse Mohamed's magazine, Garvey thoroughly understood the propaganda value of the printed page. Between late 1918 and early 1919 he founded his own newspaper, *The Negro World.*

It was a good newspaper. Even those who disagreed with

its founder admitted as much. No less a Garvey critic than the Jamaican poet Claude McKay once wrote in a magazine piece titled, "Garvey as a Negro Moses," that *The Negro World* was "the best edited colored weekly in New York." Within eighteen months *The Negro World* claimed a circulation of fifty thousand, and as it continued to grow it published sections in Spanish and French for black readers of the Caribbean and Latin America.

One of the remarkable features of Garvey's paper was that it succeeded in spite of its refusal to accept advertisements promoting hair straighteners and skin bleaches. Such was certainly not true of black newsweeklies elsewhere in the nation. The schizophrenic way in which they fought in news columns and editorials for black dignity, while simultaneously enticing black readers to look as white as possible, was normal procedure. And while such inconsistency puzzled and amused white readers, it worried most black readers not one whit. Indeed the latter were constantly scanning the pages of black weeklies in search of "miracle" products that could at least more quickly alleviate the curse of black skin and nappy hair.

The *Chicago Defender* leaned heavily upon advertisers of hair straighteners and skin bleaches. And a page from the *Baltimore Afro-American* for 1919 reveals a two-column ad for Nu-Life hair grower with an illustration of a woman having below-shoulder-length straight black hair. To the left of that is another two-column ad for Black and White Ointment. With the accent more heavy on white than black, the ad, showing a woman of light skin, entices the viewer with this caption:

> Race Men And Women Protect Your Future By Using Black And White Ointment. See What It Did For Viola Steele.

Miss Steele obviously is the name applied to the model whose pleased and not too black countenance looks appealingly out at the reader.

While Garvey's paper did carry ads for hair grower, the emphasis was on hair *growth* rather than hair straightening. It was the ad in the black press extolling the superior advantages of the light skin over the dark one that stirred in Garvey unpleasant memories of Jamaica's color caste. So disturbed was he that he found it difficult to remember that as far as American whites were concerned, it made little basic difference how light black folks' skin happened to be. Whites weren't about to accept them anyway. Moreover, the majority of black Americans were, and are, dark, not fair. Small wonder, then, that *The Negro World* so quickly found a readership among the ordinary folk in black communities of America.

As *The Negro World* attracted more readers, Garvey's preoccupation with blackness as *the* virtue became more and more apparent. Although that had great appeal to the emotions of readers whose only escape from complete obscurity lay in embracing a doctrine of black chauvinism, it limited the paper's scope. Before 1919 was over, however, Garvey had brought in William H. Ferris, a man of light complexion and a Harvard graduate, as his newspaper's editor. It was a good move. Ferris in turn brought in others, including socialist, Hubert H. Harrison, educator William Pickens, John E. Bruce, T. Thomas Fortune, and Eric Walrond. Though these were not all men of light skin, their contributions as intelligent columnists did much to promote unity among the peoples of African ancestry.

The paper's slogan, "One Aim, One Destiny," then became more meaningful to those who produced it and read it.

And during this period of its existence, *The Negro World* became a potent force. Robert Brisbane in *The Negro Vanguard*, asserts that whatever doubts one may have about Garvey's claims for the U.N.I.A., "By 1919 *The Negro World* had become the most widely read Negro weekly in America, if not in the world."

Actually, the paper was well known throughout the world. Considered by many colonial governments a seditious and dangerous organ, *The Negro World* was supressed in such places as Barbados, Trinidad, and British Guiana. The white rulers of the Italian, French, and Portugese colonies in Africa likewise banned the Garvey paper. In Dahomey a person caught reading *The Negro World* could be sentenced to prison for the remainder of his life.

What manner of news content could evoke such reactions? Well, the paper, numbering from twelve to sixteen pages, carried articles by Garvey himself in which he propounded his personal views. There was always something on African history or on the historic exploits of men of African descent. And there were the constant Garvey reminders of the highly developed and regal splendors of Africa at a time when Europeans were living in barbaric savagery.

News of what the various U.N.I.A. branches were doing contributed to the Association's being able to unify its overall program. John E. Bruce, who wrote "Bruce Grit's Column," was especially popular with the readers, and there was the page reserved for readers who felt the need to air their views. Doubtless, the most "objectionable" features of *The Negro World*, those that disturbed officialdom here in America and elsewhere, were the shafts and barbs deflating the vaunted superiority of whites and exalting that of blacks. That was deemed "racism" by the Department of Justice and the Lusk Committee of New York.

In two reports on Negro radicalism in 1919 and 1920 *The Negro World* was cited by the aforementioned agencies. It is interesting to note here that both citations followed a particularly violent period in the United States. Called "The Red Summer of 1919," we shall have a glimpse of those dreadful weeks in the next few pages.

Still it would be unfair not to say, first, that *The Negro World* survived those official attacks. In fact, it continued to be published weekly through 1933.

CHAPTER NINE

IT WAS more than mere coincidence that tied the continually rapid rise of Marcus Garvey in New York to the summer events of 1919. Black poet James Weldon Johnson had been the first to call that trying period the "Red Summer of 1919." What he referred to was the rash of race riots that covered the entire nation. Several of them were terribly serious.

Johnson, a man of judicial temperament, was not given to coining emotional phrases. An excellent scholar, lyricist, and teacher, he had also served for seven years in the American consular service in Venezuela and Nicaragua. His appointment in 1920 as the first black executive secretary of the National Association for the Advancement of Colored People attested to the esteem in which he was held. Who, then, was better qualified than the dignified Floridian to recognize and aptly label racism run amuck?

With the ending of World War I and the return of servicemen to civilian life, tensions accelerated. The need for jobs increased as the booming war years yielded to peacetime recession, and black men became white men's competitors in the labor market. Moreover, the mere sight of black males returning home in the garb of U.S. fighting men disturbed large numbers of whites. Accustomed to relegating black men to a subservient role, whites were now confronted with a new black image. Would this be a Frankenstein monster bent upon destroying its creator? It was a terrifying thought. And the touchy panic button required very little pressure indeed to set off a holocaust.

Some historians have estimated the number of race riots during the Red Summer at more than twenty. Doubtless there were quite that many around the nation but not all of them were of major import. Seven, however, were. And it is worth noting that two of the three bloodiest of them did not occur in the Deep South. The historic city of Charleston, South Carolina, is where it all started on a warm Saturday night in early May.

Following a common southern practice, two white sailors shot a black civilian to death for some obscure reason never fully explained. The murder touched off a battle between white navy men and black citizens. Blacks were attacked indiscriminately by white sailors, who charged into their district, seizing and beating victims as they looted black-owned stores. Before marines restored calm, two blacks had died and nearly twenty were wounded. White casualties numbered seven sailors and one policeman wounded.

Longview, Texas, a far smaller, east Texas town than Charleston, was the scene of a more complex riot a couple of months later. The basic trouble centered on the formation of the Negro Business Men's League by Dr. C. P. Davis. The action was taken to put an end to the exploitation of black cotton farmers by whites. The latter were further infuriated by Dr. Davis's organizing of black cooperative stores.

The spark setting off the explosion, however, was the more prosaic lynching of a young black man for allegedly raping a white woman. When the locally distributed *Chicago Defender* carried the news story that the woman and the lynched man had actually been lovers, local whites were enraged. They believed the story had reached the *Defender* through a black local teacher, Samuel Jones, and a mob formed to find and punish Jones. They got him, beat him badly, and ordered him to leave town.

Jones, instead, hid out in the home of Dr. C. P. Davis. When whites learned where he was, they formed another mob and went to the Davis home determined to finish him off. As they rushed the house a hail of gunfire erupted from inside, killing several whites outright. Such an unexpected show of fight in a community 30 percent black, filled whites with the desperation of frightened rage. For several hours they continued to flog blacks and burn their homes and shops until the following day, July 12, when the Texas Rangers quelled the fighting.

Attacks by whites on blacks in Knoxville, Tennessee, Omaha, Nebraska, and Washington, D.C., resulted from accusations of rape lodged against black men by white women. But in Chicago it was the drowning of a black boy in a beach fracas with whites that ignited a six-day battle. Thirty-six died and the number of injuries exceeded five hundred. At the root of the Chicago disaster was the need of housing by residents in the overcrowded Black Belt and the resistance of whites as blacks spilled over into white neighborhoods.

Meanwhile, the riot in Phillips County, Arkansas, was the outgrowth of an attempt by black farmers to organize against economic strangulation by white landlords. As the black farmers were meeting in their church, they were fired upon by a sheriff and his deputy. In the commotion that followed the sheriff was killed and the church destroyed by fire. That was not the end of it. Scores of blacks began to be hunted and killed like animals. Moreover, following the custom of fixing the total blame upon the victims, seventy-nine blacks were indicted and tried on charges of murder and insurrection.

R. H. Brisbane reports in *The Black Vanguard* that their trial was attended by an armed white mob, signaling the type of verdict it expected. The all-white jury condemned "twelve to death and sixty-seven to prison terms ranging from twenty years to life." But for the intervention of the N.A.A.C.P. the sentences would have been carried out. As it was, all seventy-nine were freed after a legal battle lasting five years.

While the Red Summer was a distressful period for America as a whole, it proved to be a bonanza for Marcus Garvey and his movement. For those at the very rock bottom of the nation's social and economic heap, the Garveyan ideas held a special appeal as they saw others, like themselves, lynched and set upon by mobs of whites. That the guardians of the law often looked the other way as such injustices piled upon each other only firmed the growing conviction that Garvey was right.

There were, of course, a number of Garvey critics, among them those who labeled him a foreign rabble-rouser. In a succeeding chapter some of the growing opposition to Garvey will be carefully reviewed. However, Garvey himself, ever aware of his detractors, never failed to mention their tactics against him. In addresses to the black masses he declared that "great ideals know no nationality." And using that as a theme, Garvey had this to say, as recorded in *Philosopy and Opinions of Marcus Garvey.*

> My enemies in America have done much to hold me up to public contempt and ridicule, but have failed. They believe that the only resort is to stir up national prejudice against me, in that I was not born within the borders of the United States of America.
>
> I am not in the least concerned about such a propaganda, because I have travelled the length and breadth of America and I have discovered that among the fifteen million of my race, only those who have exploited and lived off the ignorance of the masses are concerned with where I was born. The masses of the people are looking for leadership, they desire sincere, honest guidance in racial affairs. As proof of this I may mention that the largest number of members in the Universal Negro Improvement Association (of which I am President-General) are to be found in America, and are native born Americans. . . . All intelligent people know that one's nationality has nothing to do with great ideals and principles. If because I am a Jamaican the Negro should not accept the principle of race rights and liberty, or the ideal of a free and independent race; then you may as well say that because Jesus was a Nazarene the outside world should not accept His Doctrine of Christianity, because he was an "alien." Because Martin Luther was born in Germany, the world should not accept the doctrine of Protestantism.

That was Marcus Garvey, the internationalist speaking in truly catholic terms. Having chosen Catholicism, though by no means dominated by it, Garvey understood the appeal of the church to oppressed masses everywhere.

His growing U.N.I.A. membership in the United States was, as he claimed, predominantly native born. Not only were they poor working class but they were a *church-going* people. Garvey knew that the black church in America of 1919 was the *only* place its membership could call its very own.

Garvey's reference therefore to Jesus of Nazareth, along with his recognition of the Protestantism of Martin Luther struck home. Since the majority of black Americans are Protestants and their ministers could either help or hinder Garvey in his quest for U.N.I.A. strength from their flocks, he wisely chose to woo them.

Amy Jacques Garvey recalls the southern woman, who after joining the U.N.I.A. remarked, "Garvey is giving my people backbones where they had wishbones." The *Negro World*, with its weekly messages from Garvey promising hope and a fuller and more prosperous life for black people, was beginning to get around the country. And where it found fertile ground the seeds of Garveyan thought sprang alive in the form of new and burgeoning divisions of the Universal Negro Improvement Association.

It happened as a natural progression of events that along with an increase in U.N.I.A. membership there occurred also an expansion of its program. Following the close of World War I, Marcus Garvey had voiced an idea that caught the fancy of a sizable segment of the black community. Why not, he proposed, establish a black-owned and-operated steamship company. Prompted by the various reports reaching him of discrimination against black exporters, seamen and passengers alike, the idea was basically sound. Garvey had listened carefully as African seamen told of the tons of cargo left to rot on African wharves by white steamship companies. That occurred, his informants declared, whenever their African owners spoke up for better prices. Garvey lost no time. Soon his readers and listeners were, themselves, thinking and talking about the Black Star Steamship Line. Soon this new vision beckoning entry into the heretofore closed world of commerce took possession of U.N.I.A. members. And they responded. Money to support the project began to rain into the treasuries of the U.N.I.A. divisions.

Finally on June 16, 1919, the New York Assistant District Attorney, Edwin P. Kilroe, summoned Marcus Garvey to his office. Kilroe told Garvey he would either have to establish the Black Star Line as a "legitimate business enterprize" or stop collecting money. Reports on that meeting in Kilroe's office differ. E. D. Cronon asserts in *Black Moses* that Garvey complied "by securing a broad charter of incorporation from the State of Delaware, whose friendly laws had long attracted businessmen and industrial enterpreneurs." With such a charter the Black Star Line could operate its own ships and carry freight, passengers, and mail to any part of the globe.

Amy Jacques Garvey, however, makes no mention of Kilroe's offer of an alternative to closing down the operation. She states that Kilroe flatly ordered her husband to "close down the Black Star Line" and that "Garvey retorted that he had no intention to do so." Whatever actually took place in the District Attorney's office did not mark the first and last summons Garvey was to receive from there.

Garvey quickly formed a corporation. The Black Star Line capital value was fixed at five hundred thousand dollars with one hundred thousand shares of stock having a par value of five dollars per share. Garvey, himself, with four others, held forty shares of capital stock, getting the enterprise off to a start with an official capital of one thousand dollars. The sale of stock was limited to black persons; and through the pages of *The Negro World* it was made clear that no one person could own more than two hundred shares.

While this was in progress Garvey held U.N.I.A. meetings in a large auditorium he had bought in Harlem. Located at 114 West 138th Street, the structure, originally constructed as the foundation of a church, was roofed and completed as an auditorium. Seating capacity was six thousand and Garvey called it Liberty Hall. It was from the rostrum of Liberty Hall that Garvey would later thunder his messages to enthusiastic audiences. And Liberty Hall became the symbol of the general spirit of the Garveyan philosophy. Soon other Liberty Halls took root in other places where Marcus Garvey and his program had a following.

The use that Garvey made of his platform at Liberty Hall, and his newspaper, enabled him to promote the Universal Negro Improvement Association and its ventures. During 1919 the Black Star Line received more than its share of publicity. Many outsiders, not fully acquainted with Garvey's basic reason for founding the Black Star Line, did not think of it as a legitimate steamship company, hauling freight and passengers. Garvey, the visionary, saw his dream child not only as a means of providing nonsegregated services to black clients but also as a lucrative venture by blacks into intercontinental maritime commerce. Still, in the public mind the purchase of steamships by the U.N.I.A. was coupled only with Garvey's call to redeem Africa for Africans.

In such a context, Garvey's Black Star Line loomed merely as the means of transporting boatloads of black folks from America back to "darkest Africa." Much as the idea may have appealed to many whites, who saw it as a means of ridding the nation of a "problem," it was not Garvey's prime reason for establishing it. And while the redemption of Africa for peoples of African descent was, as will be seen, a part of the Garveyan philosophy, it was not to be equated solely and exclusively with the Black Star Line. Here, in part and in

Garvey's own words, is what he said, as he sought stockholders for his steamship company:

> The Black Star Line Corporation presents to every Black Man, Woman, and Child the opportunity to climb the great ladder of industrial and commercial progress. If you have ten dollars, one hundred dollars, or one or five thousand dollars to invest for profit, then take out shares in the Black Star Line, Inc. This corporation is chartered to trade on every sea and all waters. The Black Star Line will turn over large profits and dividends to stockholders, and operate to their interest even whilst they will be asleep.

Skeptics and critics saw in the proposal just another "hustle," another scheme to bilk the gullible poor out of their meager resources. The buying of a fleet of SHIPS? Whoever heard of a black man getting enough money from his people to buy *one* ship, let alone more? So the gossip went until in September 1919 Garvey announced through a circular that the first ship of the Black Star Line would be berthed at 135th Street and North River. Moreover she would be flying the Black Star Line flag and for a dollar per person she could be viewed by those caring to board her.

Within forty-eight hours Assistant District Attorney Kilroe again called Garvey into his office. It seemed that the announcement had gone out before the actual purchase of the ship had been consummated. If any stock had been sold as a result of the published circular, the company could be brought up on charges of commercial fraud. The very next day Garvey and his aides of the Black Star Line completed their negotiations for the purchase of the company's first steamship. It was September 17, 1919, and the ship, a small freighter, was named the S.S. *Yarmouth.*

She was not a new ship, having been built thirty-two years previously. Cronon writes in *Black Moses* that the price for the *Yarmouth* "was a stiff $165,000, of which the company paid $16,500 down, with another $83,500 due when the Black Star Line took possession. The balance was to be spread over ten equal monthly installments of $6,500 each at six percent interest."

The *Yarmouth's* owner was one W. L. Harriss, a New York cotton broker. Known in business circles as a shrewd Yankee horse trader, Harriss resolved, when apprised of the amount of money Garvey was collecting, that he would make a financial killing. His determination was greatly assisted by Garvey and his board of directors, who knew as much about ships as they did about interplanetary space travel. Most of all, however, Harriss was ably assisted by Garvey's black, double-dealing ship's captain, Joshua Cockbourne.

When Garvey and his aides sought the advice of Captain Cockbourne as to the seaworthiness of the *Yarmouth*, the wily seaman assured them that she was a good buy. For such testimony he had (as was later revealed) received a commission of $1,600 from the ship brokerage firm that handled the transaction. Actually the *Yarmouth* was not a seaworthy vessel, and Cockbourne and Harriss knew it.

When the Black Star Line had difficulty making its first installment payment, Harriss arranged an easier payment schedule. The price for that consideration was an added $3,500! In addition, Harriss and his North American Steamship Corporation were to retain ownership of the *Yarmouth* until she was paid for, though Garvey's Company could operate it. They could even put it in the hands of an all-black crew—for another cash consideration.

Garvey, unaware then of Cockbourne's shady character,

put him in command of the *Yarmouth.* Then declaring that he would rename the ship the S.S. *Frederick Douglass,* he announced that it would soon sail for the West Indies. But there was still a serious snag. The Black Star Line had difficulty getting sufficient insurance, and owner Harriss would not let her sail without it. Little of the behind-the-scenes difficulty was known to the general U.N.I.A. membership and the public at large.

The public did, however, read in Abbott's influential *Chicago Defender,* Robert Abbott's scathing words for this latest Garvey foray. The Windy City's swelling Black Belt, still smarting from its earlier race riot, was ripe for Garvey's thundering invective against white oppression. A Chicago division of the U.N.I.A. was formed and Garvey had gone there as its number one speaker. When the Jamaican announced the purchase of the S.S. *Yarmouth,* wealthy Robert Abbott grew scornful. He intimated that Garvey had come upon the scene much as had previously described King Sam of Oklahoma.

Garvey's response was to institute a huge lawsuit against Abbott. He received a token settlement. When Garvey, in promoting the sale of Black Star stock in Chicago, called Abbott a traitor to the race and followed that with unflattering comments in *The Negro World,* Abbott sued for libel. He proved himself a better litigator than Garvey. Moreover, according to E. D. Cronon's report in *Black Moses,* Garvey was arrested after that Chicago speech, "for selling stock illegally, a development no doubt inspired by Abbott." Back in New York Garvey met more trouble. This time it was a personal assault and it came very close to costing him his life.

CHAPTER

TEN

NEWS STORIES commenting upon exemplary human behavior, when they appear at all, rarely receive more than casual coverage. Antisocial behavior, on the other hand, is the stuff of which headlines are made. When such involves homicide or attempted homicide, the headlines become sensational. Truth becomes obscured in the maze of lurid phrases describing the deed and the principals involved therein. Persons who, prior to such involvement, were completely obscure suddenly become household names as flamboyant reports of what they did or what was done to them, are accepted as gospel. Such an occurrence took place one October day in 1919.

Reports of the attempted assassination of Marcus Garvey vary. Those of E. D. Cronon and Amy Jacques Garvey, however, seem most pertinent here. In *Black Moses*, Cronon reveals that George Tyler, described as demented, entered the 135th Street Harlem office of Marcus Garvey and began to argue with Garvey about a debt of twenty-five dollars. As the argument mounted, Tyler is alleged to have drawn a revolver and fired. Two shots, one in the leg and the other grazing the temple, inflicted minor wounds. Meanwhile, Amy Ashwood, trusted U.N.I.A. secretary and cofounder with Garvey of the association, is said to have flung herself between the two men, wrestling with the gunman and spoiling his aim.

Another version is given by Garvey's second wife, Amy Jacques Garvey, in her book, *Garvey and Garveyism.* Here there is no mention of an argument over money. The man merely loudly demanded to see Garvey, and the latter stepped from his upstairs office and identified himself. With that the attacker, looking up the stairs, shouted, "Well, I come to get you!" With that he produced a revolver and fired three shots. One creased the victim's head, drawing blood, while the other entered his leg. A vision of Garvey's mother advising her son to duck is credited with having saved his life. Meanwhile office assistants downstairs then rushed Tyler and held him until police made an arrest.

Both versions of the incident agree on one thing, however. Tyler, while in the custody of law officers, died suddenly from an alleged "fall or leap" before he could be brought to trial. Amy Jacques Garvey writes of his having confided to cell mates that he was hired to "get Garvey." The facts of Tyler's sudden death are still clouded.

There is little in the record, however, to cloud the fact that Garvey, the supreme showman, made the very most of his close brush with death. His head swathed in gleaming white bandages and his weight supported by crutches, the President-General of the Universal Negro Improvement Association presented a dramatic and heroic image indeed to his followers. Those who had teetered on the brink of indecision as they contemplated membership in the U.N.I.A.

teetered no longer. With their battered and plucky hero still shouting his war cry against the common foe, there was but one thing for them to do. Take up arms with him. Garvey's narrow escape and the publicity that emanated from it went a long way toward lifting him and his movement to heights of national prominence.

Quickly capitalizing upon his press notices, Garvey in 1919 founded the Negro Factories Corporation. He used his newspaper, *The Negro World,* to promote this new venture. Promising to "build and operate factories in the big industrial centers of the United States, Central America, the West Indies, and Africa to manufacture every marketable commodity," Garvey became the supersalesman. *The Negro World* further stated that the Negro Factories Corporation had been chartered by the State of Delaware, and was capitalized at one million dollars. This new corporation, it declared, was offering, "200,000 shares of common stock to the Negro race at par value of five dollars per share."

Garvey's plans for the Negro Factories Corporation were elaborate. He envisioned a steam laundry, millinery shop, men's hat factory, publishing house, restaurant, tailoring and dressmaking shop, and a chain of cooperative grocery stores. Even those who viewed many of the Jamaican's ideas with skepticism, favored his proposals for this new venture. That Garvey had actually gotten some of his projects under way, where their operation could be seen, was enough to convince the faithful of their leader's sincerity and unfailing ability.

Garvey simultaneously made an effort to organize the Universal Negro Improvement Association on a businesslike basis. Members were required to pay monthly dues of thirty-five cents. Twenty-five cents of that remained within the local divisions and the remaining ten cents went to the parent body, of which Garvey was the head. Still, the prompt collecting of dues could not be taken as a foregone conclusion. Because of delinquency the central treasury rarely had enough money to meet its obligations. Those included not only the paying of current expenses, but also the paying of promised sick and death benefits.

To poor working people any organization providing such practical aid in times of distress was the kind of organization they could believe in and support. Garvey knew that. Because he knew it so thoroughly, he constantly made an effort to keep the affairs of the U.N.I.A. running smoothly. To achieve that he was not loath to employ additional help. One such person was to play a significant role later in his life.

During the summer of 1919 one of the visitors to Liberty Hall was Amy Jacques, an attractive, highly trained young typist from Jamaica. Miss Jacques was a girlhood friend of Amy Ashwood, secretary of the U.N.I.A. Because Amy Ashwood had been one of the cofounders of the original U.N.I.A. in Kingston, and a constant booster of the Association, it was natural that her close associates would know about it. Amy Jacques's version of how she entered the U.N.I.A. differs from that of others who were also affiliated with it at the time. In *Garvey and Garveyism* she tells of having gone to a U.N.I.A. meeting one Sunday evening and of congratulating Mr. Garvey on his excellent oratory. She then relates how she questioned Garvey about his program and how the questions led to her being invited to his office for a more lengthy discussion. During the office visit Mr. Garvey, so the account goes, proceeded to show her about and to solicit her opinions.

According to her account, Amy Jacques was generally impressed by the potential the organization promised. She was at the same time aware of the many weaknesses in its structure. Especially in need of attention was the method of handling monies that came through the mails to the office of the U.N.I.A. Miss Jacques pointed that out to Garvey. He was grateful for her suggestion and asked if she would be willing to assist in the area of business management. Amy Jacques consented to devote evenings to establishing a better system than the one already in use. The arrangement suited Garvey well, inasmuch as his U.N.I.A. secretary, Amy Ashwood, had more than she could handle. Moreover, Miss Ashwood and Garvey were looking toward their forthcoming marriage.

In *Garvey and Garveyism,* Amy Jacques Garvey describes how she tackled the enormous task of improving the chaotic state of affairs in Garvey's office.

> A bonded mail clerk in the President-General's office received all letters. A mailing slip was pinned to any monetary enclosure, and particulars filled in: date, name, address, amount, whether cash, check or draft; to what department intended; if amount was to be divided among two or more of them, then three slips were attached. The treasurer received all monies and slips for the Black Star Line, and the chancellor received what was intended for the U.N.I.A., and *The Negro World.* They receipted the totals received. All letters were taken to the Secretary-General's department to be answered; if they were not routine, then he consulted with the President-General or the assistant.
>
> The treasurer kept in his safe stock books that were signed by president and secretary, and salesmen had to sign for same, and a record kept of all serial numbers. Cash returns were made to the treasurer, and the secretary rechecked the books. All checks were signed by president and treasurer, on the presentation of a voucher signed by president and secretary. The

head of every department sent in a daily report to the President-General's office, with remark column filled in if he had any recommendations to make. In this manner every cent that came in could be easily traced and Garvey did not handle any money.

With that plan as a guide Amy Jacques asserts she finally took over as Garvey's secretary. She writes later of having been "overworked" and having to arm herself with a hand gun because of threats from an office clerk. "He had lost a stock book of signed-up certificates and I had promptly reported this to the directors, who acted upon the matter."

Another version of how Amy Jacques came into the U.N.I.A. was given the writer by George A. Weston. Mr. Weston, who became a U.N.I.A. member in Boston in 1919, soon became an organizer and later U.N.I.A. Vice-President. Here is what he recalls of Amy Jacques and her entry in the U.N.I.A.

According to Weston, Amy Ashwood saw her girlhood friend, Miss Jacques, on the streets of Harlem one day. Amy Jacques was distraught, having been evicted from the place in which she had been living. Miss Ashwood took Miss Jacques in to meet Garvey. The meeting resulted in Amy Jacques's being employed by the U.N.I.A. as assistant secretary to her friend Amy Ashwood. Weston insists that the system of accounting for monies for which Amy Jacques Garvey takes credit was really inaugurated by Amy Ashwood herself. And even after her marriage to Mr. Garvey, Miss Ashwood continued to work as the U.N.I.A. secretary. However, Miss Jacques did serve as one of several secretaries to Garvey when he was on the road, according to Mr. Weston.

Meanwhile, Marcus Garvey and Amy Ashwood were married. It was Christmas 1919. The Yule season could hardly have been a more joyous one for the Garveys. Along with the bliss of being newly wed they saw the recently acquired S.S. *Yarmouth,* after a series of setbacks, make its first voyage. As has been already noted, the *Yarmouth* had been having an abundance of troubles. Still, during the winter of 1919–1920 the sale of Black Star Line stocks at five dollars a share rose phenomenally. Orders poured in from all over the United States and from as far away as Panama. Many were from hard-working black people with slim resources, but with such pride in the Garvey undertaking as willingly to make any sacrifice to make the Black Star Line succeed.

Little did most of them realize, however, the enormous work and responsibility involved in readying a ship for a voyage and actually putting her out to sea. Obviously Garvey and his directors didn't know either. To begin with, as soon as an old ship is purchased she must undergo a complete checkup to ascertain the extent of needed repairs. She must also have a skeleton crew aboard her. The duty of that crew is to make certain the ship is rendered seaworthy. Without such in-port servicing a ship may very well not pass the stiff inspection required before she can sail. A clearance permit and permits for the ports she will visit are issued only to inspected vessels. Nor is that all.

When a ship is contracted to carry cargo, she must sail as scheduled, otherwise she will be held in detention and her owner required to pay demurrage. And since ships earn their money carrying cargo rather than passengers, their owners have to be attentive to the regulations governing the handling of cargo.

Quite obviously the preparations preceding the three sailings of the *Yarmouth* fell far below those required of her. It has already been said that the *Yarmouth* was detained briefly for lack of proper insurance. What actually occurred was that the ship did cast off late in 1919 from her berth at 135th Street. She was loudly cheered by thousands of black well-wishers, many of whom had gladly paid one dollar each to go aboard and observe the crew making her ready. A little more than one hundred city blocks south, however, she was required to drop anchor. Black Star Line directors, having been informed that the ship carried insufficient insurance, rushed frantically about in the effort to clear the way for continuing the trip.

Several nights later, that barrier out of the way, the *Yarmouth* stealthily slipped out of New York waters. Cronon in *Black Moses* reports that her boilers were so bad, firemen were never able to raise more than sixty-five pounds of steam pressure. The ship, therefore, had to creep along at scarcely more than seven knots an hour.

Nevertheless Captain Cockbourne reported that along the way, particularly in Caribbean ports, enthusiasm for the ship ran high. The people at Havana, Cuba, he asserted, were especially anxious to pay the small fee permitting them aboard for a look. Doubtless the mere sight of the ship with her black captain boosted the sale of Black Star Line stock. And the *Yarmouth* returned to New York early in January 1920, carrying four hundred tons of log wood and a full roster of passengers.

Scarcely had Captain Cockbourne berthed his ship than he was ordered out with her again. An emergency had arisen and the *Yarmouth's* destination was Cuba. The emergency had been created by a law, the Volstead Act, introduced by Minnesota Congressman Andrew T. Volstead. Under the Volstead Act the sale of alcoholic beverages was prohibited in the United States. Whiskey distributors hastily sought ways of circumventing the law as they unloaded their supplies of spirits. The Pan Union Company approached the Black Star Line with a contract to haul a cargo of whiskey to Cuba where its sale was not prohibited. Time was of the essence. Could the new steamship company handle the order?

Though the *Yarmouth*'s old boilers had been wheezing, "NO, NO, NO!" all along that first voyage, the offer was too tempting to resist. Working with a happy feverishness, the crew managed to load the *Yarmouth* with its precious cargo of spirits and set sail before the deadline set by the Volstead Act. For what happened on that voyage, the following passage from *Black Moses* provides an interesting explanation.

> As before, the voyage was unexpectedly short. Eighty miles off Sandy Hook Light the *Yarmouth*'s engineer opened the sea cocks and an SOS was sent out that the ship was sinking. Under Cockbourne's orders, the crew immediately began to jettison the whiskey cargo, which was at once picked up by a swarm of small boats that for some unexplained reason had been following the *Yarmouth.* Considerably lightened, of whiskey but with bilges awash with sea water, the *Yarmouth* limped ingloriously back into port.

On a second try at getting the remaining whiskey to Cuba, the cargo's owner went into collusion with the ship's captain and the secretary of the Black Star Line. With a "tip" amounting to about $2,000 between them, Captain Cockbourne made port—but not before the *Yarmouth*'s crew had celebrated the final success by helping itself to a sizable portion of the cargo. When, several months later, the Pan Union Company was awarded a six-thousand-dollar judgment for its losses, the Black Star Line's assets could not cover the judgment.

Meanwhile, as the *Yarmouth* was making that ill-fated voyage with its cargo of booze, flamboyant claims were being made by *The Negro World*. Marcus Garvey grandly announced that the Black Star Line had grown from a corporation of half a million dollars to one of ten million dollars! U.N.I.A. members and supporters were ecstatic with pride. What *other* new enterprize had risen so high in so short a time?

The scholar and analyst W. E. B. Du Bois tried to induce reason as he made it clear that under the lenient laws of Delaware, the larger figure indicating a phenomenal jump in capitalization meant very little indeed.

In 1917 the fee for incorporating a five-million-dollar concern in Delaware was three hundred and fifty dollars. By paying an additional two hundred and fifty dollars the corporation could incorporate with ten million dollars authorized capital without having a cent of capital actually paid in. So the boost in the figure that Garvey used in his sales pitch had nothing whatever to do with added capital resources or the ability of the Black Star Line to meet its normal debts. But the faithful would listen to only that which they wanted to hear. And Garvey's assurances were the kind of music they craved most as they continued to pour their not inconsiderable collective resources into the coffers of the U.N.I.A.

Garvey left no opportunity to boost his program untried. Using the impressive figures for all they were worth, he ordered the *Yarmouth*'s Captain Cockbourne to return to New York from Cuba by way of Philadelphia and Boston. As the ship docked in those cities, U.N.I.A. speakers hawked Black Star Line stock with an extra-special fervor. Later there was much merriment among U.N.I.A. members and admirers in New York City. The old *Yarmouth,* meanwhile, wearily nudged into her berth, creaking and groaning under the weight of a cargo of coconuts.

CHAPTER ELEVEN

WITH THE advent of spring 1920 came also an expansion of the Black Star Line. Having declared an increase in the line's capitalization, Marcus Garvey felt he should indicate its growth in the most visible way. He cast about for, and found, two vessels to add to the Black Star fleet. The first was the S.S. *Shadyside,* an excursion boat which he acquired through Captain Leon R. Swift, a white ship-broker.

Garvey felt that the *Shadyside* would be a most welcome investment because as an excursion boat it could be used for pleasure. For many years black fraternal organizations and churches had been chartering boats for annual outings and boat rides during the summer season. Such trips provided the only chance many black families ever had to enjoy a ride up the Hudson River to cool, green, upstate recreation spots. The excursion boat lines they had used had always been white owned and operated. Here was the chance for them to make use of recreation facilities in which *they* had a share. Moreover, the *Shadyside* could, during the hard winter months, be sailed in Caribbean waters. True, the

Shadyside was nearly fifty years old when the Black Star Line Corporation bought her. With a weight of four hundred forty-four gross tons, she had been declared completely renovated according to an official report in April of 1920, and had passed local inspection. The price was thirty-five thousand dollars of which ten thousand dollars was made as the down payment. The balance was paid in monthly installments of two thousand dollars. Amy Jacques Garvey's account of the purchase asserts that the "vendor did not give the correct age of the vessel until a down payment was made, and a search of the records made by the lawyer, which revealed that it was older than represented."

In spite of her age, the *Shadyside* did make several trips up the Hudson during the summer of 1920. But she did not draw the crowds Garvey had earlier anticipated. One reason for that failure was the difficulty the Black Star Line had in securing a good upstate landing. Meanwhile, the ship's ancient boilers were consuming coal at an enormous rate.

Finally Captain Jacob Wise frankly told Garvey that the *Shadyside* was little more than a side-wheeler sponge, soaking up far more money than she was earning. The old vessel was reluctantly taken out of service at the end of the summer. A few months later during a severe ice storm one of her seams opened and the *Shadyside* sank to the bottom of the Hudson River.

In the interim the same Leon Swift who had sold the *Shadyside* to the Black Star Line offered yet another tempting maritime morsel to the corporation. The *Kanawah* was a small steam yacht that had once been the pleasure craft of oil tycoon Henry H. Rogers. It was the kind of boat that only an immensely wealthy man could afford to keep up. Surely it had never been designed to haul cargo. But Garvey and the inexperienced men around him obviously didn't know that. The outlandish asking price of sixty thounsand dollars was immediately settled upon by the corporation, who further agreed to spend an additional twenty-five thousand dollars to renovate it as a passenger and cargo vessel. Garvey then renamed it the *Antonio Maceo.*

As an economy measure and doubtless, too, as a means of keeping the new purchase easily in sight of Harlemites, Garvey had the repairs on the *Kanawah* done at her Harlem pier. Early in June 1920 it was announced that this newest addition to the fleet would make a celebration excursion up the Hudson. Tickets went on sale at $1.25. But the *Kanawah* had not been tested nor inspected and Garvey was warned by his black port captain, Adrian Richardson, to wait. That Garvey could not bring himself to do.

So the *Kanawah,* loaded with joyous passengers, had barely gotten into the waters of the Bronx, when a boiler explosion occurred, scalding one crew member seriously. After another month in port, the two hundred and twenty-five foot boat again set out for Cuba, under the command of wily Captain Swift. Again its boilers broke down in the Delaware River. Swift had the *Kanawah* towed to Norfolk, Virginia, where he wisely abandoned her. Later the *Kanawah* limped into New York under the command of Captain Adrian Richardson.

In spite of those setbacks, a meeting of Black Star Line stockholders held in Liberty Hall on July 20, 1920, was saturated in optimism. Before an auditorium packed with enthusiastic investors, Garvey was in his element. Admitting that the corporation was new and inexperienced, he assured the faithful that though theirs was a small steamship line they had much of which to be proud. The reading of the financial sheet by treasurer George Tobias revealed a capital of $610,860.00, representing sales of stock and subscriptions. Against that, $328,190.38 represented the outlay for the three steamers, *Yarmouth, Shadyside,* and *Kanawah,* along with payments for real estate and equipment. Another figure of $289,066.27 was listed merely as "organization expense." But the mood was too festive, what with ringing cheers following Garvey's fervent oratory, for anyone to question the wisdom of any transaction or the vagueness of any portion of the financial report.

The rapidity with which events had moved and the obvious confidence of those whose money was giving support to Garvey's plans was heady stuff indeed. A circular was printed reading:

> Three ships are now afloat and we must float one every three months until we build up a great Merchant Marine second to none.

Garvey then began to talk of purchasing a *Booker T. Washington* to ply the trade route between New York and South American ports. He didn't stop there. Before long, he asserted, there would be a *Phyllis Wheatley* flying the colors of the Black Star Line and sailing the seas between New York and the continent of Africa.

Such assurances, delivered with the crusader's zeal that was Marcus Garvey's style, were exactly what his followers wanted to hear—indeed, needed desperately to believe. For a long and discouraging time they had hoped for such a man who could bring to them a sense of their identity with successful ventures. Now their dreams seemed close to that grand reality they envisioned as they poured their resources into the Black Star Line and other related Garvey enterprizes.

Had they and Garvey, however, been aware of their accumulating financial difficulties and the disaster they courted, the story of the Garvey movement would doubtless have had to be considerably altered.

As informed observers constantly pointed out (and succeeding events proved them correct) the Black Star Line was never at any time of its existence in a healthy financial state. In spite of the large sums of money the organization collected, much of it was gobbled up by expensive repairs on the three decrepit vessels purchased at sky-high prices. Even with expert managerial skill the chances of emerging financially sound from such encounters would not have been good. And in the area of high finance neither Garvey nor his closest advisors, as is now all too apparent, were even remotely expert. Few, if any, had had any previous experience of the type this venture required.

The Black Star Line's treasurer, George Tobias, had been a railroad clerk. Elie Garcia, before becoming secretary of the line, had been a salesman of Black Star Line stock. And Jeremiah Certain, Vice-President of the line, came to his position from the bench of the cigar maker. His successor, Orlando M. Thompson, did have some experience in accounting. But Thompson, as future development will show, was not the most reliable of Garvey's aides. And as those who came into closest contact with him learned, Garvey's personal vanity had to be constantly catered to. Loyalty to him or at least the appearance of it, superceded both competence and integrity.

Coupled with Garvey's ignorance of correct business procedure was his suspiciousness of others. Because he found it difficult to trust anyone, he insisted upon being "the big-I-am," a trait that prevented him from listening carefully to those who could see the flaws in what he was attempting. Marcus Garvey was a difficult man indeed, as Black Star Line directors soon learned. Two vice-presidents, four secretaries, and three assistant secretaries joined and left the Black Star Line in less than three years.

To wear well with Garvey one had to be either the strong silent type or a yes-man. One could be thoroughly competent and honest and work for Mr. Garvey. Or one could be as limited as a one-legged man at a kicking tournament and as thieving as a pickpocket in a brothel full of inebriates. Whatever his basic leanings were, if he knew how to cope smoothly with the Garvey ego he could make it big with the little Jamaican. And what a great pity that was, for it allowed the onus of dishonesty to fall upon Garvey himself. With all his glaring shortcomings, few, if any, of Garvey's many critics ever seriously questioned the man's personal sincerity, dedication, and honesty.

It was during the month of May 1920 that the Executive Council of the U.N.I.A. decided to send a delegation to Liberia. Its purpose was to negotiate with the Liberian Government regarding black American colonization in that oldest West African republic. There was an urgency about the matter, since passports could not be easily obtained in a hurry, and the U.N.I.A. wanted a report to present to the delegates in the forthcoming convention in August. Fortunately Elie Garcia, with his Haitian passport, was ready and able to go. U.N.I.A. officials were delighted.

Garcia's letter to President Charles D. B. King of Liberia was polite and to the point. It read in part:

> It is the intention of the U.N.I.A. to establish trade routes through a line of steamships, etc., to encourage emigration to build up the country, to transfer its Headquarters to Liberia,

to bring with it medical and scientific units, etc. Therefore the Organization asks for written assurance that every facility will be given it to procure lands for business, agriculture, and industrial purposes. In return the Organization with its vast membership will lend financial and moral support to the Government to help her out of her present economic plight.

The idea of American colonization in Africa was not new. Carter G. Woodson made that clear in *The Negro in our History*. Said Dr. Woodson:

> In the proportion as the Negroes showed evidence of plotting insurrections in protest against the ever-increasing encroachment of slavery the idea of colonization became more pronounced in the minds of the slaveholding class. It grew in the minds of free Negroes, moreover, in the proportion as they were forced by law to leave the South for centers in the North.

Woodson then proceeded to designate Paul Cuffee, black shipowner and skipper of Massachusetts, as having made the first actual effort at taking black Americans back to Africa. Cuffee transported thirty-eight colonists in his own ship and established them on the West African coast in 1815. Liberia itself had been established as a colony by the American Colonization Society, gaining its official independence in 1848. But as Woodson stated, even though the idea of colonization had the support of an unusually large number of northern and southern American men of influence, "it failed to carry out the desired object of taking the free Negroes over to Africa."

When, seventy-two years later, the U.N.I.A. approached Liberia with its proposal it received the following response from Edwin Barclay, Liberian Secretary of State.

The President directs me to say in reply to your letter of June 8th setting forth the objects and purposes of the Universal Negro Improvement Association that the Government of Liberia, appreciating as they do the aims of your Organization as outlined by you, have no hesitancy in assuring you that they will afford the Association every facility legally possible in effectuating in Liberia its industrial, agricultural and business projects.

Garvey's man in Liberia, Elie Garcia, however had a few misgivings. In a confidential report to Garvey, Garcia described what he observed as the Liberian feudal structure. Later, back in New York City when the Convention got under way in August, enthusiastic delegates, unaware of what Garcia had seen and reported to Garvey, bestowed a special honor upon Mayor Gabriel Johnson of Monrovia. They named him Potentate of the Association and Secretary of State in the cabinet of the Provisional President of Africa. The post carried a salary of twelve thousand dollar a year.

Johnson made the mistake upon returning to Liberia of not making it crystal clear to President King that he (Johnson) was not trying to use his newly conferred title to political advantage. The result was that he was nearly done in by his aristocratic Liberian peers. Ensuing negotiations between Garvey and Liberia would shortly reveal the kind of duplicity of which Liberian officials and their supporters were capable.

Meanwhile, August 1920 ushered the first International Convention of the Universal Negro Improvement Association into New York City. A brief description of the parade and mass gathering at Madison Square Garden opened this narrative. After Marcus Garvey had delivered his address, in which he warned that black folks were tired of dying for white folks and ready to die for themselves, the delegates got down to the serious business of the convention.

First they drafted the "Declaration of the Rights of the Negro Peoples of the World." The fifty-four articles of the Declaration included demands for political and judicial equality, a free continent of Africa governed by blacks, and complete self-determination elsewhere in the world for black peoples. Their demand that the word "Negro" be capitalized did indeed take root in New York State nine years later. And the red, black, and green colors, symbolizing the blood of the race, pride in its blackness, and the promise of a new day in Africa were officially approved.

Garvey was himself declared Provisional President of the African Republic. It was implied in that declaration that his was a government in exile to which he would eventually return. Flamboyant titles were then bestowed upon various members of the group, and honorary orders such as the Distinguished Service Order of Ethiopia and Knights of The Nile were established. While this smacked of a feudal manner of creating caste and delegating comparable responsibilities with it, the effects were by no means negative.

Black porters, laundresses, and similarly employed persons could lift their heads, and leaving Liberty Hall, go back downtown to face "the man" with a hitherto unfelt pride in who and what they were. A Knight of The Nile, with a difficult-to-pronounce-name, was not as likely to indulge in petty theft as was, say, Joe Jackson, a negro nobody, trying to make it in the white man's hostile world. Conversely that same Knight of The Nile would certainly be less favorably disposed to being insulted and humiliated by insecure whites anxious to find someone they could look down upon.

Black working-class members were not the only ones to be

singled out for distinction at the 1920 U.N.I.A. convention. George A. McGuire, a well-known Episcopal minister, was elected to the position of Chaplain-General of the U.N.I.A., Henrietta Vinton Davis, an excellent actress and elocutionist, became Lady Commander of the Sublime Order of The Nile, and she was made U.N.I.A. international organizer. And two nationally known black Americans were later honored at a U.N.I.A. convention for distinguished service to the race. One was Emmett J. Scott and the other was William Pickens, a brilliant and well-liked educator working with the N.A.A.C.P. Scott became a Knight Commander of the Sublime Order of The Nile.

Reaction to that first International U.N.I.A. Convention varied in America's black communities. In New York City, one Oscar Walters, a Harlem Democrat, declared in a statement to *The New York Globe* of September 7, 1920: "As a property owner, I want to say that the better element is perfectly satisfied with conditions in America." Out in Brooklyn, the Reverend G. Miller, quoted in the *Brooklyn Eagle* said:

> Garvey is the most remarkable man of our times. He may be laughed at and ridiculed, but he has done more to emphasize the restlessness of the black people than any other man.

The black weekly, *Norfolk Journal and Guide,* in a sharp editorial of August 21, 1920, said of the Garveyites:

> They can't conquer and repatriate Africa and build up and maintain a steamship line between African ports without consulting the Christian Nations which own and dominate Africa and its ports, and Garvey and his lieutenants know that. So do we.

White press comments also varied. *The New York Times* for August 3, 1920, wrote:

> Garvey's origin probably explains the Empire scope of his ambitions—the quality of his "nerve." All through the West Indies the Jamaican Negro has a reputation for thinking well of himself, and his self-esteem, it must be admitted, is not without excuse.

The Massachusetts, *Lowell Courier-Citizen* in its September 2, 1920, editorial, had another view:

> Don't make too much fun of these earnest colored people who have a notion of an Africa for the Negro. What reads today like a libretto of an opera bouffe may tomorrow be an act in the great international drama.

Whatever the view of observers and critics, one thing is indisputable. Garvey had been seen and heard, and his presence had given the voiceless masses of blacks everywhere a sense of pride in their blackness. That marked the first time blacks in the United States and the Caribbean had, en masse, experienced such a thing. And it was extremely important to them. The rousing Garvey call-to-arms echoed and reechoed in their minds. "Up you mighty race. You can accomplish what you will!" It was not a phrase easily forgotten.

CHAPTER

TWELVE

THOSE THOROUGHLY acquainted with the Garvey movement know that it reached its zenith during 1920 and 1921. Its prestige in America was firmly established with the calling of that first International Convention, the launching of the Black Star Line, and the formation of the Negro Factories Corporation. Activities of the Universal Negro Improvement Association became a moving force in the lives of many black people in America and elsewhere. Some were sufficiently moved to affiliate themselves with the Association. Others, while lending it their moral support, never became members. None, however, could be indifferent to the force and the charisma of Marcus Mosiah Garvey.

A full thirty-five years after the first convention, an eminent black American recalled what Garveyism had meant to him. The Reverend James H. Robinson, founder of Operation Crossroads Africa, writing in the *Christian Century* for June 8, 1955, said this:

> Marcus Garvey captured the imagination of thousands, because he personified the possibility of the fulfillment of a

> dream latent in the heart of every Negro. I remember as a lad in Cleveland, Ohio, during the hungry days of 1921, standing on Central Avenue, watching a parade one Sunday afternoon when thousands of Garvey Legionnaires, resplendent in their uniforms, marched by. When Garvey rode by in his plumed hat, I got an emotional lift, which swept me up above the poverty and the prejudice by which my life was limited.

In Boston, Massachusetts, George A. Weston, a native of Antigua, was persuaded by a friend to attend a U.N.I.A. meeting at which Garvey spoke. The year was 1919, and the African Methodist Episcopal Church was packed with eager listeners on that Sunday afternoon. Later, when Garvey returned to Boston while the *Yarmouth* was anchored in the harbor, Weston met him.

> When I shook Marcus Garvey's hand, I noted that it was like a piece of boiled cabbage. He didn't have that Methodist grip at all. But he sent a thrill through me when I took his hand—a feeling I had experienced once before when I *thought* I had religion. Garvey was not at all concerned. He turned from me to shake other hands.

George A. Weston not only joined the U.N.I.A. but became a trusted worker and officer in the Pittsburg, Cleveland, and New York divisions.

Personal magnetism plus a genius for getting impressive projects underway were the great assets of Marcus Garvey up to this point. Some critics have said that U.N.I.A. strength rested upon the personal power of its leader rather than its power as a well-knit organization of many strong units. Cronon quotes an editorial comment in the *Nautical Gazette* as further recognition of the basic strength and weakness of the Black Star Line. Said the *Gazette*:

> There is nothing in the record of the black race to justify doubts as to their being capable navigators. But the success of the Black Star Line as a trading venture and as an instrumentality of disposing of goods made by Americans to African Negroes will depend on the business acumen displayed by its backers.

Implied in the *Nautical Gazette*'s editorial is the truth that black men in a setting dominated by white men can and do function well in those areas in which they are *permitted* to participate. In positions from which they have been and still are systematically barred their performances are either dismal failures or subject to some question.

A specific example of what was said to be the financial instability of the steamship transaction occurred just after Garvey had announced plans for purchasing a fourth ship. The low credit rating of the Black Star Line scarcely justified the venture and Vice-President Orlando Thompson said as much to a close friend. He did add, however, that a secret plan for expanding the steamship line was about to be unfolded. Accordingly, early in October 1920, a three-man team hurriedly crossed the Hundson River and entered Jersey City for the purpose of incorporating a new venture. They named it the Black Star Steamship Company of New Jersey.

Incorporating in a neighboring state, as they had done before in Delaware, enabled them to buy a little time. They would find it easier to get credit in New Jersey than in Delaware as they went out in search of yet another ship.

Criticism of the Garvey program, especially of its expressed intention of redeeming Africa, did not blushingly wait for an invitation to assert itself. During the summer of 1920 the Reverend A. Clayton Powell senior, pastor of the Abyssinian Baptist Church (then located downtown) conducted summer services in a tent pitched on property owned by the church and located next to Liberty Hall. On Sunday evening, August 22, Dr. Powell had invited the Reverend Charles S. Morris of Norfolk, Virginia, to be his guest speaker. The Reverend Morris, in the course of his sermon, aired his views of Marcus Garvey's plans for redeeming Africa for the African. In Dr. Morris's opinion, as reported in *The New York Age,* the Garvey plans were foolish and would prove futile. France, England, Belgium, Italy, and other European powers with interests in Africa simply would not permit it. And those nations, according to Dr. Morris, had the ability to stop Garvey cold.

It happened that sessions of the first U.N.I.A. Convention were in progress next door at Liberty Hall. And as was usual, there was not enough room in that spacious auditorium to accommodate all who wanted to get inside. The spill-over of Garveyites standing outside were well within earshot of what was being said in the tent next door. Dr. Morris obviously was a speaker who had mastered voice projection, for in a short time the gist of what he was saying about Garveyism reached the ears of the U.N.I.A. faithful. What they heard made them quite unhappy. And it was all the police could do to conduct the guest speaker to the safety of his temporary Harlem quarters. Powell himself was threatened, but no move was made to attack him physically.

Actually what was involved here were the combined emotions and experiences of a mass of rank-and-file, black, otherwise unrecognized working people. Having little faith in and even less love for the kind of cold and deliberate reasoning of the commonly accepted leaders of the race, they refused to listen to them. Dr. Morris was not responding as the Garveyites wished to their emotional yearnings and resentments. All they could hear, as he spoke, was what to them was a repetition of the old, well-worn you-shun-that-devil-and-follow-us-to-the-promised-land doctrine. That they had tried before. It hadn't worked for them, though they noted how well, indeed, the preachers were doing. The expensive suits and cars were being paid for by many who, like themselves, were not well dressed and who had no cars. Meanwhile they were convinced Garvey was offering them far more for their money. Shares in the Negro Factories Corporation and the Black Star Line were more meaningful to them than all the rosy promises of a good life in the hereafter. Besides, Garvey had even offered them a religion—a version of the deity they wanted to accept, as shall shortly be shown.

So from the viewpoint of the Garveyites milling just outside the gospel tent, Dr. Morris was pulling their last hopeful prop from beneath them. He had delivered a blow at their trusted leader. And anyone knocking their leader had to be dealt with quickly and not gently. Criticism of Garvey continued, meanwhile, to come from other sources.

The Messenger, a monthly magazine published in New York City by a group of black Socialists, was *the* radical periodical of its day. Chandler Owen was its editor. Contributors included A. Philip Randolph and George S. Schuyler. *The Messenger* minced no words, as was evident in an editorial appearing in its issue of September 1920. Its title was "Africa for the Africans." Without once naming Garvey or any of his disciples *The Messenger* stated:

> Certain elements of American Negroes, as well as similar elements of West Indians in their native lands, in Central

> America and in the principal cities on the Atlantic seaboard of the United States, are enthused over the idea of ousting all non-Negroes from Africa. The plan is variously and euphemistically described as "redeeming Africa," "back to Africa," and "getting a place in the sun." The *modus operandi* for the attainment of this end is extremely simple—transparently so. It involves neither politics nor cooperation with the native races of Africa. All that is necessary is unity—magic word!
>
> Viewed seriously this state of mind must be regarded as being indicative of two things: a desire to end the oppression of the black race by Caucasians and a lack of understanding of the basic causes of that oppression.

The writer then outlined the basic causes of the oppression of black people. Moreover, he named a few of the oppressors in the following quote:

> It is Alfred Beit and the Duke of Fife, brother-in-law of King George, and the directors of the National City Bank of New York City who profit from the robbery of native lands and the serfdom of their rightful owners. And these men form the powerful and respectable of England and America. They are dignified statesmen, liberal philanthropists, devout Churchmen and prominent social and political leaders.
>
> The freedom of Africa from alien exploitation, if that is what is meant by redeeming Africa, must comprehend a defeat of these men and all the moral and physical resources they control.

For the next few issues *The Messenger* dispassionately analyzed the U.N.I.A.'s political, economic, social, and international program. Under its cold analysis Garvey and his movement did not score impressively. Moreover, *The Messenger* made it quite clear that while its editors, Chandler Owen and Philip Randolph, had shared the platform with

Garvey at one of his mass meetings several months before, *The Messenger* and its staff were in no sense a part of the U.N.I.A.

A little later Truman Hughes Talley, a reporter writing in the December 1920 issue of *World's Work*, presented the first of his two-installment profile titled: "Marcus Garvey—The Negro Moses?" Talley's articles, falling in the area of routine reporting, nevertheless revealed the author's amazement that Garvey and his followers could organize a U.N.I.A., establish business ventures, and conduct a month-long convention in New York City. There was nothing suggesting a critical probing into the movement in Talley's writing. Certainly he showed not the slightest understanding of how or why there could have ever been a Marcus Garvey in the first place.

Then came an appraisal of Garvey written by W. E. B. Du Bois in the *Crisis*.

Following in the wake of what many writers have described as the irreparable feud between the two men, the Du Bois piece was surprisingly objective. Much was made, on the other hand, of two later Du Bois writings, one appearing in the February 1922 issue of *Century Magazine* and the twenty-eighth edition of *The Crisis*.

In the first, Du Bois described Garvey as "a little fat black man, ugly, but with intelligent eyes and a big head." In the second article Garvey was described by Du Bois as "either a lunatic or a traitor." Because of the choice of words both descriptions were far better remembered than the more restrained (and doubtless less emotionally inspired) Du Bois comments. The harsh words infuriated Garvey and his followers to the point where they ascribed them to the theory that Du Bois, because of his African-French ancestry, considered himself superior to Garvey, the man of unmixed blood.

However, keen observers less emotionally involved knew that Du Bois was above such nonsense. They knew also how typical it was (and is) of powerful inside vested interests to keep "outsiders" constantly fighting among themselves. In that way the combatants' attention is diverted from both the real issues at stake and those who stand to gain most from such constant infighting. A close look at the more thoughtful Du Bois appraisal of Garvey reveals what could have been the former's truer feelings toward the latter. Under the title "Marcus Garvey" Du Bois wrote his impressions in the December 1920 and January 1921 issues of the N.A.A.C.P.'s official organ. After briefly reviewing the well-known facts of Garvey's early life and phenomenal success in America, Du Bois posed three questions. Is Garvey's movement honest? Are its industrial and commercial projects businesslike and effective? Are its general objects plausible and capable of being carried out? Of the first, here was the Du Bois conclusion:

> It is a little difficult to characterize the man Garvey. He has been charged with dishonesty and graft, but he seems to me essentially an honest and sincere man with a tremendous vision, great dynamic force, stubborn determination, and unselfish desire to serve; but also he has very serious defects of temperament and training: he is dictatorial, domineering, inordinately vain and very suspicious.

Du Bois then cited the numerous changes of personnel in the organization, Garvey's lawsuits, his "fistfights with subordinates," and his brief marriage to Amy Ashwood. While Du Bois admitted that such deportment militated against Garvey, he had "not found the slightest proof that his objects were not sincere or that he consciously diverted money to his own uses."

Calling Garvey "an extraordinary leader of men," Du Bois further declared that "he is able to stir them with singular eloquence and the general run of his thought is of a high plane."

Of Garvey's industrial and commercial ventures, Du Bois had misgivings. He was not impressed by the incorporating of the Black Star Line in Delaware, whose loose laws required no financial statements. And he mentioned having written to Garvey requesting "such financial data as he was willing for the public to know." The request was never answered.

Du Bois suggested that Garvey's refusal to publish a financial statement, while not necessarily indicative of dishonesty, proved that Garvey was ill advised, or that his enterprises were not financially sound. And Du Bois, studying one Garvey balance sheet published July 26, 1920, and describing the financial state of the Black Star Line, concluded the following: "It has cost nearly three hundred thousand dollars to collect a capital of less than half a million. Garvey has, in other words, spent more for advertisement than he has for his boats!"

The Du Bois feeling was that Garvey was being forced because of heavy expenditures to use the money from stock sales to meet current expenses. He also observed that the boats were being used more as advertisements than for shipping. Heavy mortgages on property were necessary to the Garvey method, as were more grandiose schemes designed to bring in desperately needed ready cash.

Still Du Bois did not strip Garvey's efforts bare of merit

and some success. Indeed he declared that the basic idea of the accumulation and ministering of capital by black Americans was workable. With their own capital they could organize industry and join the black centers of the south Atlantic by commercial enterprise. In such a way they could, said Du Bois, "ultimately redeem Africa as a fit and free home for black men." He saw such a plan as both "feasible" and "practical."

But, seen by DuBois, that was not a job to be done by one man or one organization. It would demand time, skill, and self-sacrificing effort. And though the idea was not original with Garvey, he had made of it such a living vocal ideal as to sweep thousands into the belief of its accomplishment. Then Du Bois, declaring that American black leaders were not jealous of Garvey's success, but fearful of his failure, concluded with this statement.

> He can have all the power and money that he can efficiently and honestly use, and if in addition he wants to prance down Broadway in a green shirt, let him—but do not let him foolishly overwhelm with bankruptcy and disaster one of the most interesting spiritual movements of the modern Negro world.

Like most superstar performers whose words and acts are under constant public scrutiny, Marcus Garvey kept up with what was being written about him. Little, however, in his deportment immediately after the *Crisis* profile by W. E. B. Du Bois indicated that he had taken the scholarly warnings with any degree of seriousness. Within a month he was seeking additional money with which to enlarge the Black Star Line. Orlando M. Thompson announced that the corporation would soon be negotiating for the purchase of the S.S. *Tenny-*

son. A British vessel, the *Tennyson* was reported to be just the kind of ship needed for the transatlantic voyage to Africa.

With this new venture in the offing, Garvey set out in February 1921 for the West Indies. There, and all along the route, he intended to promote the sale of Black Star Line stock. He left New York by train and traveled that route all the way to Key West, Florida. From there he went to Cuba, stopping long enough to be greeted by President Menocal and to address West Indian workers in various cities of the island. He had arranged to board the *Kanawah* at Santiago and make a triumphant landing at Kingston.

Since having undergone repairs amounting to nearly forty-five thousand dollars (more than two-thirds of her original cost), the *Kanawah* was still having her troubles. Captain Adrian Richardson had inadvertently damaged her stern, the fan engine was in poor shape, and engineer Charles Harris had used salt water in her boilers. By the time the *Kanawah* reached Santiago, she was far from being in first-rate condition. She did, however, make the trip to Kingston.

There Garvey's presence alarmed the American officials considerably. Aware of the Garvey plan to include Central America in his promotional tour, Secretary of State Charles Evans Hughes cabled American consular officers advising them not to aid Garvey as he sought visas. But it was useless. Garvey not only got into Costa Rica, Guatemala, and Panama, but turned his visits into not inconsiderable triumphs. Garveyites in the banana republics flocked to see and hear him and to support his movement with their money. One estimate of thirty thousand dollars, collected from black laborers in Costa Rica alone, is reported by Cronon in *Black Moses.*

Although the Canal Zone barred Garvey from entry, he visited and addressed huge throngs in Bocas-del-Toro, Panama City, and Colon. Returning to Jamaica, Garvey was again detained. For two months he waited for a visa, spending the interim speaking and visiting with old friends. His ship the *Kanawah,* meanwhile, continued to run up bills.

Garvey, convinced that she was being deliberately sabotaged by her officers, Captain Richardson and Engineer Harris, lodged charges of "destructive management" against them. The American Consul, Charles L. Latham, was completely unsympathetic to Garvey's proceedings, however, and charges against the two men were finally dismissed. So Garvey was compelled to continue supporting the officers and the ship as he, his visa finally granted, started for home.

Taking a banana boat, he was permitted to reenter the United States through the port at New Orleans. Toward the end of July he sent enough money to Kingston to pay off the *Kanawah*'s debts and the luckless lady left Jamaica for her voyage home. She got only as far as Antilla, Cuba. Her boilers were gone again and Garvey, who hated to admit defeat, was forced to abandon his optimism about the ship. Reluctantly he threw in the towel and doomed the *Kanawah* to a rotting death in Cuban waters. In addition to the $60,000.00 it had originally cost, the ship had run through an additional total of $134,681.11 in less than a year and a half! Its reported operating income was a mere $1,207.62.

Troubles continued to plague the Black Star Line. Garvey's aforementioned announcement just before leaving for Jamaica that the S.S. *Tennyson* was being bid for, while sincerely made, precipitated more embarrassment for him. No sooner had he left the country than the offer of the *Tennyson* was suddenly withdrawn. Vice-President Orlando Thompson

Marcus Garvey.
Drawing by Elton C. Fax

The New York Times

Garvey's first wife, Amy Ashwood, photographed in New York City, 1969.

Except where otherwise indicated, all photographs are from the James Van Der Zee Institute.

Marcus Garvey on parade in New York City.

The S. S. Yarmouth *of the Black Star Line.*

Spectators of a Universal Negro Improvement Association (U.N.I.A.) parade in New York City.

Gathering for a U.N.I.A. parade in New York City, 1924.

U.N.I.A. women on parade.

U.N.I.A. Black Cross nurses.

Marcus Garvey in the reviewing stand, 1924.

Youth contingent of the U.N.I.A. on parade in New York City.

U.N.I.A. Black Legion, 1924.

U.N.I.A. Black Legion and spectators.

Marcus Garvey in full uniform.

BELOW: *Garvey's second wife, Amy Jacques, with portrait bust of her husband, photographed in Kingston, Jamaica, 1971.*

was on the spot. *The Negro World* had already published a photograph of the *Tennyson* and readers had practically accepted the purchase as fact. Something would have to be done—quickly.

Anthony R. Silverstone was the operator of a small ship brokerage in lower New York City to whom the desperate Thompson turned for help. Silverstone was all teeth and bland assurances as he convinced the directors of the Black Star Line that they had come to the right man. As a white broker he could, he confidentially whispered, negotiate for them without encountering color prejudice. Silverstone was, of course, right about that, and he was immediately given the green light.

A few weeks passed before Silverstone came up with an old British tramp steamer, the S.S. *Hong Kheng*. Though the ship was still operating in oriental waters, Silverstone declared he would have her in New York shortly after mid-May 1921. The new Black Star Steamship Company of New Jersey agreed to the price of three hundred thousand dollars, with a deposit of three thousand seven hundred dollars and an additional sixteen thousand three hundred dollars held in escrow until delivery.

When the date of delivery came and passed with no sign of the *Hong Kheng*, Black Star Line directors grew anxious. They had exerted a lot of pressure to raise the twenty thousand dollars down payment through the various U.N.I.A. divisions. Finally, when it was learned that the *Hong Kheng* was not on its way to New Jersey, but in dry dock in Indo China, Silverstone clamly explained that the ship would not have been a good purchase anyway. Moreover, he had something much better for them, a German ship, the *Orion*.

The deposit on the *Hong Kheng* could be applied to the *Orion*.

Given the power of attorney to negotiate for the German vessel, Silverstone went ahead with his business. The Black Star Line directors may just as well have done it all themselves. In spite of all Silverstone's glib talk of fronting for them to avoid the pitfalls of racism, he deliberately told the United States Shipping Board (owners of the *Orion*) who the prospective buyers were. When the Board demurred at Silverstone's offer of two hundred and twenty-five thousand dollars, the latter cried "race prejudice."

The Board replied by asking to see a complete financial statement of both the U.N.I.A. and the Black Star Line. Obviously satisfied with what they saw, the Board accepted Silverstone's offer. A down payment of twenty-two thousand five hundred dollars was made and an agreement to monthly installments at 5 percent interest was reached. Of the more than twenty thousand dollars Vice-President Thompson had handed over to Silverstone, the latter had paid only twelve thousand five hundred dollars to the United States Shipping Board. The balance he claimed as having gone toward his "expenses."

Marcus Garvey was to learn all about this upon his return from the Caribbean and Central America. The President-General of the U.N.I.A. must have sighed heavily as he contemplated the staggering cost of a dream transformed into a maritime nightmare. Then, squaring his shoulders, he turned to the more pleasant prospect just ahead. The U.N.I.A. was about to convene its second International Convention in New York City.

CHAPTER THIRTEEN

THE CONVENTION opened in August with all the expected dramatics so characteristic of the Association. There was the morning prayer meeting followed by a parade. And that Fifteenth Regiment Band made famous by its conductor, James Reese Europe, led the procession. The opening mass meeting took place at the Twelfth Regiment Armory where messages sent to Ghandi, De Valera, and George V of England were read to the assembled delegates. Following sessions were held at Liberty Hall for the remainder of the month. Some of them grew hot and heavy.

Expressions of dissatisfaction with official vagueness surrounding the promised new ship, *The Phyllis Wheatley,* burst out in the open. Where was the ship? It was a natural enough question. After all, the boat had been talked and written so much about within the Association and in the pages of the press. The head of the Los Angeles division of the U.N.I.A., Noah Thompson, was particularly sharp in challenging what he viewed as unwarranted secrecy. He said as much upon his return to California. A story appearing in the *Chicago Defender* for November 19, 1921, announced Thompson's withdrawal from the U.N.I.A. and his founding of an independent group.

Garvey and the Black Star Line responded by issuing a reassurance to its members through a circular reading in part:

> Whatever might have been the errors of the past, the present administration of the Black Star Line is composed of trained business men and specialty service help, unquestionably equal to their responsible tasks.

Then Garvey himself began to put pressure on his Vice-President, Orlando Thompson. Thompson passed the pressure on to broker Anthony Silverstone. The deal for the *Orion* would have to be consummated—or else! Silverstone borrowed ten thousand dollars on a promissory note of two months and Thompson signed the note in the name of the Black Star Line. The interest on it was a stiff 10 percent. Still the Shipping Board, who owned the *Orion*, refused to release her in spite of advance contracts for hauling freight Thompson had managed to obtain.

When Garvey demanded a reason for the Shipping Board's reluctance, he learned that only twelve thousand five hundred dollars of the required twenty-two thousand five hundred dollars deposit had ever been received. Not until December, four months later, did the missing check for ten thousand dollars reach the Board through an associate of Silverstone. Even then Silverstone's fine, light hand was still at work. He later tried to claim the money as his own!

Another reason given for the Shipping Board's slowness in releasing the *Orion* was the charge by the Federal Bureau of Investigation that the U.N.I.A. was an arm of the Communist party. A more hysterical conclusion is hard to imagine in view of the relationship of the U.N.I.A. to American Communists. Of that more will be said shortly.

Criticism of Garvey continued, some of it even coming from foreign sources. A near riot erupted in Harlem during the second week of the convention when a South African black took public exception to Garvey. Mokete Manoedi, a native of Basutoland, while addressing a street crowd on upper Seventh Avenue said the following:

> We are not favorably impressed with the unmitigated presumption of this man, Garvey, in electing himself provisional President of Africa.

Garveyites in the crowd fumed. Within minutes a free-for-all ensued and police rushed to the scene from the nearby West 135th Street Precinct, restored calm before the fracas got out of control. The South African speaker was allowed to continue his criticism as Garveyites, under police restraint, glowered and growled their resentment.

As the second Convention continued its sessions in New York, another meeting of black men was simultaneously taking place across the Atlantic. It was a far smaller and less hectic gathering, composed of representatives from all parts of the world. The American representatives were headed by Dr. W. E. B. Du Bois. In her book, *Garvey and Garveyism*, Amy Jacques Garvey bitterly describes that congress in the following manner:

> In order to get the help of European colonial powers in his campaign to get rid of Garvey, Du Bois called a Pan-African Congress in Paris, timed with the opening of the Second International Convention of the Negro Peoples of the World, in New York City. He sent out a press release as to number of delegates and the purpose of the conference.

Mrs. Garvey then quotes excerpts from four leading New York daily papers describing Du Bois' repudiation of Garvey and his program.

It is entirely true that the programs of Marcus Garvey and W. E. B. Du Bois, while directed at liberating the peoples of Africa and of African descent from white domination, differed vastly. In an article on Pan-Africanism appearing in an early edition of the *Crisis,* Du Bois said:

> The problems of the American Negro must be thought of and settled only with continual reference to the problems of the West Indian Negroes, the problems of the French Negroes and the English Negroes, and above all, the problems of the African Negroes. This is the thought back of the Pan-African movement in all of its various manifestations.

Du Bois, often called "the father of Pan-Africanism," had met previously in Paris with prominent Africans, West Indians, and other colonials. Together they had discussed their economic, social, and political problems. They then adopted a petition requesting the victorious allies of World War I to place the former German colonies of Togoland, Cameroons, South-West Africa, and Tanganyika under international supervision. Their inhabitants, according to the terms of the proposal, were to have their territories held in trust for them as future self-governing countries.

During that first Pan-African Congress in 1919 it was agreed that the affair should be biennial. Between the first and second congresses much had happened in America. The dreadful "Red Summer of 1919," for one thing, along with the rash of lynchings sparked by Ku Klux Klan terror, occupied the attention of all decent Americans. Du Bois had thrown himself fully into the fight to eliminate those domestic evils. With an easing of the postwar tension he regathered the threads of his design for an even larger Pan-African Congress—one that would include black Americans. Arrangements were finally completed. The next meeting would take place in London, Brussels, and Paris in August and September 1921.

Trying to evoke interest in Africa and her problems among his liberal white associates was not easy, Du Bois learned. The N.A.A.C.P.'s board of directors was not especially interested. He found black colleagues for the most part hostile to anything suggesting their relationship to Africa. Many had developed a mistrust of schemes to deport all ex-slaves or free-born blacks to Africa, and coupled the Pan-African concept with those misgivings. To hear a black American of the middle class loudly proclaim his American roots and ties was the rule and not the exception. Such attitudes confronted Du Bois as he sought domestic support for the second congress.

In the interim another significant movement in the United States had taken place with the phenomenal rise to prominence of Marcus Garvey. No two men could have been more different. Each suited the purpose to which he was unswervingly dedicated. And as George Padmore has written concerning the reactions of black Americans to each leader:

> The American Negro was caught between two irreconcilable programmes: that of the N.A.A.C.P., which stood for "equal rights for blacks in America," and that of the U.N.I.A., which advocated mass migration back to Africa on the ground that Negroes would never get racial equality in the United States.

Both Du Bois and Garvey were Pan-Africanists. The difference separating them was this: Du Bois' Pan-Africanism was designed as an aid to African national self-determination under African leadership for the benefit of Africans themselves. Garvey's Pan-Africanism envisioned the movement as one in which Africa would be the place where black peoples of the Western world would colonize, and where Garvey and his U.N.I.A. would head the program of colonization, with the consent and cooperation of African leaders.

Garvey had an edge on Du Bois. It was an edge the great scholar was not hesitant to acknowledge. The Garveyan movement was a *people's* movement, encompassing masses of followers, lettered and unlettered, while Du Bois appealed solely to intellectuals. Moreover, Garvey's movement was more disturbing to the powers in Europe and America because it was greatly strengthened by the disenchantment with colonialism and white racism exhibited by restless blacks in their territories. Simultaneously, the weakness of Garvey's movement lay in what Du Bois described in *The World and Africa*, as "its demagogic leadership, poor finance, intemperate propaganda, and the natural apprehension it aroused among the colonial powers."

The latter had certainly been proved true by the manner in which Garvey's newspaper, *The Negro World*, had been banned in so many colonial territories. And one is forced to believe that charges of official persecution of the U.N.I.A. here in the United States were solidly founded. Take, for instance, the alacrity of the office of the assistant district attorney for New York in dealing with Marcus Garvey.

Cronon reports in *Black Moses* that between the summers of 1919 and 1920 Assistant District Attorney Edwin P. Kilroe called Garvey into his office three times. The first summons was to warn Garvey not to sell stock until he had properly incorporated the Black Star Line. Attorney James Watson, who was later to become a judge, helped Garvey with that detail.

A few weeks later Kilroe again summoned the Jamaican to his office to warn that he could be prosecuted for commercial fraud. Garvey and his directors quickly complied with the legal requirements. But Garvey did not hesitate during the following few days to say what in his opinion the real difficulty was. Here quoted from the second volume of *Philosophy and Opinions*, is a portion of Garvey's own statement of his tiffs with Kilroe:

> To have built up a new organization which was not purely political, among Negroes in America was a wonderful feat, for the Negro politician does not allow any other kind of organization within his race to thrive. We succeeded, however, in making the Universal Negro Improvement Association so formidable in 1919 that we encountered more trouble from our political bretheren. They sought the influence of the District Attorney's office of the County of New York to put us out of business.

Having linked his opposition within the black community to the political environment of New York County, Garvey then proceeded with this statement:

> Edwin P. Kilroe, at that time an Assistant District Attorney, on the complaint of Negro politicians, started to investigate us and the association. Mr. Kilroe would constantly and continuously call me to his office for investigation on extraneous matters without coming to the point. The result was that after the eighth or ninth time I wrote an article in our newspaper, *The Negro World,* against him. This was interpreted as criminal libel, for which I was indicted and arrested, but subsequently dismissed on retracting what I had written.

What Garvey had written stated, in essence, that "certain sinister forces" were making political use of Kilroe and his office in persecuting the U.N.I.A. He concluded that it was obviously the white man's intention "to scatter the sheep by striking the shepherd." If Garvey's charges of official harassment in New York could be termed weak and exaggerated, more than the same could be said of charges of communism leveled against his organization by the F.B.I. in Washington. Here, indeed, the facts overwhelmingly disputed the allegations.

Garvey was far from vague in expressing his opinions of Communist activity among black American working-class people through this statement appearing in *The Philosophy and Opinions of Marcus Garvey.*

> If I must advise the Negro working man and laborer I should warn him against the present brand of Communism or Workers' Partizanship as taught in America, and to be careful of the traps and pitfalls of white tradeunionism, in affiliation with the American Federation of white workers or laborers.

Such a statement not only alienated Garvey and his U.N.I.A. from Communists but from labor-conscious Socialists as well. That is why *The Messenger* was not one of Garvey's supporters. The Jamaican leader further cited what he saw as the great menace of communism in countries where the black man is a minority. To Garvey it was simply a selfish and vicious attempt of the Party to use the black vote and black numbers in the violent overthrow of a system injurious to *white* underdogs. Once accomplished, the revolution would still leave whites in power. In Garvey's opinion the new order would be no better for blacks than the one overthrown.

Nor did his warning against communism signal Garvey's full endorsement of American capitalism. Here, in the same essay, is what he had to say about that:

It seems strange and a paradox, but the only convenient friend the Negro worker or laborer has, in America, at the present time, is the white capitalist. The capitalist being selfish —seeking only the largest profit out of labor—is willing and glad to use Negro labor wherever possible on a scale "reasonably" below the standard white union wage. He will tolerate the Negro in any industry (except those that are necessarily guarded for the protection of the white man's material, racial, and assumed cultural dominance) if he accepts a lower standard of wage than the white union man; but if the Negro unionizes himself to the level of the white worker, and in affiliation with him, the choice and preference of employment is given to the white worker, without any regard or consideration for the Negro.

Garvey's earlier experience as a printer's foreman in Kingston and his observations in Latin America and the United States bore testimony to the basic truth of his brief for and against capitalism as it still affects the black worker. And even as he condemned communism in America he was not loath to recognize Nikolai Lenin respectfully as the leader of Russian masses, whose hunger Lenin had tried to feed and whose ignorance he had tried to enlighten. The Garvey who would send a cablegram of tribute to the memory of Lenin would still not permit American Communists to take over his U.N.I.A. or make use of its membership to further its aims.

It was George Padmore, however, who most succinctly summarized the relationship between Communists and black organizations. Writing in *Pan-Africanism or Communism*, Padmore said the following of those who accused Garvey of being a Communist.

These reactionaries ascribe to the Communists the inspiration for everything Africans and other colonial peoples ever try

> to do to improve their status. And such intolerance has done more than all the Communist propaganda in the world to create in the minds of Africans and other Colonials the idea that the Communists are the only white people in the world who are sympathetic to their legitimate aspirations. . . . The Pan-African Movement, like the N.A.A.C.P. and Garvey's U.N.I.A.—whatever people may think about them—have absolutely no connection officially or otherwise with Moscow. . . . In fact . . . the attitude of most white Communists toward Negro organizations has been one of contempt. If they cannot control them they seek their destruction by infiltration.

So amid the confusion in certain quarters of America about Garvey and the Communists, the final sessions of the second U.N.I.A. convention were called at the Harlem Liberty Hall headquarters. Simultaneously the meetings of the second Pan-African congress opened on August 28 and 29 at London's Central Hall.

A modest 113 delegates, men and women from Africa, the United States, Europe, and the West Indies, listened to the presidential address by Dr. Du Bois. They then conducted discussions and joined in endorsing their "Declaration to the World." That document affirmed their dedication to the doctrine of complete racial equality. In addition, the delegates listed eight demands which they directed at the colonial governments. Those demands included: local self-government for backward groups; freedom of religion and social customs; education in self-knowledge, science, and industrial technique coupled with the arts; and "The return of Negroes to their land and its natural fruits and defense against the unrestricted greed of invested capital."

From London the congress moved on to Brussels, Belgium, where, for a time, it was feared they would not be allowed to meet. Belgium's desperate dependency upon the wealth of the Congo was evident in the hostility to the congress of the Belgium press and certain wealthy companies having interests in the Congo. Still, the Belgium police permitted the Pan-African Congress to assemble and to endorse the resolutions they had adopted in London. Paris played host to the final sessions.

There a delegation headed by Du Bois drew up and presented a petition to the Mandates Commission of the League of Nations. Again stressing its stand on the full equality of all races, the delegation asked that the Mandates Commission appoint qualified men of color, including black men, to its membership. That, on the surface of it, was all the second Pan-African Congress seemed to accomplish in 1921. But was that *really* all?

Back in New York Garvey could not have been too concerned that the Du Bois-led group would ever achieve any of its aims. One recalls the Jamaican's own words that mere petitions for justice presented to powerful governments by politically and economically weak subject groups are without meaning. True enough. But to what extent did that apply to the work of the second Pan-African Congress? Hardly any at all. The analogy is invalid because what that gathering of black intellectuals started did not begin and end with mere talks in London, Brussels, and Paris.

Nearly thirty years later a seemingly sudden political development in West Africa startled the world. A new group, the Convention People's Party, was formed in what was then the British-controlled Gold Coast. American- and British-trained Kwame Nkrumah was the founder of the Convention People's Party, a group made up primarily of poor working people of the Gold Coast. They had no army, no navy, and little formal schooling. What they did have going for them were their numbers; the fact that they were occupying their own indigenous land; the determination to be free; a leader in whom they believed; and the power of the vote.

Their political party was the outgrowth of another African federation started thirty years earlier in 1920 by a group of middle-class Gold Coast intellectuals and scholars. Similar in purpose to the group of Africans assembled a year earlier in Paris by Du Bois, this African federation called itself the West African National Congress. Its leader was the Honorable Joseph Casley Hayford, mentioned earlier in this narrative as one of Marcus Garvey's heroes during the latter's early residence in London.

In 1951, two years after the founding of the Convention People's Party, Dr. Nkrumah, following a well-organized general Gold Coast strike carried out by his party members, was swept into the office of prime minister by an overwhelming vote. And even though still in prison, where the British had put him, Nkrumah had become his country's first African to be so elected by his people. As Nkrumah picked his first cabinet ministers he did not neglect to include Archie Casley Hayford, the son of Joseph Casley Hayford. And as Padmore has written in *Pan-Africanism or Communism,* "Pan-Africanism had taken root in African soil. Dr. Du Bois' dream had been fulfilled."

Marcus Garvey never lived to see that complete evolution of events envisioned and begun by W. E. B. Du Bois. However, following the close of his own second International Convention in 1921, he busied himself with the immediate work at hand. Having consistently stressed the glory of pride in the black man's past, Garvey extended that feeling to religion. He made it known that the black man in ending his subservience to the white man should cease to worship a white God. The idea, of course, was not new or unique with Garvey. In African countries it is commonplace to find that visual interpretations of the Deity resemble Africans in color and facial features. The same principle operates in areas of the Orient.

So Garvey, with his concept of a black deity, declared the following as quoted in *Philosophy and Opinions.*

> If the white man has the idea of a white God, let him worship his God as he desires. If the yellow man's God is of his race let him worship his God as he sees fit. We as Negroes have found a new ideal. . . . We Negroes believe in the God of Ethiopia, the everlasting God—God the Father, God the Son, and God the Holy Ghost, the One God of all ages. That is the God in whom we believe, but we shall worship Him through the spectacles of Ethiopia.

An important figure in the promulgation of the Garvey concept of the black deity was the Reverend George A. McGuire. A little more than a year previously the Reverend Mr. McGuire, an Episcopal minister, had left his church in Boston to become Chaplain General of the U.N.I.A. It seemed natural enough that Garvey, himself of Roman Catholic faith, and accustomed to its formal ritual, would be drawn to McGuire, the Episcopalian.

In September 1921 McGuire was ordained a bishop and consecrated as head of the new African Orthodox Church. The ritual he wrote for the new church resembled that of both the Episcopal and the Roman Catholic faith. Marcus Garvey, the bombastic black nationalist leader, was also a surprisingly religious man. Three years later he was to enlarge even further upon his concept of a black deity.

CHAPTER FOURTEEN

THE STORM clouds gathering and hovering over Marcus Garvey and his movement were matched by those settling over the nation at large. Ku Klux Klan activity had reached a dangerous peak. Nor did it confine itself to the South. During the latter part of October 1921 residents of Portland, Oregon, were horrified by an attack upon a black woman resident of a white neighborhood.

The Reynolds family had created a stir when they moved into their Roselawn Avenue home. However, the excitement their presence created subsided as it was seen that the new residents were attractive and desirable neighbors. Several anonymous warnings to get out of the area were ignored as the work of cranks. Then one night two men clad in K.K.K. robes and hoods forced their way into Mrs. Elise Reynolds' home. After beating her, one of them, using acid, branded the letter "K" on the left cheek.

From Denison, Texas, came the story on December 9 of a standard Klan ritual. Dave Mitchell and Prince Lee, two aged black citizens, were summoned from their respective homes by a mob of robed and hooded klansmen. They, along with W. W. Willis, a black grocery-store owner, were driven in a car by the mob to a wooded area. There Mitchell and Lee were charged by the mob with "disorderly conduct," tied to a tree, and flogged with whips. Willis was forced to witness the ceremony and to "Go tell your people to clean up their homes. This is only the beginning. The worst is yet to come."

As 1921 approached its end a disturbing news report under the byline of Charles T. Magill and datelined New York, December 23, appeared in the *Chicago Defender*. The Democratic administration of Woodrow Wilson, widely hated by black Americans, had been replaced by the Republican victor of the 1920 campaign, Warren Gamaliel Harding. Expectations of a new era in race relations had been high as the party of Lincoln was restored to power. The following are the first two paragraphs of Magill's story:

> The advent of 1921 found our people in a most hopeful frame mind. Not in a decade had a new year been more auspiciously welcomed than was 1921. Did it not mark for our group the entrance of a new administration and the death of a Race-baiting, color-hating one? Things, said our people, would be different.
>
> The close of 1921, freely prophesied as the year that would mark the dawn of a new era for our people, finds them how situated? For the East, and probably for the entire country, that question may be answered thus: The close of 1921 and the advent of 1922 find our Race disillusioned, bitter, vengeful.

The writer elaborated with these details. Since the Republican victory had been decisive and since 99 percent of the black vote had been cast for the winner, it was expected that economic, political, and industrial advancement for blacks would follow. Magill charged instead that in that first year not one black person had been confirmed by the Republican Senate for an appointment.

Specifically, Henry Lincoln Johnson, nominated for the post of Recorder of Deeds in the District of Columbia, had been turned down by the Senate. The reason given was that Johnson was "personally unacceptable" to the senator from his state. Investigation revealed that the objection had come from Senator Tom Watson of Georgia. During 1921 Georgia had led the nation in lynchings, with a total of fourteen against thirteen for Mississippi. When asked their views of Johnson's rejection, several prominent New Yorkers cynically intimated a unanimous opinion. Had the Republican administration *wanted* Johnson confirmed he would have been.

Magill then took note of both the Secretary of the Navy and the Secretary of War. He reminded readers that the latter had "bombastically defended the conduct of the United States Marines in Haiti"; and that both the Marine behavior and Navy Secretary Denby's defense of it had never set well with black Americans. Of War Secretary Weeks, the writer decried Weeks's action before the House Military Committee. Mr. Weeks had protested to that body the release of the imprisoned men of the Twenty-fourth Infantry convicted in the previously mentioned rebellion of black soldiers in Houston, Texas.

Finally, writer Magill commented bitterly upon the Dyer antilynch bill which he described as "smouldering somewhere in the House of Representatives while lynching in the South goes merrily on." As could be expected, the South was vociferous in its condemnation of the Dyer Bill and joyful that it was being buried in the heap of national bureaucratic hostility.

It came as a surprise to many, however, that *The New York World* would show opposition to the bill. So piqued was the black press as to carry copies of a *World* editorial condemning the antilynching measure as a federal infringement upon the rights of the states. *The Chicago Defender* for January 14, 1922, reprinted the editorial with the terse comment that the New York daily gives a "punk opinion" of the Dyer Bill.

Meanwhile, as such unpleasant news items appeared in the nation's press, Marcus Garvey's troubles were accelerating rapidly in New York City. Foes were taking great delight in demanding to know what had happened to the *Orion,* soon to be rechristened *The Phyllis Wheatley.* What had happened was that the United States Shipping Board was now asking an unreasonable performance bond of four hundred and fifty thousand dollars before it would release the ship. That was far more than the Black Star Line could possibly meet. Then Cyril V. Briggs, editor of *The Crusader,* a periodical not friendly to the U.N.I.A. delivered a mortal blow. Still smarting from a statement by Garvey that he (Briggs) was "a white man passing for a Negro," Briggs did a little investigating of the Black Star Line on his own.

In response to his letter of inquiry to the Department of Commerce he was informed by the Navigation Bureau that it had no records of either the *Antonio Maceo (Kanawah)* or *The Phyllis Wheatley, (Orion).* Briggs was elated. In the November 1921 issue of *The Crusader* he demanded to know why the Black Star Line had been selling passage on a nonexistent boat. Some observers, including E. D. Cronon, say it was partly through editorial agitation in the press and partly because of complaints of Black Star Line stockholders that postal authorities arrested Garvey and charged him with using the mails to defraud. Amy Jacques Garvey's version differs.

She makes no mention in *Garvey and Garveyism* of Cyril Briggs and *The Crusader*'s "exposé" of the Black Star Line. Instead, she tells of Garvey's having written the United States Shipping Board in 1921 and of being told in reply that twenty-two thousand five hundred dollars was indeed on deposit with them for the *Orion*. In Decemmber, however, the Massachusetts Bonding Company informed Garvey that it had eleven thousand dollars due. Orlando Thompson had borrowed that amount to make the deposit with the Shipping Board. Garvey then began to investigate the entire matter and simultaneously attempted to recover the remaining balance of thirteen thousand five hundred dollars from Anthony Silverstone.

It was at that point, Mrs. Garvey declares, that her husband also sought to learn to what extent Thompson was negligent or involved in a deal with Silverstone. Perhaps, she suggests, Thompson was trying to conceal the deficit by borrowing from the bonding company. And she adds this cryptic comment:

> But to his (Garvey's) amazement, instead of getting help from the District Attorney's office in the matter he was indicted in January for using the mails to defraud.

Actually Garvey was merely arrested in January. The indictment did not come until late in February when Garvey, Elie Garcia, George Tobias, and Orlando M. Thompson were indicted on twelve counts of fraudulent use of the mails. The defendants were released on twenty-five hundred dollars bail each, pending trial. Meanwhile the office of the District Attorney seized books and records of the Black Star Line as well as some of those belonging to the U.N.I.A. and the *Negro World.* Garvey's protests of what he felt were illegal seizures of materials not related to the Black Star Line were brushed aside with threats of contempt charges.

As could be expected, the Garvey foes were highly pleased at news of the cocky Jamaican's misfortune. "U.S. AGENTS SEARCH FOR 'MYTH' SHIP" was the headline of a *Chicago Defender* front page story on January 21, 1922. The story related how Garvey was "swooped down upon" at his home on West 126th Street by agents who had received complaints from investors in Black Star Line stock. Cyril Briggs was so overjoyed he brought out an extra edition of his *Crusader.* Especially cruel was his headline in the *Crusader Bulletin* for February 18, 1922. "GARVEY BUNK EXPOSED," it shrieked, following with, "Faker who defrauded Negroes with worthless stocks and false tickets on fake steamships now poses as 'martyr'!"

Marcus Garvey, meanwhile, was forced to announce the closing down of the Black Star Line. It was a sad day indeed for the proud Jamaican and one of painful irony, too. The issue of *The Negro World* in which that unhappy announcement appeared was dated April 1, 1922!

In May, Edward Orr, a holder of Black Star Line stock, sued Garvey for one hundred and five dollars. Though the amount was small and the trial in Bronx Superior Court not the most serious in Garvey's stormy brushes with the law, it threw the spotlight directly on the structural weaknesses of the organization. Marcus Garvey was cornered into admitting that there were no corporation assets. Actually the Black Star Line held mortgaged interest in two ships it did not have, the *Kanawah* left in Cuba, and the *Shadyside* that had sunk a year earlier. Moreover, no dividends had been paid any stockholders.

Again, Garvey was publicly rebuked by Judge Jacob Pankin for not having kept a strict accounting of monies. More than half a million dollars had been spent in the steamship ventures and still two hundred thousand dollars was owed with nothing to show for the effort. The obviously angry judge not only reprimanded Garvey for exploiting the gullibility of his followers, but added: "There is a form of paranoia which manifests itself in believing one's self to be a great man."

As if that were not enough to beset him, the Jamaican leader was also having domestic problems. His marriage to Amy Ashwood was not working well. Shortly after a year he sought a divorce, but dropped the suit in the spring of 1921. However, during the summer Mrs. Garvey herself sought a separation. Her husband and Amy Jacques, her lifelong friend, had, it seemed, become more than business associates. Mrs. Garvey decided she needed a change of scenery. While she was in England her husband sought and obtained a divorce in Kansas City, Missouri, on June 15, 1922. He and Amy Jacques were married the following month.

Caught completely by surprise, Amy Ashwood returned to the United States and filed a countersuit seeking to invalidate the proceedings in Missouri and naming Amy Jacques as correspondent. The court action provided just the kind of grist the gossip mills loved to grind.

All of Garvey's old enemies of the press, particularly Robert Abbott, whetted their knives. Their hated quarry had at last ripped his underpants, fore and aft, and they were delighted to hold him up to public exposure. The bad journalistic taste of some of the stories revealed as much that was uncomplimentary about their writers and editors as about the misadventures of Marcus Garvey. And in spite of it all, the marriage of Garvey and Amy Jacques was not only legally sustained, but it lasted for the remaining twenty-seven years of Garvey's life.

Meanwhile the third International Convention of the Universal Negro Improvement Association assembled in New York. It was August 1922, and the unrelenting Garvey critics stepped up their efforts to destroy him. An editorial in the July issue of *The Messenger* and A. Philip Randolph's "Reply To Marcus Garvey" in the August issue of the same magazine set the pace. *The Messenger* for July took Garvey to task for remarks he was charged with having made in New Orleans before a contingent of the Ku Klux Klan. Here, as quoted in *The Messenger*, is an excerpt from Garvey's ill-considered comments.

> This is a white man's country. He found it, he conquered it, and we can't blame him if he wants to keep it. I am not vexed with the white man of the South for jim crowing me because I am black.
>
> I never built any street cars or railroads. The white man built them for his convenience. And if I don't want to ride where he's willing to let me ride then I'd better walk.

Garvey had committed a mortal error and his foes were quick to react. Using the remarks (that could broadly be interpreted as either an endorsement of the doctrine of white supremacy or a challenge to blacks to produce their own accommodations), *The Messenger* chose the former interpretation. After praising other "splendid, courageous, intelligent West Indian men and women," the editorial concluded:

Here's notice that *The Messenger* is firing the opening gun in a campaign to drive Garvey and Garveyism in all its sinister viciousness from the American soil.

In its August issue, appearing during the U.N.I.A. convention, *The Messenger* continued to belabor the man from Jamaica and his program. Randolph's "Reply To Marcus Garvey" was buttressed by a reprint editorial from *Ryan's Weekly,* a Tacoma, Washington, periodical. Garvey had spoken at Tacoma's Valhalla Hall and the editorial was an appraisal of his lecture. Concluded *Ryan's Weekly*:

> Garvey's lecture was a disappointment to many of those who expected to hear something of the land of which he prates so much and seems to know so little.
>
> The sensible thing for the Negroes of America to do is to leave Garvey severely alone.

Pursuing the line that Marcus Garvey had aligned himself with the Ku Klux Klan, William Pickens declined an invitation to be honored by the U.N.I.A. at its convention. In reply to a request from Garvey that he be present to accept the honorary title, Pickens in a lengthy letter said in part:

> Now, I believe in law and civilized government, and am therefore against the Klan and all of its principles, *yesterday, now, and tomorrow. I would not therefore accept any special honor from even black people who believe in Klan-principles.*

W. E. B. Du Bois, writing in *The Century* magazine for February 1923, charged Garvey with planning to get the Klan to finance the Black Star Line. He further said that "the Klan sent out circulars defending Garvey and declaring that opposition to him was from the Catholic Church." In that context one must recall that Garvey was a Catholic and that the Ku Klux Klan was opposed to power in the hands of Jews, Catholics, and Negroes.

Then there were some unexpected fireworks at the Convention itself. The *Chicago Defender* for the twenty-sixth of August reported that during a Liberty Hall meeting of the nineteenth, Garvey surprised everyone by tendering his resignation as President-General. "I refuse," he is reported as saying, "to associate any longer with a body of men on the executive council who are not honest enough to do business above board. I am tired of this plotting and intrigue."

Garvey's resignation was immediately followed by that of Elie Garcia, auditor general, F. Wilcom Ellegor, Henrietta Vinton Davis, Rudolph Smith, and R. L. Preston. There ensued a general debate and formal acceptance of the resignations. The action on the part of those who resigned was, according to the news account, meant as a prelude to a plan of Garvey's to reorganize the U.N.I.A. Of the new group Garvey, it was said, would be the sole director.

The *Defender* story also mentioned a tense moment when Garvey publicly accused James W. H. Eason, a former clergyman of Philadelphia, who was named U.N.I.A. Leader of American Negroes, of double-crossing him and trying to ruin Garvey and the association. It appeared for a moment that the two men would exchange blows. But a violent disturbance was averted by alert officials who kept the pair apart and by police stationed outside Liberty Hall. Eason supporters insisted that the "resignation" of Garvey was not genuine but merely a maneuver to pave the way for Garvey's reelection by the general membership.

Amy Jacques Garvey's version of the convention makes no mention of the internal organizational strife. She deals instead in *Garvey and Garveyism* with the general elation created by the reading of a message from the King and Queen of Abyssinia (Ethiopia). The message, read by H. H. Todakyn, Consul General of Persia, was interrupted by wild cheers when the reader reached that part of it inviting the association's members to "come back to the homeland." Mrs. Garvey further states in her account:

> The convention unanimously voted thanks and cabled congratulations to the King and Queen of Abyssinia. Marcus Garvey was reelected Provisional President of Africa.

The issue of *The Messenger* that appeared in September 1922, after the U.N.I.A. convention, carried the editorial by Chandler Owen. "Should Marcus Garvey Be Deported?" After briefly reviewing who, under the law, is eligible for deportation, Owen castigated Garvey, his movement, and all of his followers, concluding with this statement:

> The die is cast, Marcus Garvey *must go*. Every self-respecting Negro is called upon to rescue the race from the Black Kluxer's disgrace. Garvey must get out of Negro life everywhere. There is no place in America for a black race baiter, one time reviling all white men; and a "good nigger" race traitor, at another time selling out the rights of all Negroes.

The October issue of *The Messenger* called Garvey and his organization "thoroughly anarchistic." It cited the acts of violence of Garvey supporters in dealing with opponents of U.N.I.A. activities. It also mentioned the near-violent scenes pervading the August convention as proof of Garvey's anarchy. *The Messenger* then rushed to the defense of Garvey victims. Cyril Briggs, J. W. H. Eason, J. Austin Norris, Noah Thompson, W. Ashby Hawkins, and Dr. Le Roy Bundy were all named among those who had been threatened by "anarchistic Garveyites." Several of the afore-named had themselves been affiliated with the U.N.I.A.

Though thoroughly understandable in terms of human inconsistency, it was ironic, nonetheless, that *The Messenger* would take such a stand against Marcus Garvey. By its own definition of anarchistic acts on the part of Garveyites, *The Messenger* had inadvertently implicated itself in anarchy. Only two years previously, in its September 1919 issue, the radical magazine had run an inflamatory cartoon advocating anarchy.

Actually there were two cartoons, one facing the other on opposite pages. The first was a drawing depicting three black leaders (Du Bois flanked by two others) admonishing readers to be forgiving, patriotic, and modest. In the background Liberty holds the torch high as black civilians fall before attacks of whites wearing the uniform of the United States Army. The drawing is titled "Following the Advice of the 'Old Crowd' Negro."

The other drawing depicts a black man, armed to the teeth, hurtling through a crowd of whites, firing a pistol and other armaments mounted upon the speeding motor vehicle he is driving. The vehicle is labeled "The New Negro" and it flies a penant labeled "Longview, Texas, Washington, D.C., Chicago, Illinois?" The black man shooting his way through shouts, "Since the Government won't stop mob violence I'll take a hand!" Above the drawing is a Woodrow Wilson quote urging, "Force, Force to the Utmost . . . Force Without Stint or Limit!"; and below is the caption, "The 'New Negro' Making America Safe For Himself." It is not the kind of propaganda one expects to find in a publication accusing Marcus Garvey or anyone else of anarchy.

Still *The Messenger* pressed the attack. Calling attention

to a grisly package containing a human hand and sent ostensibly from the Ku Klux Klan in New Orleans to A. Philip Randolph, the publication was relentless in its determination to break the back of Garveyism. It formed "The Friends of Negro Freedom" which said in part:

> . . . The attorneys for The Friends of Negro Freedom are instructed to take steps immediately to bring about the dissolution of the organization, the arrest and prosecution of any American Negroes guilty of conspiracy in the incitement of crime, and the deportation of any foreign Negroes guilty of any overt anarchistic acts.

A. Philip Randolph wrote his opinions of African redemption titled, "The Only Way to Redeem Africa" in *The Messenger* for November and December 1922. It bore little resemblance to or sympathy for the Garveyan approach. And, finally, *The Messenger* devoted three pages of its December issue to "A Synposium on Garvey" by Negro leaders. It posed the following three questions:

1. Do you think Garvey's policy correct for the American Negro?
2. Do you think Garvey should be deported as an alien creating unnecessary mischief?
3. Remarks?

The letter went to twenty-five persons around the nation. Fourteen replied. Twelve expressed the belief that Garvey's policy was not good for the American Negro. Carter G. Woodson said he had given so little attention to Garvey's work he could not offer an opinion. Du Bois preferred to make his assessment later. Five felt Garvey should be deported, seven that he should be allowed to remain.

As the furor continued to rage around the determined

little vortex of anti-Garvey hate created by *The Messenger* and other foes, 1923 stormed on stage. The infant year was about to unfold an act of violence that would make all other U.N.I.A. scandals appear bland by comparison.

CHAPTER

FIFTEEN

JAMES W. H. EASON, former U.N.I.A. official named by Garvey the Leader of the American Negroes, formed his own group following a break with the Jamaican. He called it the Universal Negro Alliance. After the convention of August 1922, Eason spent a lot of time traveling about the country speaking against what he regarded as the evils of the U.N.I.A. One such lecture tour took him to New Orleans, Louisiana, at the beginning of 1923. It was Eason's last trip.

Under the headline, "EASON ASSASSINATED," the *New York Amsterdam News* for Wednesday, January 10, 1923, carried the following brief story:

> New Orleans, La.—Reverend J. W. H. Eason, a former leader in the Garvey movement and founder of the Universal Negro Alliance, who was shot here last Monday night by one of three men who opened fire upon him as he was leaving the Bethany Baptist Church where he had been speaking against the U.N.I.A. died at Charity Hospital last Friday. Three bullets pierced the body, two in the back and one in the right temple. He was rushed to Charity Hospital where

every effort was made to save his life, but he died early on Friday morning.

Dr. Eason was unconscious most of the time that elapsed between the attack and his death. He rallied sufficiently to swear before the police authorities that two of the men who sprang out at him from an alley in which they had been laying in wait for him were Frederick Dyer, forty-two, a longshoreman, and William Shakespeare, twenty-eight, a painter. Both men are said to be prominent members of the U.N.I.A. in this city.

In a *New York Times* story appearing on January 13, 1923, Dyer and Shakespeare were described as "minor officials" of the U.N.I.A. Dyer was referred to as "patrolman" and Shakespeare as "Chief of Police of the U.N.I.A." Both were said to be Jamaicans whose arrival in New Orleans coincided with that of Eason. However, *The New York Times* reported that the victim failed to live long enough to identify the two alleged assailants.

The *Chicago Defender*'s story paralleled that of *The Amsterdam News*. It added, however, that,

> Eason told a *Defender* reporter that he was shot by "hired assassins," and that it was the second attack made on him since he broke with the Garvey movement and denounced it as a fraud.

The *Defender* report also quoted Eason as declaring his assailants were sent to kill him in order to prevent his testifying at Garvey's trial in New York's Federal Court.

That part of Eason's alleged deathbed statement is supported by Amy Jacques Garvey's comment on Eason in her biographic study of her husband. She describes Eason in this manner:

Among the renegades from the black race, the one whom the prosecutor listed as his star witness "to testify against Garvey" was J. Eason—the first American U.N.I.A. Leader.

Mrs. Garvey then quotes Eason as admitting he is not a saint but that his love for his people is unassailable. She further declares that Eason forced the U.N.I.A. to pay him the maximal amount of back salary, after which he campaigned against Garvey and the U.N.I.A. he had sworn to protect even with his life. Her final words about Eason are these:

> After one of these denouncement meetings in New Orleans, in January [*sic*] 1924 he was shot to death in an alley. The prosecutor said he had rendered valuable service.

In New York, Marcus Garvey in a *New York Times* news story appearing January 21, 1923, emphatically denied that the U.N.I.A. was a radical organization or that it had any part at all in Eason's slaying. Garvey's enemies, however, refused to believe him. Indicative of the depth of anti-Garvey feeling was the promptness with which the opposition rallied to a fresh let's-get-rid-of-Garvey effort. The Committee of Eight, a group of prominent black citizens, seven men and a woman, drafted a letter to United States Attorney General Harry M. Dougherty.

The letter protested the length of time it was taking the government to bring Marcus Garvey to trial. In twenty-nine paragraphs it called the Attorney General's attention to "a heretofore unconsidered menace to harmonious race relationships." The letter went on to say:

> There are in our midst certain Negro criminals and potential murderers, both foreign and American-born, who are moved and actuated by intense hatred against the white race. These undesirables continually proclaim that all white people are

enemies to the Negro. They have become so fanatical that they have threatened and attempted the death of their opponents, actually assassinating in one instance.

From that opening paragraph the letter took off on a flight of condemnation of Garvey and all his enterprises. At some points it rose to a high pitch of hysteria, as in the following:

> The U.N.I.A. is composed chiefly of the most primitive and ignorant element of West Indian and American Negroes. The so-called respectable element of the movement are largely ministers without churches, physicians without patients, lawyers without clients, and publishers without readers, who are usually in search of "easy money." In short, this organization is composed in the main of Negro sharks and ignorant Negro fanatics.

At other points it sank to the piteous and grovelling tone of this statement:

> An erroneous conception held by many is that Negroes try to cloak and hide criminals. The truth is that the great majority of Negroes are bitterly opposed to all criminals and especially to those of their own race, because they know that such criminals will cause discrimination against themselves.

Rehashing all the charges of fraud, corruption, and terror already lodged against the U.N.I.A. the letter concluded:

> The signers of this appeal represent no particular political, religious or nationalistic faction. They have no personal ends or partisan interests to serve. Nor are they moved by any personal bias against Marcus Garvey. They sound tocsin only because they foresee the gathering storm of race prejudice and sense the imminent menace of this insidious movement, which cancerlike is gnawing at the very vitals of peace and safety of civic harmony and interracial concord.

The eight signers were Harry Pace, Robert S. Abbott, John E. Nail, Julia P. Coleman, William Pickens, Chandler Owen, Robert W. Bagnall, and George W. Harris. They represented the limited world of the black business entrepreneur, publisher, civil-rights worker, and local politician. Each had arrived at his position by grace of the paradox of racism that allowed a few to prosper above the many who did not. And each, fully aware that the official heat was about to be turned on Garvey, wanted to make certain not one of them would be caught up in the back draft.

But what they really feared was not Marcus Garvey and his vociferous followers, but an irate and vengeful white populace and what it could do by way of stripping all Negroes, *including them,* of the few gains they had made. Indeed, they brought that fear clearly forward in their letter.

No one understood the Committee of Eight better than Marcus Garvey. However, his point-by-point reply to their appeal to the Attorney General lost much of its power as Garvey himself fell into the use of invective. His point, for instance, that true leaders seek to "reform and improve their criminals" rather than oppose them because such criminals will cause discrimination against leadership, was well taken. So also was his criticism of the Committee's effort to link him with the Ku Klux Klan. Here Garvey tried to allay the Committee's fears as he reminded everyone that first, last, and always the K.K.K. was an organization of *white* supremacists, committed to the suppression of black aspirations. Said the Jamaican leader:

> Garvey would be illogical and foolish if on the one hand he preached ill-feeling and hatred between the races and then

went back on all that and allied himself with the Ku Klux Klan.

Such logic was all but submerged, however, as Garvey, employing the invective of his adversaries, tried to better them at their game. His hot retaliations, studded with such epithets as "good old darkey," "selfish dogs," and "barber shop rat," obscured the clarity of his thinking and weakened the power of his stance. While the Committee of Eight in its offensive position might have received a few bouquets for slinging mud in Garvey's direction, Garvey was considerably less securely anchored in the eyes of most people. Squirming in the defensive hot seat, he needed as much public support as he could get. Bombastic name-calling was not the way of winning it. Garvey's temper, fed by an inflated ego, was overriding his better judgment, and the results were not helping him.

Still, the responsible historian will not permit the intemperate Garvey tongue to destroy the many basic truths inherent in much that he said. In less emotionally charged statements Garvey provided completely sensible replies to many of the charges placed against him. More than that, he revealed, along with his suspicious and domineering nature, an almost childlike idealism.

Up to now we have heard very little from Garvey himself about the deficiencies of business management in his organization. All of the criticism of such weakness has come from others. And one gets the impression that Garvey never made any verbal or written criticism of his association's flaws. Such is not so. In *The Philosophy and Opinions of Marcus Garvey* one finds an enlightening section in which Garvey was refreshingly frank about certain such organizational flaws. Under the heading, "Salaries to Officers of the

Universal Negro Improvement Association—The Conflict of Ideals," one learns a great deal more about Marcus Garvey than that he was stubborn, hotheaded, impractical, and that his presence annoyed many contemporaries. Some of that information is apropos at this juncture.

One of the errors committed during the first U.N.I.A. convention was the voting of large salaries to newly elected officers with insufficient capital in the treasury to cover expenses. Salaries ranged from twelve thousand dollars to three thousand dollars per annum, the top figure going to His Highness, the Potentate. Next came Garvey's salary of ten thousand dollars equally matched by that of the Leader of the American Negroes. The Surgeon General and Counsel General were voted seven thousand dollars each.

The Deputy Potentate, Assistant President-General, Secretary General, High Chancellor, International Organizer, and two Leaders of the West Indian and Central American Provinces, received six thousand dollars each. Salaries of five thousand dollars were voted the Chaplain General, and the Auditor General. To The High Commissioner General, the Assistant Secretary General, and the Minister of Labor and Industry went the salaries of four thousand dollars. Finally, the lowest figures for officers of three thousand dollars each went to the Minister of the Legion and the Speaker-in-Convention.

By present day inflationary standards such salary figures are not impressive. In 1920, however, they were high, and an annual payroll of one hundred twenty-two thousand dollars for executives' salaries alone was expensive for such an organization with no endowment funds. But as Garvey had said, "We were glad to cut away from the old venal and corrupt leadership." Moreover, the delegates' oral and written reports of their past experiences with black organizations riddled with hustlers and thieves prompted the U.N.I.A. to try a new approach.

> With this in mind, and the desire to remove the new leaders from theft, graft, and alien influences, a sufficient salary was voted to each to make him independent and true to his trust.

Garvey had naïvely believed that good salaries would promote good organization and hard, earnest work, which would automatically guarantee the success of his program. He was in for a number of stunning surprises, as he later admitted in these words:

> Subsequent experience proved that all the majority of these men wanted were the offices with the titles and the privilege to draw large salaries.

Garvey cited Sidney De Bourg from Trinidad. A man past sixty, De Bourg came to the U.N.I.A. with a woeful tale of persecution and improverishment at the hands of the British for trying to help his people in Trinidad.

Garvey made him Leader of the Provinces of the West Indies at six thousand dollars a year. Yet, because Garvey demanded efficient work from him, De Bourg, in the spirit of vengeful resentment, became the first U.N.I.A. official to sue for twelve thousand dollars after one year of unsatisfactory work. In addition, the old man, according to Garvey, "was the principal witness against me for the Government in 1923."

Only two officers, Garvey found, actually did the work they were paid to do. They were Bishop George Alexander McGuire, Chaplain General, and Mrs. Henrietta Vinton Davis. The rest have been described by the President-General as not "worth more than $1,200 a year as an office boy or lackey." Calling them together and seeking to appeal to their sense of race pride was futile.

Meanwhile, to make up for the lack of capital, Garvey and his officers unanimously agreed to float a loan of two hundred thousand dollars from the membership. Sixty percent of the money so borrowed was on short notes of one year, and it was agreed that each man would do his part in raising the money. On the short-term loans the effort to repay by year's end had to be conscientiously made. Garvey suggested that each officer make a loan to the organization. They finally agreed to lend from five hundred to a thousand dollars, to be deducted from their salaries. At the completion of payment the notes were to be given for a period of five years.

But because Garvey was on the road much of the time he could not keep up with what was happening. "A group conspired," he asserted, "to issue their notes for one year so they could collect from the Association more quickly." Garvey was unaware of their tactic until they began to sue the Association in the New York courts. The service they actually rendered the U.N.I.A. amounted to very little indeed.

Even greater difficulties developed, as Garvey later discovered during his 1921 trip to the Caribbean.

> I was not out of the country twenty-four hours before my enemies, some of my own executive officers and associates, especially of the Black Star Line, started to plot for my exclusion from the United States. Instead of being out of the country for thirty days, I was kept out for five months. Through great effort I was readmitted to the country just in time to attend the convention in August. During my absence the Council had absolute power. They paid themselves regularly,

as usual, doing very little, if anything, constructive to enhance the work of the organization.

The young woman hired to supply Garvey with private and confidential information was in love with the man seeking to keep such information from him. When word reached Garvey in the West Indies that the ship planned for trips to Africa had been purchased, he was elated. But the fires of elation turned to ashes of despair when, upon returning to New York, he learned the truth. Instead of finding the much-hoped-for ship, he encountered his many critics both inside and outside the U.N.I.A. Worse still, he was greeted shortly thereafter with the charge of having used the mails to defraud.

Bitterness became intensified for Garvey when, after reducing his salary by 50 percent, he found that the others were selfishly clutching the full amount of theirs. That persisted in spite of an official resolution adopted at the second convention in 1921 when a salary cutback was deemed necessary to the health of the U.N.I.A. treasury. The resolution provided that:

> All officials and high officers of the Universal Negro Improvement Association shall be paid their salaries at the minimum which shall be half of the maximum, and each shall be allowed to earn the maximum by ability and fitness, which maximum shall be paid at the end of each month according to the record of such official.

However, Garvey asserted that the secretary whose job it was to edit the resolutions and insert them in the constitution had neglected his work. Wittingly or not he had omitted this most important law from the constitution for two consecutive printings. Garvey never knew this had happened until the officials who were fired or who resigned began to institute law suits. Upon making the discovery, Garvey immediately requested the official minutes of the convention for the lawyer to examine. No minutes could be found. As Garvey said, "They were wickedly destroyed in anticipation of the legal fights to extract money from the Association."

When, after the 1921 convention, some of the U.N.I.A. executives realized their maximum salaries would not be forthcoming, they resigned. At the same time they knew they had borrowed heavily from the membership to pay their own salaries. They knew they were morally obligated to repay those members whose notes were falling due. The more cunning of them remained to the last minute before leaving to sue for maximum salaries. It is significant that of the fifteen who sued the U.N.I.A. and received judgments, five were clergymen.

The Reverend Bishop George A. McGuire was not one of them. Both he and Mrs. Henrietta Vinton Davis remained faithful throughout the difficult days. Of his own salary here is what Garvey has written:

> My salary of five thousand dollars I have received in no one year. As the amounts accumulate I have continued to reduce same by making the Association a present of the balance. When I was first imprisoned I left my wife with a bank balance of only thirty-five dollars.

That is the substance of Marcus Garvey's own assessment of an area of his operations that became the focal point of much speculation and free expression by others. Since in this narrative views of his financial difficulties have been aired by others, it is fitting that Garvey's, too, be offered for whatever they may be worth.

CHAPTER SIXTEEN

THE TRIAL of Marcus Mosiah Garvey opened in New York's Federal Court on Friday, May 18, 1923. Three codefendants went on trial with him. They were Elie Garcia, former auditor general of the U.N.I.A.; George Tobias, Treasurer; and Orlando Thompson, Secretary General. The charge against the four was using the United States mails to defraud.

Assistant District Attorney Maxwell S. Mattuck represented the United States Government's prosecution. Garvey was represented by two black attorneys, the very able Cornelius W. McDougald and Vernal Williams. Garcia, Tobias, and Thompson were represented by three other attorneys. The trial judge was the Honorable Julian W. Mack.

Garvey had tried at the outset to have Judge Mack disqualify himself because of the jurist's membership in the N.A.A.C.P. Recalling that several of the "Committee of Eight" were closely associated with the famed black civil-rights group, Garvey, ever alert and suspicious, felt that the judge would be too prejudiced against him to rule fairly in the trial. Judge Mack disagreed. Though freely admitting his contributions to the N.A.A.C.P., he stood firm in declaring his intention to see that justice was done fairly and impartially. He refused, therefore, to step down from the case.

After a delay occasioned by the challenging of several prospective jurors, the panel of twelve white men was finally selected. And the mechanism of justice began its slow and tortuous grind. Prosecutor Mattuck opened with the statement that he was "not concerned with any fool's dream, however foolish it may be, for the social advancement and betterment of a people." He also declared his willingness to help any oppressed group attain its rights. The question to be considered, however, involved funds fraudulently obtained through the use of Garvey's paper, *The Negro World.* It was the jury's duty, Mattuck insisted, to find out if, in the process of collecting a million or more dollars, a large number of poor persons had been victimized.

Mattuck's first witness was Edgar M. Gray, former U.N.I.A. Secretary General. Gray asserted that Garvey had from the outset intended to defraud. He said the Jamaican incorporated the Black Star Line only after having been forced to do so by Assistant District Attorney Edwin B. Kilroe. Furthermore, Gray insisted that money collected from the sale of Black Star Line stock had been used to support other ventures not subsidiary to the steamship line.

The witness also declared that 51 percent of the stock was owned by the U.N.I.A., even though that Association had not paid for it. For every dollar the Black Star Line invested, fifty-one cents went to the U.N.I.A. According to Gray, he, as a corporating member of the Black Star Line, received forty-five shares of stock which in reality belonged to the Universal Negro Improvement Association. Finally Gray declared that as secretary general his salary was fourteen dollars a week. For his other duties he received merely a promise.

Assistant District Attorney Kilroe, as the second witness for the prosecution, repeated the story of having called the defendant into his office several times. He also told of a complaint by Edgar Gray and Richard E. Warner that a stock book had been lost; and Kilroe asserted that not once had Garvey offered to show his books or account for money.

> I had the case from June sixteenth to September sixteenth, 1919, and although I asked for the books I did not get all of them. I got some at one time, some at another, but I never got them all.

Richard Warner's testimony paralleled that of Gray's with respect to his status as an incorporator of the Black Star Line. In addition, he spoke of Amy Ashwood as "the power behind the throne" who accompanied Garvey on a business trip to Virginia when, in Warner's opinion, her place should have been taken by the treasurer. Said Warner, "I was supposed to control the accounts but Miss Ashwood was dominant and wouldn't let anybody look in her books." He testified that he soon afterward resigned his position.

Shortly after the opening of the trial a disagreement between the defendant and his chief counsel, C. W. McDougald, evoked a startling change of procedure. Garvey, who had read law in England but was no lawyer, decided that his counsel was not defending him adequately. Casting aside the adage that any layman who defends himself in a court of law has a fool for a client, the irrespressible and suspicious Garvey took over his own defense. Attorney McDougald, refusing to act merely in the capacity of Garvey's advisor, withdrew, leaving the defendant to carry on alone.

Judge Mack, meanwhile, acknowledged Garvey's right to defend himself. He added, however, that the defendant need not expect special consideration because of his inexperience and that he would be bound by the regulations governing the deportment of the professional legal counsel. To this Garvey readily agreed. Toward the end of the trial, however, realizing his need for expert assistance, he accepted the sideline aid of the experienced white attorney Armin Kohn.

As could be expected, it soon became clear that Marcus Garvey was far less than adroit and precisionlike in the role of his own defense counsel. Press reaction to his courtroom decorum ranged from the crisp, sparse, and impersonal reporting of *The New York Times* to the more personally involved commentary of the black New York *Amsterdam News*. Said that weekly in its edition of May 30, 1923:

> Mr. Garvey is acting as his own counsel, with the result that there is a distinctive atmosphere about the trial. Peal after peal of laughter rocks the court at frequent intervals, and Judge Mack, on one occasion, threatened to clear the court if another outburst occurred. But even the judge himself—grave, serious and patient as he appears to be—cannot help laughing at times. Reporters from all the leading papers throng the court on the lookout for comic copy.

That the *Amsterdam News* was not without a feeling of concern for Garvey is apparent in this comment appearing in its edition of June 13, 1923.

> With its entry into the fifth week, the Garvey case is beginning to simmer down to the question: Who will win? Will

the Government, with its well-organized, ably presented case; its corps of experts, prompt and efficient in every detail, and its short, sharp and masterly cross examinations; or will Garvey with his loose rambling defense; his elementary knowledge of legal ways; his stumbling, irrelevant, often pointless cross-examinations, and his force, tragic seriousness, and thorough knowledge of the details of the case?

Given equal chances can mere good intent, however dynamic, win against organization and skill?

Interim days of testimony made public many of the adventures and misadventures of the Black Star Line already mentioned in this narrative. Captain Joshua Cockbourne testifying as a witness for the prosecution, declared that his ship, the *Yarmouth,* was not used as had been promised. Instead of carrying freight and serving eventually as a passenger vessel for those wishing to journey to Africa, the *Yarmouth* made cruises between large Eastern seaboard cities. There Garvey called mass meetings at which he urged the buying of Black Star Line stock. Cockbourne declared that as an inducement to stock buying Garvey had him appear at meetings in the uniform of ship's captain.

In cross-examining Cockbourne, Garvey was himself accused by the witness of being jealous of Amy Ashwood. When Garvey tried to impugn Cockbourne's moral character, Judge Mack sustained the prosecutor's objection.

During his two days on the stand Captain Cockbourne bared details of the *Yarmouth*'s voyage with the eight-hundred-ton cargo of whiskey. Admitting that he received a bonus of two thousand dollars for promptness in getting the whiskey on board, he protested the low freight rate of nine dollars per ton. And for the loss of the whiskey, Cockbourne said the Green River Distilling Company got a fifty-two-thousand-dollar judgment from the Black Star Line. Garvey, acting as his own counsel, was unable to shake the witness's story.

Leo H. Healy, attorney for the owner of the *Yarmouth*, proved to be a man of puzzling contradictions. Under Garvey's cross-examination his words were a mixture of condemnation of both Garvey and himself. They then quickly turned to words of seeming praise for Garvey. Of the first, the following exchange is a sample.

GARVEY: Isn't it a fact that Harriss McGill and Company did everything they could to influence the purchase of the *Yarmouth*, Mr. Healy?

HEALY: No, they were not anxious. I know you'd have paid $200,000, you were so anxious to get the boat.

QUESTION: Do you know of any reason why Garvey wanted a ship?

ANSWER: I heard that Kilroe was forcing him to buy one.

QUESTION: When you negotiated a contract for $165,000, did you believe the ship was worth it?

ANSWER: I did not.

Still under Garvey's cross-examination, Healy stood fast by his contention that the latter was far more anxious to buy than his clients were to sell. He even admitted that Harriss had confided to him that Garvey had access to six million Negroes from whom Garvey hoped to collect one dollar each. Harriss then instructed Healy to get as much as he could out of the deal.

Healy's courtroom exchange with Garvey then abruptly assumed an entirely different tone. He freely admitted being favorably impressed by the U.N.I.A. leader. The impression Garvey made upon him was so great "that it almost made me feel that I wanted to buy some stock." Apparently the temptation was short-lived, as Healy gave no indication that he yielded to the impulse. He did, however say to Garvey on the witness stand:

> You impress me even now. I have read many evil things about you, but to be candid, I don't believe half of them, even now.

Attorney Healy's ambivalent feelings toward Garvey were certainly not shared by Adrian Richardson, captain of the ill-fated *Kanawah*. Richardson's description of the U.N.I.A. leader summarized him as a "good orator, poor businessman, and a highway robber." With Garvey cross-examining the outspoken and unshakable Richardson, the exchange between the two grew understandably sharp, personal, and irrelevant to the case before the court. Not only did Richardson accuse Garvey of "robbery" but of denying burial funds to a crew member who died during a period of delinquency in the payment of his U.N.I.A. dues.

At another point Richardson testified that he and Garvey had already engaged in a fist fight over salary allegedly owed the former, and that when the case was over he'd fight him again—if he could get by Garvey's heavy bodyguard. Garvey, according to news reports, "shook with laughter" at Richardson's threat.

Other witnesses told of being "deceived" by Garvey, of having been quizzed by prosecutor Mattuck prior to the trial, and of having purchased Black Star Line stock without ever receiving dividends. Garvey was alternately accused of turning all monies over to his secretary, who had become his second wife, and of accounting to no one for those and other monies. He was said to have high-handedly run things to suit himself.

Garvey was further accused by witnesses of squandering money at the race track in Kingston, of having his treasurer issue him signed blank checks at will, and of accusing those who raised objections of conspiring to overthrow him. Such charges, along with those of having deliberately sought to defraud stock investors and of using the ships for propaganda purposes, summed up the prosecutor's case.

It is important here not to forget the overall charges upon which Garvey had been indicted. He was, in fact, twice indicted. The first indictment charged Marcus Garvey alone, "for using the mails to defraud in the promotion of the Black Star Line and the Universal Negro Improvement Association." That indictment, however, having been deemed faulty, was withdrawn. It was withdrawn because the Black Star Line was a corporation and not a private enterprise. Garvey was then placed under two new indictments, and this time his Vice-President, Secretary, and Treasurer shared the indictments with him.

The two new indictments, referred to during the trial as "the first and second indictments," were based upon replies to questionnaires sent out to all stockholders of the Black Star Line. Those questionnaires, soliciting opinions of Marcus Garvey and his operation from stockholders, were issued by the prosecution. That, in itself, was said to be "unusual." Moreover, they were sent out following the first indictment and the seizure "by the government of all the books, records and documents of the Black Star Line and the Universal Negro Improvement Association."

Such a procedure, over Garvey's objection, was a violation of the defendant's constitutional right under Article IV of the United States Constitution. By admitting such documents in evidence, Garvey was being forced to give evidence against himself. Under such circumstances the government was legally weakening its case against the defendant.

Garvey, acting as his own lawyer, proceeded nonetheless to carry on his own defense. In a conference preceding the defense, Judge Mack requested, and Garvey agreed, that the proceedings would not prevent the judge from keeping an engagement in Chicago on June 14. They had about a week in which to make it. So anxious was Garvey to establish his innocence of the many allegations leveled against him that he had to be restrained several times by Judge Mack. Testimony by witnesses who worked in the offices of the Black Star Line and the U.N.I.A. indicated that Garvey never personally handled money. Nor was he seen by them to sign "whole rows of checks" over to himself or pocket blank checks. Then, even though Judge Mack had initially ruled Garvey's wife an "incompetent witness under the law," he allowed her to testify later that morning.

Amy Jacques Garvey, nervous at the beginning, soon settled down to her testimony. Asserting that she wrote out orders for *all* checks including those for Garvey, she contended that all accounts of the various U.N.I.A. activities were kept "separate and distinct." Mrs. Garvey related how she had taken a trip to the West Indies aboard the *Yarmouth.* Someone, she said, was obviously trying to sink the vessel. At one point an explosion occurred in the engine room, creating panic among the passengers, who were then threatened with being tossed overboard by the inebriated chief engineer. The following morning, according to the witness, she heard someone yell, "My God! They've opened the sea cocks!" Water was rushing into the hold, and all on board were ordered to man the pumps.

When asked about circulars sent through the mail, Mrs.

Garvey said that her husband had never personally done such a thing. Those chores were handled by the office workers "upstairs." Amy Jacques Garvey left the witness stand far more composed then when she had taken it.

For the next few days the case droned on with little of the kind of excitement courtroom spectators flock to see and hear. It was revealed that Marcus Garvey had sent an envoy to the League of Nations in Geneva. His purpose was to introduce the Black Star Line to that international body and thereby stimulate trade between the United States, the West Indies, and Africa. Witnesses Frederick Augustus Toote and George O. Marks, both affiliated with the U.N.I.A. and the Black Star Line, expressed their confidence in Garvey and his endeavors.

The U.N.I.A. leader tried to link witness James E. Amos to a former British ambassador in Washington, Lord Reading. Amos, a black man and former bodyguard of President Theodore Roosevelt, was an agent of the Department of Justice. Garvey was sure that Amos had been "planted" by the British to "get Garvey." He tried unsuccessfully to establish that such a conspiracy existed.

The Jamaican then attempted to have a mistrial declared on the ground that Prosecutor Mattuck had accused him of lying. The court ruled against him. Garvey then charged that Mattuck was deliberately keeping some of the exhibits introduced by the defense from being shown. After a heated denial by the Prosecutor the papers under dispute were located. Garvey's pique was further roused by Orlando Thompson whose attitude on the stand seemed less friendly than the U.N.I.A. felt it should be. The Court had to step in and admonish Garvey for his line of questioning.

Further aggravation came to Garvey on the following day

of the trial. A newspaper report that Judge Mack, Prosecutor Mattuck, and the jurors had received letters threatening their lives if Garvey were convicted had come to Garvey's attention. In view of the murder of J. W. H. Eason in New Orleans and the jailing by Judge Mack of Garveyite Charles Linous on contempt charges, talk of further threats was serious. During the trial Linous had been accused by Hugh Mulzac, a former Black Star Line captain and a United States Government witness, of threatening the lives of Mulzac and Sidney De Bourg if they testified against Garvey.

This new alleged threat against judge and prosecutor, whether real or fancied, would not set well with an all-white jury. Garvey knew that and he was not alone in his concern. Indeed the rash of scare stories of alleged violent plots by Garveyites against government witnesses during the trial induced repeated attempts on the part of the Garvey defense to have a mistrial declared. District Attorney Haywood, seeing that as a possibility, asked newspaper reporters not to endanger the Government's case by playing up the mere allegation of such threats upon life in the public press. Apparently the District Attorney knew, as shall shortly be shown, just how wobbly the government's case against the Jamaican actually was.

If Marcus Garvey's floundering and often irrelevant questioning of witnesses marked him a poor defense lawyer, his summation to the jury, in spite of its great length, was a far better effort. In essence it reviewed the charges brought against him and how, in his opinion, those charges were never proved true. Castigating each of those who had borne major testimony against him, Garvey then concluded with an analysis of what it meant to be a Negro with purity of intent regarding the welfare of his people. Even Garvey's bitterest press enemy, *The Chicago Defender,* was moved to comment grudgingly in its editions of June 16, 1923, "At times even a degree of admiration must be felt at the nerve of the man in shattering court customs."

Judge Mack then charged the jury. It was a legal formality described by the New York *Amsterdam News* of June 20, 1923, as "a model of balance and lucidity swerving by not one scintilla either to the side of the government or to that of the defendants. It was a reflection of the unexampled patience he has shown throughout the trial." According to the *Amsterdam News* report, Judge Mack asked the jury not to be swayed by Garvey's pleading of his own case.

Admitting that the procedure had prolonged the case, he nonetheless said he did not believe such to be Garvey's deliberate intention. "The only thing you have to consider," he continued, "is the guilt or innocence of the defendants—nothing else whatsoever." The jurist further reminded the jurors that neither the Black Star Line nor the U.N.I.A. was on trial and that black-white antagonisms should not enter their considerations. The case, he reminded them, centered solely upon the issue of the guilt or innocence of the defendants of the charges mentioned in the indictments.

At 12:30 P.M. on Monday, June 18, 1923, the jury began its deliberations. Eleven hours later Judge Mack sent for the twelve men and delivered to them, without their having requested it, a further set of instructions. Details of that second charge will be discussed in the next chapter. Thirty minutes later the jury returned with its verdict. Elie Garcia, Orlando Thompson, and George Tobias were declared "not guilty." Only Marcus Garvey, alone, was found guilty as charged.

The New York Times of June 19, 1923, reported that the

eleven hours of jury deliberation was occasioned by two jurors who were holding out for the conviction of one of the freed defendants. It did not identify the defendant, however. Following Judge Mack's second charge to the jury the two hold-outs agreed with the others that the defendant in question should be freed. He was, they decided, merely an employee of Garvey, who had complied with the instructions of the head man. The trial of Marcus Garvey, after a month of wrangling, was finally over.

CHAPTER SEVENTEEN

JUST HOW fair a trial did Marcus Garvey receive? The answer depends upon one's interpretation of what constitutes fairness and justice in a courtroom trial. To those convinced of the rightness and, yes, even the unquestionable *righteousness*, of the law-and-order authority that tried and convicted Marcus Garvey, the fiery leader received full justice. But one learns after a time that courts controlled by human beings do not dispense justice with impartiality. Judges, prosecutors, defending lawyers, witnesses, and juries are neither always right nor righteous.

One learns also that honesty and fair play can never be compatible with racism. Fair play and racism are a contradiction in terms. Such has already been clearly seen in the shameless behavior of those whose involvement in Marcus Garvey's activities just happened not to bring them to trial with him. We have had a clear look at many of the weaknesses of the complex President-General of the Universal Negro Improvement Association. A critical look at key parts of the mechanism that judged and condemned him is now in order. To preface that, however, with two paragraphs about Mrs. Marcus Garvey may well add illumination to Garvey's decision, unwise though it obviously was, to act as his own defense counsel.

Marcus Garvey's second wife, Amy Jacques, was no tyro in the general area of legal proceedings. As a young woman in high school she persuaded her father to let her study shorthand and typing. Though Mr. Jacques objected to the idea of his daughter being "exposed to the wiles of men in an office," he consented. He stipulated, however, that Amy use such skills only in the nursing profession he had chosen for her. Amy completed the course and received an offer from the legal firm to which her teacher was attached. Her father's "No," though firm, was not final. He died shortly thereafter and Amy went to work as a clerk in the office of the family's lawyer where she was able to look after her father's estate.

Four years in the law office prepared her, in her own words, to "attend to every legal phase of the work including that of a fire insurance agency." Amy Jacques Garvey has never pretended to be an attorney. Still, her general acquaintance with certain routine legal procedures was conceivably helpful to her husband from time to time. Doubtless her suggestions, for better or for worse, cast an influence upon many of his decisions.

As has been said earlier, Marcus Garvey's legal rights under the United States Constitution were violated when his seized records, books, and documents were admitted in evidence at the trial over his objections. The Bill of Exceptions filed in Garvey's behalf after the trial contained ninety-four alleged trial errors, according to the record cited in *The Philosophy and Opinions of Marcus Garvey*. The following three took place during the trial itself. Still others were committed later.

1. The Court erred in not declaring a mistrial after articles and stories of threatening letters to Judge, Prosecutor, and Jury appeared in New York newspapers. This held if a verdict adverse to the Plaintiff-in-Error (Garvey) had been returned and the publication of such articles and stories had been called to the attention of the Court.
2. The Court erred in not declaring a mistrial after the Prosecutor called the Plaintiff-in-Error a "liar" in the presence of the jury. That occurred when Prosecutor Mattuck asked Garvey to turn over certain papers and Garvey replied that he had previously done so.
3. The Court erred in refusing to comply with the request of the Plaintiff-in-Error to restrain persons attached to the Court from giving out news to the press that was prejudicial to the Plaintiff-in-Error.

There were still other violations of Garvey's rights. Take Judge Mack's second charge to the jury—the one for which the jury itself never put in a request. The twelve men had been in deliberation for eleven hours when they were called back by the Judge, who gave them the following instructions:

> Some men feel that having given their view in the beginning, it is an indication of their firmness of character, their sound judgment, if they stick inalterably to it. . . .
>
> Now the effect of a disagreement, whether it be as to one count, two or three or four of them, as to any particular count, means that as to such count or as to such defendant, or both, as to which you may disagree, the government is put to the expense, the public is put to the loss of time, and the Court and jury, and the witnesses and the defendants are put to the expense of having to go through the whole thing again.

In simpler and briefer language Judge Mack told the jury to hurry up their deliberations. They were already taking up the Government's money, the public's time, and subjecting him, the jury, and the witnesses, to the possibility of a hung jury and a costly retrial. Obviously Judge Mack had hoped for a quicker decision. He got one, thirty minutes after that second charge. What Garvey got, of course, was the guilty verdict.

Another courtroom item worth remembering, as one considers bias or lack of it, is that, while four men were on trial, the Assistant United States Prosecutor indicated he felt otherwise as he asked this in his closing remarks to the jury.

> Gentlemen, will you let the tiger loose?

"The tiger" of course was Marcus Garvey. That he, alone, was singled out by the prosecution for such grave consideration by the jury gives a strong hint of the Government's preference for bagging what it regarded as its big quarry in the case.

But if one chooses to bypass that issue, there is still the basic one of exactly what it was that the defendant had been convicted of. We are told that it was "the third count of the second conviction." Precisely what was that?

The indictment of Marcus Garvey and the three other aforementioned officers of the Black Star Line charged a single scheme to defraud. The various counts charging the substantive offense of using the mails in executing such a scheme were based upon the separate mailing of letters to different addresses. Each mailing, then, became the basis for a count.

Garvey was acquitted of all the charges in both indictments except the charge contained in the third count of the second indictment. The substance of that count was as follows:

> That on or about December 13, 1920, "for the purpose of executing said scheme and artifice," Garvey placed in a post office in the Southern District of New York "a certain letter or circular enclosed in a postpaid envelope addressed to Benny Dancy, 34 West 131 Street, New York City."

Mr. Dancy, a porter at Pennsylvania Railroad Station, was the prosecution's prime witness. A reading of the verbatum transcript of his testimony reveals that after giving his name and occupation, Dancy asserted he had bought fifty-three shares of Black Star Line stock. When asked if he had received a letter from the Post Office Department, he replied that he had not. When asked how the Government came into possession of his mail he said that agents came to his home in Brooklyn where he handed it over to them.

Prosecutor Mattuck then produced an empty envelope which Dancy recognized because the back of it bore the stamp, "Black Star Line." Under continued questioning by Mattuck the witness could not recall what the envelope had contained. He asserted that he had received numerous letters from the U.N.I.A., the Black Star Line, and the Negro Factories Corporation. Some he had read and some he had cast aside without reading. The letters, he said, had been too numerous for him to recall any single one. Dancy did recall, however, that "some of the letters said invest more money in the Black Star Line for the case [*sic*] of purchasing bigger ships and so forth."

Under Garvey's cross-examination, Dancy again recalled receiving circulars in "some letters." When Garvey persistently asked for positive and specific information of the contents of the letters, Dancy ended his testimony by declaring: "I can't remember all of them; I got so many letters I couldn't remember all the letters."

Four legal conclusions have been drawn from Benny Dancy's testimony. First, he was not charged in either of the indictments as one of the persons whom it was intended to defraud (fol. 860). Further, he could not have been one of those included in the description, "divers other persons whose names are to the Grand Jurors unknown," appearing on the face of the indictment. Dancy was known to the Grand Jury.

Second, though Dancy was a Black Star Line stockholder, there is no mention of when he bought his stock. In order to determine whether any letter or circular addressed to him was in execution of the scheme to defraud, one would have to know when Dancy became a stockholder.

Third, Dancy never testified that he *received* the envelope (Exhibit 112) shown him in the courtroom. He merely testified that he *recognized* the envelope (fol. 2582). Fourth, the envelope was offered in evidence with no testimony other than that of Dancy who said he recognized it. Mr. Mattuck, the prosecuting attorney, offered it in evidence with the following comment:

> I offer the envelope in evidence, on the ground it bears on the back a stamp, "Black Star Line" and it is a reasonable assumption that envelope contained matter from the Black Star Line (fol. 2585)

A reasonable enough assumption. But is it an equally reasonable assumption that the empty envelope exhibited by prosecutor Mattuck was placed in the mail by Marcus Garvey on or about December 13, 1920, and that it contained matter designed to perpetrate a fraud upon Benny Dancy? Hardly. Yet that was the core of the United States Government's case against Marcus Garvey. It does therefore become apparent that Garvey was actually convicted and harshly sentenced for reasons other than contained in the legal charges against him.

Joel A. Rogers, black historian and newsman, who covered the Garvey trial, offered an explanation. Rogers, himself a Jamaican, had known Garvey as a boy. Though he had never been a U.N.I.A. member, Rogers had written for *The Negro World.* He had talked many times with Garvey, often disagreeing with him, but without ever joining the hostile anti-Garvey camp. In his book, *Great Men of Color,* Rogers observed that in view of contemporary offenders whose crimes were worse, Garvey's sentence was considered harsh. Besides, Rogers said, only five or six stockholders of thirty-five hundred testified against Garvey, and they did so only after much prodding by the prosecution. Then Rogers revealed this:

> There were reasons which had undoubtedly influenced the judge, Julian W. Mack, however. During the trial Garvey had indulged in several bursts of anti-Semitism, and when called before Judge Mack after the jury had found him guilty, he shouted, "Damn the Jews!"

Rogers further explained that Garvey's unhappy dealings in the *Yarmouth* affair had been with Jews, and he had blamed all Jews for the disastrous results. Judge Mack, Prosecutor Mattuck, and other Jews sitting in the jury box were quite understandably not kindly disposed to Jew-baiting. Moreover, as Rogers pointed out, Judge Mack's N.A.A.C.P. affiliation, plus his Jewish faith, did not cotton to Garvey's unhappy alliance with the Ku Klux Klan, a group as disdainful of Jews as of blacks and Catholics. So there Marcus Garvey stood, damning the entire feline family to hell with his head thrust deep in the lion's mouth.

The hardening of the attitude of Judge Mack and Prosecutor Mattuck in denying Garvey concessions after that courtroom outburst lends an air of compassionate astuteness to Roger's observation. The honest, sensitive, black reporter understood the feeling and reaction of the Jew publicly ridiculed. It reveals also that the three men, Judge Mack, Prosecutor Mattuck, and the U.N.I.A. President-General each had his Achilles heel.

E. D. Cronon offered yet another explanation for the harsh punishment meted out to Garvey. He attributed it to the Jamaican's "bumptious activities in the courtroom." The author of *Black Moses* took the view that Garvey's efforts to vindicate himself and the entire black race were inspired by belligerence, and they doubled the length of the proceedings. That, the writer concluded, was "not calculated to impress favorably a jury of restless businessmen" even though the Government's case was, in Cronon's words, "admittedly weak."

Dr. Cronon's acknowledgement of the weakness of the Government's case might well have been followed by an explanation of *why* Garvey's bumptious courtroom behavior disturbed the all-white jury and unquestionably had great bearing on its decision to punish Garvey with severity. Unlike historian-reporter Rogers, who saw the courtroom events through the eyes, and more important, the *feelings*, of a black man, Cronon was handicapped from the start.

Indeed he acknowledged as much in the preface to his well researched study. He can therefore be forgiven for failing to grasp fully and express freely what racism has done to its victims on both sides. And it is essential for one to know that if he hopes really to understand what motivated the principals engaged in the human drama that was Marcus Garvey's trial.

White participants in that drama—trial personnel and spectators alike—felt no discomfort or inconvenience with those elements of the proceedings affording them the luxury to which they were accustomed, of feeling superior to the black participants. That was particularly true when black participants were, inadvertently or not, providing amusement or entertainment.

It should be added here that black spectators also found some humorous aspects of the trial easy to take. They were far more uncomfortable than whites, however, whenever one of their own, particularly the defendant, Marcus Garvey, found himself in an embarrassing position. White laughter at what to them is the wildly humorous bumbling of the black buffoon sounds to blacks like the mocking echo of the white man's assertion that he is supreme. That is a fact many white Americans have never fully understood. And they haven't understood it because they have forgotten that an important pillar in the structure of American racism was the traditional function of the black man as the white man's entertainer before the former developed his own theatre.

It began during slavery. Black slaves entertained one another as well as their owners and they did it without pay. After slavery, minstrelsy moved from the plantation to the professional stages, and the earliest minstrels were ex-slaves and freedmen who performed for pay all over the United States. White performers, seeing them, were captivated not only by their artistry but by the great commercial possibilities inherent in the art form.

They copied the routines, blackened their faces, and put on minstrel shows. Black minstrels, in order to survive in a business controlled by whites, followed suit. They were, ironically, forced to transform themselves into superblacks (blackened face and exaggerated speech) in order to be acceptable as representative of what whites fancied blacks to be. Thus was born the image of the hilariously funny, eye-rolling, grinning, singing, and dancing darkey. The die was cast, the stereotype fixed. Wherever black men were put on public view it was assumed they would provide some form of entertainment.

So the role of the black man in the American theater, or even in that most tragic of theaters, the courtroom, was assumed to be, however unwitting, that of the entertainer. He was there, it was believed, to provide at some point a measure of comic relief. The frightened, confused, genuinely funny, or just plain nondescript black man or woman in court was quite in the pleasant American tradition. Such witnesses did take the stand in the Garvey case. Some of what they did and said evoked general laughter. Reporters and photographers packed themselves off daily to the trial automatically looking for a show. Many of their stories revealed the carnival spirit they carried with them.

Witnesses from the disgruntled ranks of ex-Garveyites provided occasional verbal fireworks highly entertaining to those enjoying the spectacle of angry conflict. Carried on in the dialects of the participants, such exchanges amused the spectators. They were especially funny to those white persons whose subconscious sense of inate racial superiority was never threatened by such shenanigans.

The thing that marred it all, making it difficult to swallow completely, was the personality of Marcus Garvey. So thoroughly has racism brutalized and dehumanized its perpetrators as to make it impossible for most whites to cope rationally with blacks who do not fit neatly into the mold they have designed for them.

Marcus Garvey definitely did not fit the mold. While his black skin and stocky build may have suggested the funmaker, he was not one to keep folks laughing. In fact his precise West Indian speech, good diction, and generally excellent grammar, while a source of pride to black people, was a source of irritation to most whites. The latter in search of a jolly black man oozing simple goodwill and primitive charm did not find what they had hoped for in the leader from Jamaica.

Garvey was an example of the kind of tense anger and frustration, directed not altogether inward at himself and his people but also outward toward whites. Racism breeds many such blacks. Garvey's force lay not alone in his anger and frustration, but in the way he harnessed them to a brilliant mind and a tremendous gift for leading masses of people. Cronon was not incorrect in calling Marcus Garvey, "bumptious," "arrogant," and "belligerent." That is how racism had brutalized *him.* The blacks who fought him so bitterly were by so doing giving expression, in their own way, to what racism had done to dehumanize *them.*

Take a long, hard look at Robert S. Abbott and the Committee of Eight whose hatred of Garvey was so great. Obviously they were motivated by fear and envy, with the former overshadowing the latter. As black Americans they were no less disenchanted with the condition of the unequal existence they were required to endure than was Marcus Garvey himself.

The difference that separated them from him was this.

They had decided that the solution lay in playing it safe and going along with the system, and Garvey had resolved to gamble by trying to establish an independent system for blacks alone. For a few, flickering instants it appeared that Garvey might succeed in at least bringing the status quo into serious question. White opposition stiffened. Garvey's black opposition, sensing that his loosely structured schemes would collapse, loudly proclaimed their stand against him. They wanted no association with a failure who was also subject to being severely punished by dominant whites determined to teach blacks to stay in their proper place.

But Garvey was tough. A measure of his toughness was seen in his refusal to roll over and play dead when to do so would have made things considerably easier for him. As an adversary he was at once a nagging, hated, and awe-inspiring gladiator. He was of that breed that a truly worthy opponent wanted to defeat but never to destroy.

CHAPTER EIGHTEEN

With the announcement of the verdict by the jury foreman, Garvey's attorney, Armin Kohn, made an appeal for another trial. Judge Mack promptly denied the appeal. Kohn then asked for a postponement of the sentence. His motion was answered by Prosecutor Mattuck, who after declaring he had no objection to such a postponement, asked that Garvey be remanded to the Tombs to await sentence. Said Mattuck:

> I have evidence to prove that money is being used in the purchase of guns, arms, and ammunition, and his Legion will stop at nothing to defend him. He is a menace to the community, and at this time, more so than ever, I ask that Marcus Garvey be remanded without bail.

Judge Mack then ordered the convicted man to jail to await sentence on the following Thursday. Garvey requested that bail be granted so he could clear up his business. He said:

I know what the prosecutor says about my followers being armed is only malice. No one knows better than he that is false.

Judge Mack stood firm in his ruling and Garvey, still protesting, was led off to the Tombs just a short distance away.

A group of Garveyites waiting meanwhile at a nearby elevator had prepared for a celebration as they were certain their leader would be acquitted. Their stunned dismay transformed itself into frenzied action, however, as they swiftly rallied and began organizing efforts legally to gain the Jamaican's freedom. On June 21, 1923, Marcus Garvey was sentenced by Federal Judge Mack to five years' imprisonment and a fine of one thousand dollars. The Court recommended that the condemned prisoner be sent to the federal prison at Atlanta, Georgia. While bail was not fixed, the Judge did grant a stay of execution of the sentence. Garvey then made this conciliatory statement:

> We regard America as the greatest friend of the Negro. If I have said during the trial what may have been interpreted as an insult to this court, I never intended it as such. I accept my sentence and will do my best for the Negro race.

Several applications for bail were turned down, and when the judge left for Europe another effort yielded results. Bond was set at fifteen thousand dollars. But the city's leading bonding companies backed off as soon as Garvey's name was mentioned, openly admitting their fear of being blacklisted. One did, however, consent to aid if Garvey's supporters could raise part of the money. At the last minute that company reneged. Garveyites finally raised the money from U.N.I.A. members and found a willing bonding company.

There was much celebrating when, three months after his incarceration, the U.N.I.A. leader walked out of the Tombs in September 1923. There had been no effort made to hold a third convention while Marcus Garvey was in jail. The newly released leader lost no time, however, in taking to his rostrum at Liberty Hall. The fires of organizational morale, still flickering, had to be blown to a roaring flame.

In that first speech since his confinement, delivered to a beaming audience on September 13, Garvey assured all present that news of his "trial and so-called conviction" had gotten all over the world. Even those in "the remotest parts of our homeland, Africa," he declared, had formed their opinion of white man's justice in America.

Garvey insisted that he was tried and convicted not for fraud but for seeking black emancipation. Then, speaking with the wounded emotion of the embittered patriarch set upon by wayward sons, Garvey added this:

> I was convicted because an atmosphere of hostility was created around me. I was convicted because wicked enemies, malicious and jealous members of my own race, misrepresented me to those in authority for the purpose of discrediting and destroying me.

The depth of Garvey's hurt and its accompanying tortured confusion was evident in this outburst:

> I would not blame the few white persons who contributed to my conviction, neither would I blame the Government and the illiberal of the white race who had prejudices against me. They know no better than the information they received from treacherous, malicious, and jealous Negroes who, for the sake of position and privilege, will sell their own mothers.

Garvey's understandable angry disappointment at black treachery seemed temporarily, at least, to dim his view of total reality. It was a great deal easier, of course, for the personally uninvolved outside observer to see what Garvey's anguish would not allow him to see. An editorial in the *Planet*, a southern newspaper published in Richmond, Virginia, took a view less conciliatory to the United States authorities.

In its issue of July 21, 1923, it likened the federal action in Garvey's case to that of the same government toward "men of Communistic and Soviet tendencies during World War I." The *Planet* charged United States officials with blind prejudices that regarded such people as being outside the protection of the United States Constitutional guarantees. It further charged them with "extending repressive measures to mild-mannered men" and of thus making a mockery of their rights. Said the *Planet*:

> Now comes this foreigner, Marcus Garvey, convicted of the tentative charge of using the mails to defraud, based upon a letter sent to one of the citizens of this country relative to the sale of stock in the Black Star Line Corporation.

In short it was more and more beginning to appear to many that the attitude of the United States Government officials toward Garvey was at the root of his conviction and harsh sentencing. But if Marcus Garvey was crushed by such a probability, his actions belied it. Instead of sitting nervously idle to wait for the outcome of his appeal he organized the Black Cross Navigation and Trading Company.

This new outfit, modeled after the old Black Star Line Corporation, had a charter permitting it to trade between the United States and other areas of the world populated by blacks. Garvey also envisioned that his new line would serve as a transport for those who wished to sail to Africa as colonists.

With undaunted aplomb the Jamaican contacted the chairman of the United States Shipping Board in Washington, D.C. Mr. Garvey was coming to confer with him on June 6 to discuss the purchase of another ship! A few days later Garvey's new company submitted an offer for the purchase of the steamship *Susquehanna.* Though he promised to pay one hundred forty thousand dollars by August, the Board, recalling past dealings, declined to sell.

Garvey then went to the Panama Railroad Company, who sold him the *General G. W. Goethals* for one hundred thousand dollars. With an additional sixty thousand dollars invested in refurbishing the vessel, the *General Goethals* was by far the best such investment Garvey had made. When Garvey announced he was changing the name of his newest acquisition to the *Booker T. Washington,* his followers grew ecstatic with joy. And though critics were snide, the Garvey faithful were more convinced than ever of the wisdom and genius of their irrepressible leader.

The *General Goethals* was mastered by Captain Jacob R. Hiorth, a white skipper sworn by Garvey to avoid all the errors so fatal to the vessels of the ill-fated Black Star Line. It seemed to U.N.I.A. members that Garvey had at last made the right maritime move.

Late summer and early autumn of 1923 brought a revival of interests linking Liberia to black American leadership. Previously a brief mention was made of Garvey's sending Elie Garcia to Liberia in 1920 to negotiate an agreement between the Liberian Government and the Universal Negro Improvement Association. The specific Garvey proposals as set forth in Garcia's letter to the then Liberian President,

Charles King, appear in that portion of Garica's letter previously quoted.

Basically they requested that Liberia grant land to those black immigrants who desired to colonize in Liberia. They also suggested Liberia as the headquarters of the U.N.I.A. In return the U.N.I.A. promised the establishment of a trade route linking "Mother Africa" to her black offspring in other areas of the world. Moreover, Garvey promised capital to aid Liberia in her struggle to become a stable black republic in Africa.

With a favorable reply from President King's Secretary of State, Edwin Barclay, Garcia went to Liberia to negotiate. Meanwhile Garvey, at his first U.N.I.A. convention, had conferred such lavish honors upon Monrovia's mayor, Gabriel Johnson, as to rouse the envy of President King back in Liberia. Upon returning home poor Johnson was exiled to a minor post on the Island of Fernando Po where he could no longer be considered a menace to his President.

As if that Garvey *faux pas* were not enough, suspicious Liberian officials intercepted a letter written by Garcia to his chief in New York. The letter contained Garcia's confidential and most unflattering report on conditions then existing in Liberia.

Details of that confidential report will be described shortly. What made it so damaging to Garvey's relations with Liberia was its suggestion that guile be used in dealing with Liberian officials. After revealing his findings, Garcia had cautioned Garvey to be very cool but no less deliberate in getting a foothold in Liberia. Once that was achieved, Garcia suggested that the liberation of the indigenous Liberian hinterland folk from the repressive Americo-Liberian aristocracy could be effected.

Unfortunately for Garcia and Garvey the interceptors of the report were themselves members of that repressive Americo-Liberian aristocracy. As past masters of the art of intrigue, they acted as though they knew nothing of Garcia's criticism or Garvey's plans. They simply sat back and played a shrewd and patient game of waiting—and watching. As they did so Garvey's plans for Liberia were being neutralized by yet another independent project.

At the very time the U.N.I.A. leader was in the Tombs awaiting bail, his adversary, W. E. B. Du Bois, was invited by the Liberian Government to attend the second inauguration of President King. A short study by Professor Frank Chalk of the history department of St. George Williams University at Montreal provides revealing information. Titled "Du Bois and Garvey Confront Liberia," Professor Chalk's paper was prepared for the Fifty-second Annual Meeting of the Association for the Study of Negro Life and History, held in 1967. Chalk reported that Du Bois shared his decision to attend the King inauguration with William Henry Lewis. A Boston attorney, Lewis, a leading Massachusetts Republican, had been an assistant Attorney General during the presidency of William Howard Taft. On October 4, 1923, Lewis proposed to President Coolidge that Du Bois be sent to Liberia as a special envoy.

Such a gesture, said Lewis, would yield valuable dividends. It would insure the Republicans of the support of the *Crisis* with a massive black leadership and possibly apply brakes to the runaway black vote aligning itself with the Democrats. Coolidge promptly accepted Lewis's suggestion. And Du Bois was endowed with the rank of Envoy Extraordinary and Minister Plenipotentiary. The title, an honorary one, carried no salary.

Just before Christmas 1923, Du Bois, following the meeting of the third Pan-African Congress in Portugal, boarded a ship for Liberia. So thrilled was he by the sight and the feel of Africa and those who entertained him that Professor Chalk made this comment:

> It appears that Du Bois was completely misled about the reasons for his appointment. In April 1924 he called the day of the inauguration one of the great days of his life and referred to his appointment as an "epochal" act, "a great and significant action" through which President Coolidge meant to express the concern of the American people to Liberia.

Du Bois wrote a report on his visit for Coolidge and Secretary of State Charles Evans Hughes. In it he suggested an aid plan for a study of Liberia's agricultural, industrial, and educational development. His report indicated that he sincerely believed what he said as he wrote:

> Nothing would go further to reassure the colored peoples of Africa, Asia, and all America, particularly the eleven million in the United States, than to see the United States . . . eschewing the temptation of conquest, domination and profit-making and seeking to be a guide, friend, and protector.

Chalk then described how, upon his return to America, Du Bois tried to encourage the investment of American capital in Liberia. He wrote Harvey Firestone, who reportedly was interested in creating an American supply of rubber in Africa. Du Bois cautioned Firestone against putting his operation "under the control of officials who despised the natives." Obviously thinking of the Belgian operation in the Congo, Du Bois suggested that blacks themselves, local and immigrant, should be put in charge of Liberia. Firestone never replied.

Marcus Garvey, meanwhile, proceeded with his own plans for Liberia. Early in 1924 a committee of distinguished Liberians, including former presidents Arthur Barclay and Daniel Edward Howard, prepared to receive a group of colonists in the fall. Garvey sent seven experts—three engineers, a shipwright, master carpenter, commissioner, and paymaster to Liberia. Their job was to build temporary housing for the colonists who would follow. Then in the following harsh language Garvey accused Du Bois of duplicity.

> W. E. B. Du Bois, of the National Association for the Advancement of "Colored," "Light" People got himself appointed as Ambassador Extraordinary of the United States, to attend the second inaugural, in Liberia, of "Black" President King.

Garvey also mentioned the arrival of Mrs. Helen Curtis, wife of the late Consul General to Liberia and an active N.A.A.C.P. member. Mrs. Curtis was the guest of President King while Du Bois was the guest of "other parties." Garvey then said cryptically: "What transpired then against the interest of the Universal Negro Improvement Association can be imagined." In view of what happened shortly thereafter to the U.N.I.A. group in Liberia as a result of Liberian interception of Elie Garcia's report, Garvey's charges were especially pathetic.

In May 1924 Du Bois took open issue with Marcus Garvey's assertions that the position of Negroes in America was hopeless. Writing in the *Crisis* for May 28, he declared:

> Marcus Garvey is, without doubt, the most dangerous enemy of the Negro race in America and in the world.

He further characterized Garvey as "either a lunatic or a traitor" who "should be locked up or sent home."

Meanwhile, the ill-will toward the U.N.I.A. that had been

quietly smouldering in official Liberian circles on account of Elie Garcia's report to Marcus Garvey suddenly leaped aflame. No sooner had the seven U.N.I.A. experts debarked at Monrovia than they were arrested and immediately deported. Moreover, Liberian police seized and held the fifty thousand dollars' worth of construction material intended for use by the American colonists to follow.

Ernest Lyon, Liberian Consul General, curtly informed Washington that Liberia was "irrevocably opposed both in principle and in fact to the incendiary policy of the Universal Negro Improvement Association headed by Marcus Garvey." United States Assistant Secretary of State William Castle went so far as to see communism in the U.N.I.A. And he envisioned American suppression of Garvey as an aid to the Republicans in the forthcoming elections.

At his fourth convention in August Garvey again tried to woo the Liberian Government away from "the man W. E. B. Du Bois." He also tried to defeat a bill granting a land concession to the Firestone Tire and Rubber Company. But Liberian officials stood firm. They had already received protests against Garvey from the British and French Consuls in Sierra Leone and the Ivory Coast, and they were not about to risk intervention by either government in the internal affairs of their country.

The the *Liberian News* came out flatly during August and September with the real crux of its Government's feud with the U.N.I.A. It declared that the Government had been adhering to its policy of "irrevocable opposition to the U.N.I.A. ever since it learned through the intercepted Garcia report of the Association's revolutionary purposes in Liberia."

That the Garcia report presented an uncomplimentary

view of Liberia is undeniable. And the wrath of Liberian officials upon discovering that Garcia had written it testified to the truth of his report. One needs but read the first two short paragraphs to grasp the damning force of Garcia's description.

> Liberia although a very rich country in natural resources is the poorest place on the face of the earth and actually the people are facing starvation.
>
> This condition is due to many facts, first the strong repulsion of the Liberians for any kind of work. There is no cultivated land in the Republic and RICE which is the National food is imported from England and other places and sold at a fabulous price, although it can be produced in enormous quantities there.

Garcia then touched upon a very sore spot among the Liberian elite with this statement:

> Class distinctions—This question is also a great hindrance to the development of Liberia. There are at the present time two classes of people; the Americo-Liberians also called "sons of the soil" and the natives. The first class, although the educated one, constitutes the most despicable element in Liberia. Because of their education, they are self-conceited and believe that the only honorable way for them to make a living is by having a "Government job." The men of this class having been most of them educated in England or other European places, are used to life which the salaries paid by the Government do not suffice to maintain. Therefore, dishonesty is prevalent. To any man who can write and read there is but one goal, a Government office, where he can graft.

Harsh as those words sounded to elite Liberians they were mild in comparison with the paralyzing pronouncements of the next few lines.

> For the same reason, they are absolutely hostile to "immigration" by American or West Indian Negroes, that is, if said Negroes show any tendency to take part in the political life of the Republic. This fact is of great importance and I dare suggest that words must be given to anyone going to Liberia in the interest of the U.N.I.A., to deny firmly any intention on our part to enter into politics in Liberia. This attitude will remove any possible idea of opposition and will not prevent us after having a strong foothold in the country to act as we see best for their own betterment and that of the Race at large.

The phrases quoted above, far more than anything W. E. B. Du Bois could ever have said or done, killed any chance Garvey might have had in Liberia. Indeed it is questionable that he could have made any headway there even if Garcia had never written such a report. The powerful American and European interests in control of Liberia's vast rubber plantations, iron ore deposits, and diamonds, had no plans for vanishing as a courtesy to Marcus Garvey and the Universal Negro Improvement Association.

Still, the back-to-Africa aspect of Garvey's program persists, even today, in dominating the thinking of most outsiders who have ever heard of Garvey and his movement. As has been suggested earlier, that was but one element of the Garveyan philosophy. The Jamaican leader was far too intelligent to envision conducting a wholesale exodus of blacks from this hemisphere back to the "motherland."

To begin with, he knew that the majority of Afro-Americans were no more interested in such a move than the majority of Euro-Americans were interested in returning to Europe. But Garvey never gave up on the idea of setting up a state in Africa completely free of white domination.

Ideally it would be a productive and self-supporting "Zionist" refuge for those in other areas of the world who wanted to go there.

That Southern racist politicians and the Ku Klux Klan readily embraced the idea meant only that they and Garvey had agreed upon the same thing for entirely different reasons. Marcus Garvey's alleged "union" with the Ku Klux Klan was not nearly as damaging to him and his program as was his intemperate rhetoric. With all of his native intelligence Garvey had an uncanny faculty for making public statements that did him no earthly good. Publicly declaring himself to be the first Facist for instance, was as nonconstructive as it was impulsive and inaccurate.

Marcus Garvey took his setback in Liberia in his usual stride. Even with the impending prison sentence hovering over him, he went ahead with the development of another interest. This involved his concept of a fitting deity for black religionists. Spectators viewing the parade of the fourth International U.N.I.A. Convention in 1924 saw marchers bearing a large portrait of a black Madonna and Child. At that convention Bishop McGuire urged his listerners to hasten the day when they would replace the traditional white Christ and white Madonna with black ones.

Bishop McGuire did not stop there. Since God had an adversary who was constantly needling him and his children, McGuire decided it was high time the world knew what the devil really looked like. Black people of the Western world, he exhorted, were the only ones who didn't seem to know the devil was not black, but white.

In supporting the contention of a black Christ, sympathetic black clergymen all over the nation quoted freely from the Book of Revelation. There, according to their interpretation of the Scripture, John, the revelator, writing on the Island of Patmos, saw an image of Christ resembling a black man with white wooly hair and feet like polished brass. Though the interpretation of the written word was quite liberal, it served the purpose. And Garveyites set a trend in a religious concept among Afro-Americans that still exists in many places and many minds.

But even having a black deity with a two-edged sword emanating from his mouth to look out for their interests did not render black Americans immune to the ravages of white racism. The year 1924 had brought little appreciable respite from the pressures of the continuous fray.

CHAPTER NINETEEN

A BRIEF MENTION of three news items of 1924 and their bearing upon the thinking and feeling of black Americans may help explain why Garveyism did not collapse after the trial and conviction of the Jamaican leader. Indeed they may well indicate why the principles and practices of Garvey's philosophy and teachings are still very much with us. These half-century-old news reports were occasioned by the same racism that still exists.

More than that, however, national events concerning Afro-Americans that developed from 1924 through 1927 have a related significance. They designate why the clamor to free Garvey that rose to a near crescendo in America's black communities was echoed in some white quarters also. Some of that clamor emanated from sources that formerly had offered bitter vocal opposition to Marcus Garvey and everything he sought to accomplish.

The first news item, international in character, was a proposal to Brazilian Government authorities by Brazilian writer Lauro de Nantes. Permission to reprint the essay, published originally in the Gazeta de Noticias, Rio de Janerio, December 4, 1923, was acquired by Robert Abbott, who had it translated and republished in his *Chicago Defender* of January 12, 1924. Under the headline, "South American Lands Go Untitled for Want of Labor to Work Same," the Nantes essay became front page *Defender* news. Abbott's own editorial note above the author's byline offered a statement of caution, however.

Acknowledging the suggestion that black Americans be encouraged to emigrate five million strong to Brazil, editor Abbott, who had recently toured South America, suggested that "it is better for us to send fewer men and women in order that we may send our best." He warned that Brazil was not in need of "handymen and loafers" but the best-trained professional people, industrial artisans, and cotton growers in the black communities of the United States. He further warned that each person going should be able to take with him five thousand dollars to finance himself until full establishment was achieved. Said Abbott's foreword to the Brazilian writer's appeal:

> These people will be the advance guard in opening up this wonderful country for their children, who will have everything before them that any white child has in this country.

Author Nantes opened his appeal by citing a controversy in Brazil over the admission of large numbers of nonwhite immigrants to the country. Opponents of the open-door policy, he said, were concealing their fear of colored United States immigrants behind a dodge. They were alleging that the United States would unload its "undesirable" black citizens upon Brazil. Their real concern, asserted the author, was that an increase in the already larger nonwhite Brazilian population would corrode the political power and national control exerted by the white minority. Nantes cited the contribution of the African slave to Brazil's development, before adding:

> It is possible, no doubt, that with the entrance of the North American Negro the mixed race would predominate here, because the United States Negroes would be Americans—to wit: men of initiative and hard workers.

Declaring the superiority of the Negro and other mixed races in the area of agricultural work, Nantes appealed for the admittance of at least half a million black agricultural workers from the United States. Their need was imminent in the cultivation of Brazilian cotton. He appealed also for more Japanese workers such as had settled and become small land owners in Sao Paulo. Nantes then concluded his article with a denunciation of the indolent merchant class and this appeal to national practicality:

> . . . And it is to the Negroes and Japanese, to these inoffensive and heroic Titans of work and progress, that some people would like to impede the entrance into our country.

Viewed in broad terms, the Nantes essay lent substance to Marcus Garvey's contentions. Garvey had been telling listeners that the descendants of African slaves generally occupied the bottom rungs of the economic ladder all over the Americas. He had observed that in earlier travels in Central and South America. And he had declared that the low place on the totem pole was deliberately assigned to non-whites by Europeans fearful of losing the political and economic power they had usurped through force and terror.

In its narrower and more restrictive sense the Nantes story was morale lifting to *Defender* readers in 1924. It signified something positive to them that the talents of black agricultural workers were not only held in high esteem but solicited by a writer in South America's largest nation. The mere knowledge of being wanted and needed in Brazil, a nation more than half colored, was a relief from the negative news stories coming out of Washington, D.C., about Walter L. Cohen.

Cohen, a black man, had been appointed to the office of comptroller of customs for the New Orleans district by President Calvin Coolidge. For weeks his appointment had been opposed, blocked, and delayed, by politicians who obviously rejected him on the grounds of color. Chief opposition had come from two Louisiana senators who objected to Cohen on "personal grounds." At one point during the lengthy arguments they were joined by another pair of southerners, Joe Robinson of Arkansas and Tom Heflin of Alabama, in an effort to talk the confirmation to death.

The plan failed, however. With the aid of liberals La Follette of Wisconsin, McCormick of Illinois, Shipstead of Minnesota, and Walsh of Massachusetts, the southern Ku Klux Klan influence was considerably subdued.

Meanwhile, the Lincoln League, led by Roscoe Conklin Simmons and backed by the *Chicago Defender,* did much to prevent the appointment from becoming buried in the Senate. After many harrowing weeks and two ballotings in which Cohen was rebuffed, a third attempt on March 17, 1924, squeaked the confirmation through. The final vote was 39 to 38. Cohen, in a telegram to the *Defender,* declared that his victory was due in large measure to the "indefatigable efforts of its representative, Roscoe Simmons."

A major political significance of Cohen's confirmation was that it succeeded in destroying a rule going back to the violent days of Andrew Jackson. It killed the infamous rule of "senatorial courtesy," that hypocritical regulation providing legal sanctuary for those who formerly had freely maligned and destroyed those they didn't like. Another element of Cohen's victory was the valiant action of Senator Henrik Shipstead of Minnesota in moving for reconsideration of the second vote against the appointee. It was Shipstead's move that opened the gate leading directly to Cohen's confirmation.

The third news item indicated that even the arts could not escape the virus of racism. Following the success of *The Emperor Jones,* in which Charles Gilpin starred with phenomenal success, playwright Eugene O'Neill wrote *All God's Chillun Got Wings.* The latter is the story of eight persons, four black and four white, growing up in New York City.

Jim and Ella are childhood sweethearts. Jim is black and Ella white. With advancing physical maturity they drift apart as Ella takes up with a white boxer. The couple aren't happy together, however, and Ella, tiring of being brutalized by the fighter, returns to Jim, whom she entices into an elopement. The mixed couple returns to live in their old neighborhood with Jim's mother and sister.

As studious Jim prepares himself for a career in law, Ella, fearful of losing him, suffers a mental breakdown. The climax of the play occurs when Jim, after failing to pass his bar examination, is showered with gratified affection by a happy and quietly relieved wife.

O'Neill's play was chosen as one to be done by The Provincetown Players at their own theater in New York. The producers chose a promising young unknown black singer and actor for the role of Jim. He was Paul Robeson, Phi Beta Kappa Rutgers graduate, all-American football great, and ex-law student at Columbia University. Even before the actress to play Ella was chosen, speculations with ugly racial overtones sprang alive and ran rampant in the pages of the nation's press. What *white* woman, columnists openly wondered, would *dare* accept such a role?

Reporters frenzidly and almost pathologically, scurried about questioning and staging advanced interviews with actresses not even remotely being considered by the play's producers.

Finally it was announced that Ella would be played by Mary Blair, who had previously worked with the Provincetown players. Miss Blair had appeared opposite Louis Wolheim in O'Neill's, *The Hairy Ape*. Neither Miss Blair nor the producers of *All God's Chillun Got Wings* would do much talking, preferring, no doubt, to concentrate on the work ahead. Outsiders fumed. Some even suggested that the play should not be done—that the police department should prevent its showing.

Journalist Heywood Broun, writing in *The New York World* for March 4, 1924, took issue with an editorial in the very newspaper that hired him. Said Broun in part:

> I do not intend to raise the question as to whether or not O'Neill's play indicates approval of the characters whom he portrays. But I do want to protest against the theory that a playwright must be limited to law-abiding drama.

Broun pointed out that in the theater Raffles was a thief, Jimmy Valentine a safecracker, Cleopatra a courtesan, Tristan a violator of the Mann Act, Rip Van Winkle a wife deserter, Oedipus incestuous, and the Pied Piper a flagrant kidnapper. Why then, he wanted to know, all the hue and cry over a pair of miscegnationists? Broun concluded his column with this thought:

> If *All God's Chillun Got Wings* is a good play I think it should be produced. If it is a bad play it won't last long.

The play, by no means O'Neill's greatest, nevertheless enjoyed fine moments, what with its strong performances. It had its run. And the nation somehow managed to survive it. Such were but three of the scores of vignettes so meaningful to black Americans during 1924. With the advent of the new year they were braced for any eventuality that presaged yet another violation or suppression of the black man's human rights. And the case of Marcus Garvey versus the United States Government was fully alive in their consciousness.

Garvey's activities at the beginning of 1925 gave not the remotest hint of the prison sentence hanging over him. Having acquired the steamship *General G. W. Goethals,* which he planned to rechristen the *Booker T. Washington,* the U.N.I.A. leader hoisted the flag of the new Black Cross Line and prepared the ship for a voyage to the West Indies. Along with Captain Hiorth, Garvey sent the Secretary General of the U.N.I.A., G. Emonei Carter. The latter's job was to raise money to pay the vessel's running expenses through the sale of stock as they put in at various ports. Late in January and amid much fanfare, the *General Goethals* departed on its Caribbean voyage.

Garvey had been advised by legal counsel during January that his appeal was due to come up in March. He therefore had a little time to get out and raise money to help defray legal costs. Confident of his ability to draw crowds and much needed money, the Jamaican, after leaving a complete itinerary with his lawyer, set out on a Midwest speaking tour. Scarcely had he reached Detroit than he was ordered to return immediately to New York. His appeal had been rejected on February 2, 1925, by the United States Circuit Court of Appeals. Garvey's lawyer had quickly contacted the District Attorney, advising that he, personally, would deliver Garvey on the following morning.

But the law could not wait. No sooner had Garvey's train pulled into the elevated station of the New York Central at 125th Street, than the Jamaican, accompanied by his wife, was seized by two United States marshals. Theatrically handcuffing their prisoner, they hustled him off the train as bystanders gaped in amazement.

Garvey's attorney, when informed by Mrs. Garvey of her husband's arrest aboard the train, was amazed. He said he had been previously assured that his offer personally to bring the U.N.I.A. leader in had been verbally accepted. The Garvey defense immediately prepared an appeal to the United States Supreme Court, and on the following morning the prisoner was brought, handcuffed between a pair of towering guards, into the courtroom.

There, after being denied additional time for setting his affairs in order, Garvey was formally committed to the Federal Penitentiary at Atlanta. An order for his deportation upon release from Atlanta would be sent along with him. The prisoner was then taken to the Tombs to await the train that would deliver him to Atlanta.

Amy Jacques Garvey tells in *Garvey and Garveyism* of being informed by the District Attorney that her husband had forfeited his bail of fifteen thousand dollars.

> We had to engage counsel to fight in the courts for months until the amount was released, every cent of which we returned to the lenders.

Mrs. Garvey also tells of being aided by sympathetic redcaps who kept her well hidden before spiriting her, at the last minute, aboard the train carrying her celebrated husband to Dixie.

Perhaps for reasons of "security," the hour of Garvey's departure was not publicly announced in advance. Members of the U.N.I.A., however, kept a constant vigil outside the prison. An eyewitness account of that departure from the Tombs was given the writer by George A. Weston, one of Garvey's trusted aides. Said Mr. Weston:

> When Mr. Garvey was on his way to the penitentiary we had more than one thousand Negroes from Harlem down there at the old Federal Building at Park Place. Garvey was handcuffed and I saw all that I counted of value being sent away.
>
> Each marshal kept a hand in his pocket. It was as though they were expecting trouble from the crowd. When they got near the car I saw Garvey's mouth working but I couldn't hear what he said to the marshals who seemed to be rushing him toward the vehicle. So they slowed up a bit as Garvey himself slowed as much as to suggest that they need not be frightened of the crowd. The marshals were obviously nervous.
>
> One woman asked me why we didn't take Mr. Garvey from the officers. And I reminded her that Mr. Garvey had taught us to respect the law at all times. That was a part of the Garveyan philosophy. At one point I raised my hand to quiet the crowd. When a reporter asked me to repeat the gesture for the photographers I refused to comply. A woman in the crowd was particularly incensed that a reporter would ask me to do such a thing. Then they took Marcus Garvey away.

Two days after his arrival at the federal prison, on February 8, 1925, Garvey wrote a message to his supporters outside. He explained what had happened prior to being summoned from Detroit and seized upon his return to New York. His counsel, he told them, had estimated there would be a period of ten days or two weeks before the court mandate would be handed down. In the interim, Garvey planned speaking engagements in Detroit, Cincinnati, and Cleveland. All had to be cancelled.

He even related how he had been declared a "fugitive" within ten hours of his departure from New York. Garvey then castigated Du Bois and the N.A.A.C.P., warning his followers to beware of them. And his call for even firmer fidelity during his imprisonment was coupled with a reassurance of ulitmate success.

On the same day Garvey wrote that message the *General Goethals* docked in Kingston. She had been delayed at Havana by creditors seeking to attach her for old debts incurred by the Black Star Line. Escaping that embarrassment, the *General Goethals* was, nevertheless, unable to pay her way along the route, as had been hoped. Then dissention erupted among the members of the crew, and it wasn't long before Captain Hiorth admitted his inability to maintain ship's discipline. Lack of funds tied the vessel up in Panama for a month. There is no record of the ship's ever managing to return home to New York.

Four months after entering prison, Marcus Garvey filed application for a pardon. In the lengthy document dated June 5, 1925, and addressed to The President of The United States, several noteworthy facts emerge. One was that prosecutor Mattuck had summoned Edward Young Clark, Imperial Wizard of the Ku Klux Klan, to New York from Atlanta, Georgia. Clark, himself under federal indictment at the time, was questioned by Mattuck about Garvey's alleged membership in, or close relationship to, the Klan. Garvey contended that such questioning was irrelevant to his indictment for allegedly using the mails to defraud.

His letter to President Coolidge also revealed that Garvey had applied for and secured his first naturalization papers. He charged later that as soon as news of that become known "my political enemies hurried up and forced my indictment."

Still another revelation of that letter was that the prosecution both during and after the trial had "threatened to suppress" both Garvey newspapers, the weekly, *Negro World*, and the daily, *Negro Times*. Garvey stated in his petition for pardon that the editors of both papers were so intimidated by Prosecutor Mattuck "as to prevent their reporting his conduct during the trial for public information." A further charge was that the Prosecutor seized and retained the subscribers' mailing list of the *Negro World*.

Finally, and this is most significant, the largest holder of Black Star Line stock was none other than Marcus Garvey himself. Of that Garvey had this to say:

> The record shows that I had no financial advantage to gain. . . . I am the largest stockholder in the Black Star Line, and did subscribe my money at all and every time when other Negroes were asked to do so for the good of the cause of African development; and it is illogical to believe that I would commit a fraud against myself . . . The salary I received during the short period that I accepted it was less than five thousand dollars, while other officers were paid continuously and consistently, and they were in no way censured by the Court.

Press reaction to the imprisonment of Marcus Garvey was by no means unanimous in its approval of the decision of the courts. The black press for the most part assumed a we-told-you-so attitude. Their condemnations of Garvey, the "gigantic blunderer," "cunning promoter," and "self-convicted criminal" were quite consistent with their treatment of him all along.

But there were other viewpoints, too. Led by Dean Kelly Miller of Howard University, several of Garvey's severest black critics, as will be seen, did an about-face. And while the reactionary daily, *The New York World,* continued its harsh sniping, other dailies refused to follow suit.

The *New York Evening Bulletin,* a maverick white daily whose life span was relatively short said the following:

> Garvey is a Negro, but even a Negro is entitled to have the truth said about him.

Stating that the Jamaican had been ridiculed and made to look like a buffoon by New York newspapers ever since he had arrived in the city, the *Bulletin* acknowledged that many of Garvey's acts were "strange." But the *Bulletin* saw nothing strange or abnormal in his offering an ideal to his people. Nor did it find anything objectionable in the leader's proposal that Africa should be controlled by its indigenous people. Moreover, it was the *Bulletin*'s opinion that the Garvey ideal would eventually be realized and that Africa would no longer be the pawn of France and Great Britain.

> Garvey's troubles—asserted the *Bulletin*—began when he stepped on the toes of these nations . . . And so hireling journalists, acting at the bidding of their foreign masters, painted Garvey as a joke and a trickster.

The *Bulletin* concluded with the opinion that had Garvey "been given half a fair deal," his plans may have materialized, and his disastrous misfortunes would never have brought him into the courts.

Along with the *Bulletin* the *Buffalo Evening Times* for February 25 was far from convinced that justice had been done. "White hostility" feared the effects of Garvey's race consciousness upon the masses of black people, in that paper's opinion. The *Evening Times* also noted Garvey's legal disadvantage as his own counsel vying with a trained prosecutor in a federal court. The upstate paper concluded its editorial statement with this sentence.

> What we regretfully point out, in the consideration of comparative justice, is the fact that this colored man is given a sentence of five years when so many greater offenders are sentenced to but two years, and still others are enjoying complete immunity from any punishment whatsoever.

While Marcus Garvey must have derived a measure of satisfaction from reading such comments, he was not of a disposition to wait for them or to lean upon them for survival. His critics had complained of his "arrogance," "conceit," and "nerve." They were not wrong. He possessed all three in liberal measure. And right or wrong, he, the true leader, gave no indication of surrendering them now.

CHAPTER TWENTY

It was 1926 when, in the vernacular of ancient legends, the once proud Universal Negro Improvement Association began to come upon evil days. A major disappointment hit the Association in the early spring, by way of a court decision in British Honduras. Preliminaries culminating in that decision began four years earlier in New York City when Isaiah Morter, a native of Honduras, met Garvey at the U.N.I.A. convention.

Mr. Morter had come from Belize to attend that gathering as the guest of the Garveys, as well as to seek medical aid for himself. So impressed was the Honduran visitor by what he saw and heard at the convention that he willed two-thirds of his entire estate to the parent body U.N.I.A. The property included a small island producing mahogany, bananas, coconuts, and chicle. The bequest was valued at a hundred thousand dollars by Garvey himself. Other estimates ranged between one hundred and fifty thousand and three hundred thousand dollars.

When the ailing benefactor died the following spring his

widow contested the will. A legal battle lasting fully fifteen years ensued, and final disposition of the case was made then. But it was in 1926, with its treasury so empty and its leader imprisoned, that the U.N.I.A. needed a financial lift. And it was in that year that the first of several legal rulings was handed down in the case.

The court ruled then that the principal objective of the U.N.I.A. was the redemption of Africa. It further ruled that the means advocated for the attainment of Africa's redemption were more violent and militant than peaceful. Then the British Honduran Supreme Court cited the lyrics of the U.N.I.A. official anthem as proof of the Association's proclivity for violence. Following that, the chief justice of the court issued this ruling as reported in the *Amsterdam News* of May 5, 1926:

> I find that the residuary devise and bequest in the will to the parent body of the U.N.I.A. is for an illegal purpose and contrary to public policy and consequently that such a devise and bequest is void and of no effect and that the testator died intestate as to such residuary devise and bequest.

It was a tough blow to the hopes of a financially crippled organization. The relatively tame opening of the fifth U.N.I.A. Convention in August 1926 was, therefore, accurately reflective of the Association's somber mood. Gone were the pomp and color of former gatherings. Such glamour was as noticeably absent as was Marcus Garvey himself. Not more than two hundred delegates had registered by the second day, though representatives from as far as South Africa, Sudan, Egypt, Cuba, and Puerto Rico were present.

Sunday's traditionally restrained and quiet prayer services quickly gave way to the rough-and-tumble sessions that began on Monday. Supreme Deputy Potentate George O. Marke of Sierra Leone was instructed by a vote of 27 to 2 to take legal steps against any other group calling itself the Universal Negro Improvement Association. It was further ruled that a convention held five months previously in Detroit had been illegal.

George A. Weston, the elected chairman of the convention, delivered an interpretation of the constitutional rights of each officer. His action was appropriate inasmuch as debate had grown heated over the authority vested in the higher officers of the association. U.N.I.A. Secretary Wesley McDonald Holder, while making a point of declaring the group's loyalty to the imprisoned Garvey, added this:

> We still respect Garvey as the man who gave the idea for the African program, but we admit at the same time as a business man he is a failure. We feel that the association needs most at this time an economic program which we are not willing to submit to Marcus Garvey.

Secretary Holder then continued by declaring that as a propagandist Garvey ranked with Toussaint L'Ouverture, but the Jamaican was not able to "weave events and thoughts into some organic reality." Holder further regretted that Garvey's methods lent themselves too readily to outside injustice and intolerance. He concluded with the statement that the convention was not called to dethrone Garvey but, to carefully limit his powers. Moreover the future work of the U.N.I.A. would stress building from the ground up as opposed to what had been happening—and stress would be placed upon a sound industrial and educational program.

It was apparent that with its charismatic leader behind bars in Atlanta, smouldering unrest in the U.N.I.A. was now beginning to assert itself openly. Even as early as the autumn of 1925 the New York *Amsterdam News* for September 23 had published a denial by the then acting President, Dr. J. J. Peters, of a rift over leadership in the U.N.I.A. New York division. Peters vehemently denied any challenge to his authority.

A different story, however, was told by James A. Brown, leader of a dissenting Harlem faction. Mr. Brown cited "discord, scandal, and turmoil" between officers of the U.N.I.A. parent body and George A. Weston, its acting president. Weston, the story alleged, began an investigation of Harlem property of the U.N.I.A. that revealed it to be so heavily mortgaged as to be irretrievable. The exposure, so the news story stated, irked Garvey, who brought Peters in from the South to replace Weston.

With the family squabbles getting a public airing at a time most trying for the beleaguered U.N.I.A., several black spokesmen began to substitute reason and compassion for emotion and vitriol in their discussions of Marcus Garvey. One of them was the brilliant sociologist and teacher E. Franklin Frazier. His brief interpretative sketch of the Jamaican leader appeared in *Opportunity* magazine dated November 1926 under the title "The Garvey Momement."

Frazier saw Garvey martyred by his imprisonment. Not only that, he saw a justification for the contention that Garvey was martyred, especially as he recalled the crime of mail fraud for which Garvey had been imprisoned. In that context Frazier reminded readers of the energetic businessmen who flood the mails with promises of eternal youth and beauty to hopelessly old and ugly women. The prisons would be overflowing, declared the sociologist, if the Government punished all who use the mails to defraud.

"Garvey's promises were modest by comparison," declared Frazier.

He also made the point that Garvey's movement attracted not only the ignorant but those intellectuals who had not found the acceptance their education entitled them to.

> Instead of blaming themselves—and they were not always individually responsible—they took refuge in the belief that in an autonomous black Africa they would find their proper place.

In describing the importance of the titles conferred by Garvey upon the most humble of his followers, Frazier recognized the reason for the ready acceptance of extravagant titles and claims among the lowly. He found them to be "based upon the deep but unexpressed conviction in the minds of most Negroes that the white man had set certain limits to their rise in this country."

Garvey himself was seen by Frazier as having raised himself above mortals with his promise of returning after his death "in the whirlwind or the storm" to aid his followers in their fight for liberty. The injection of the messianic element in his program did indeed transform the man Garvey into the "Redeemer of the Black World."

That Garvey's schemes were often unfeasible and still acceptable to the masses was, as Frazier saw it, not unusual. Such was but another evidence that "tests of reasonableness cannot be applied to schemes that attract crowds." Marcus Garvey gave *his* crowd the chance to "show off in colors, parades, and self-glorification." Neither the N.A.A.C.P. nor the Urban League offered that.

In discussing Garvey's sincerity, Frazier compared him with other evangelists, though he found the U.N.I.A. leader's appeal more permanent. Nor with the evidence available would he classify Garvey as a swindler. In the following concluding phrase of his essay, the eminent sociologist summarized his assessment of Garvey's achievement.

> He has failed to deal realistically with life as most so-called cranks, but he has initiated a mass movement among Negroes because it appealed to something that is in every crowd-minded man.

It was likewise during the month of November that newsman and historian Joel A. Rogers interviewed Garvey in prison. Number 19359, as he was designated, was, after nine months of confinement, in good health and strong spirits. Because Garvey had ample time for reading and study, Rogers found him to be alert to events taking place outside. Garvey, pleased that his old friend Rogers had recently returned from Europe, was piqued that he had been refused admittance to Africa.

When asked how he felt about the N.A.A.C.P., Garvey replied that it was an excellent organization, but that its leaders were interested only in succeeding themselves in office and handling only cases that brought them plenty of notoriety. Of Liberia the prisoner felt that the Liberian Government should try to get the Firestone Company under its direct control.

Garvey squashed rumors that he would never be allowed to return to Jamaica or that President Coolidge had offered him a pardon if he would leave the United States. And when asked if he had any regrets about having tried his own case, the irrepressible Jamaican replied without hesitation that had it been left to his lawyers his sentence would have been even stiffer! Before the guard signaled the end of Rogers' verbal interview, Garvey assured him that when he was released he would "do a thousand times more" than in the past to advance the cause of the race. "The Tiger," it seemed, had been neither declawed nor defanged.

Kelly Miller was another who wrote on Garvey during his imprisonment. Miller, dean of the Junior College at Howard University, had been one of those black leaders to receive the aforementioned query about Marcus Garvey circulated in 1922 by *The Messenger*. Dr. Miller had then said that "the redemption of Africa through Negro initiative and genius" was certainly worth striving for—even if it took a thousand years. He felt there were good and bad aspects of Garvey's program; that the stimulation of black self-realization and initiative was good, though the raising of impossible hopes among simple people was bad. Dean Miller was unalterably opposed then, however, to the idea of deporting Garvey for publicly expressing his views.

Five years later, *The Commentary Review* for April 1927 published Dr. Miller's essay, "After Marcus Garvey—What of the Negro?" In that brilliant assessment, marked by a magnificent use of the English language, Miller's critical and humanely balanced critique of Garvey missed none of the pomp, bombast, and showmanship of Garveyism. Nor did it seek to transform foolhardy investments of money into coups that went wrong because somebody *else* "goofed." Dr. Miller knew precisely what Garvey's weaknesses were. He also recognized his prodigious strengths.

Wrote Miller:

> The Garvey movement attracted the attention of the nation and caused no little apprehension . . . No other Negro, not even Booker Washington, ever received such national notoriety.

In summarizing the effect of Garvey on the black race, Dr. Miller unhesitatingly noted the quickening of the sense of self-dignity among the common black folk all over the world. Here is what he observed of that phenomenon:

> The National Association for The Advancement of Colored People, with its capable and consecrated leadership, so far has been able to make no great impression on the hearts and imagination of the proletariat. But Garvey arouses the zeal of millions of the lowliest to the frenzy of a crusade.

Kelly Miller recognized that the "caging of the Tiger" would not erase the memory of his teachings—that "philanthropy paralyzes the energies of the black peoples of the world and pauperizes their spirit." He knew also that Garvey's promotion of the idea of black colonization on the mother continent was not new—that other black leaders had dreamed it and tried it before. But Kelly Miller saw in Marcus Garvey a man whose influence would be felt many years after he departed the scene.

A measure of the great educator's respect and esteem for the best he discerned in the imprisoned man was expressed in these two simple sentences:

> He has an unfathomable faith in the possibilities of his people. No greater vision has ever haunted the human mind.

It was Kelly Miller who actually took the initiative in publicly calling for clemency for Marcus Garvey. Four months after his essay was published in *The Contemporary Review* he wrote again—this time under the caption "Garvey Should Be Pardoned." The essay, published in the New York *Amsterdam News* of August 24, 1927, was another brilliant example of his combined scholarship, statesmanship, and literary prowess.

Dr. Miller opened that appeal to reason on the astute premise that where legal technicalities are involved in social propaganda, the situation loses its clear-cut character. Citing Mohandas K. Gandhi as a modern national leader imprisoned by the British, who considered him a troublemaker, Miller came closer home as he recalled idealists imprisoned in America.

Eugene V. Debs, jailed for speaking out against the Espionage Act during World War I, was pardoned by President Harding. Never once did Debs recant a single word or retreat a step from the position that indicted and condemned him. Nicola Sacco and Bartolomeo Vanzetti preached a doctrine distasteful to many who nevertheless believed the men were condemned and executed for their *doctrine* rather than for their imputed crime. Said Miller:

> The trick is as old as political cunning and chicanery. Accuse the advocate of detested doctrine or some technical violation of the law and impose upon him a sentence of imprisonment and banishment or death; thus society rids itself of the agitator and his agitation by due process of law.

On the matter of deporting Garvey, a procedure strongly recommended by *The Messenger,* Miller reminded readers that William Lloyd Garrison, Wendell Phillips, and Frederick Douglass would have met swift extermination in the South simply because their views differed from those of that provincial area of the country. To the editors of *The Messenger* Dean Miller was especially chiding. He pointed out (as did this writer in an earlier chapter) that *The Messenger*'s writers and editors were themselves deemed dangerous by those who disagreed with their social and political gospel. "This," said Miller, "was an instance of carrying inconsistency to the 'Nth' degree."

Dr. Miller was eloquently scornful of the "Negro Intelligensia" who furnished information to the United States Government leading to Garvey's conviction. The measure of his scorn for them was seen in the studied paucity of the words he employed in rebuking them. "Truth," he declared, "can well afford to contend with error without taking sinister advantage."

His concluding paragraph issued a call to the "Negro race to join in one united petition for the pardon of Marcus Garvey." Dean Miller recommended that the combined black newspapers of the nation open their columns for signatures in the gigantic petition. And those who had any part in Marcus Garvey's imprisonment should, asserted Miller, be the most active in seeking his release.

In the same issue of the *Amsterdam News* carrying Dean Miller's article, there appeared a story from Wilmont, Arkansas, about the lynching of twenty-year-old Winston Pounds. The young man, accused of "attacking a young married white woman," was taken from a posse of deputy sheriffs by a mob of fifty armed men. Pound's body was found later hanging from a tree.

Editions of the *Chicago Defender* for September 24, 1927, carried the story from Panama City of a new law affecting the citizen status of black residents of Panama. The item stated that few of the West Indians who had come to Panama during the construction of the Canal had become citizens. The new law threatened to make citizenship an impossibility for them. The law did provide, however, that Panama-born West Indians automatically became citizens if they remained in Panama until the age of twenty-one. The object of the law was to "keep the country for Panamanians of the Spanish type."

In New York's Harlem a white Ford car dealer told William Harris, a black salesman who lived in the community, that the Caswell Motor Company would not permit him to sell cars in its 125th Street showroom. Harris, an authorized thirty-six-year-old representative, had been sent by the East Side office to the sales job in his home community. "The only way you'll get me out of here is to *put* me out." Harris declared. Two hours later Mr. Harris was out of the showroom.

From Washington, D.C., the Department of Justice on October 2, 1927, through Attorney General John G. Sargent, announced that Marcus Garvey's plea for parole had been rejected. So also was Garvey's petition for a pardon denied by the President. Sargent's report stated that the charge of falsifying his income tax for 1922 was also pending against the prisoner.

The rules of the Justice Department prevent the consideration of petitions for clemency while other charges are pending against the applicant. Garvey had otherwise been eligible for parole two weeks prior to the announcements. President Coolidge, when approached directly about the White House denial of a pardon, replied that the matter was in the hands of the Justice Department.

Continued demands by black citizens for leniency for Marcus Garvey, though not nearly as loud and showy as Garvey's own demonstrations had been, nevertheless began to accumulate. In a matter of weeks they had grown to a swell. Even the hostile *Chicago Defender* for November 26, 1927, came out editorially with a demand for the Jamaican's release. The *Defender* made the following boast two weeks later in a story datelined Atlanta, Georgia, December 2, 1927:

Through the intervention of the *Chicago Defender* with the U.S. Department of Justice, Marcus Garvey who was sentenced to the Federal Penitentiary here for using the mails to defraud, was freed last Thursday by President Coolidge.

It seemed that Kelly Miller's writings, coupled with the ceaseless acts of white racism all over the nation, served as a sober reminder to all black Americans. White America was making no pretense at showing that whatever their training or conduct, blacks were not the equals of whites and need not expect to be treated as such. Obviously some key black leaders who had strongly opposed Garvey got the message. They began to see that they too were occupying the racist bag labelled with that well-known epithet containing six letters and and beginning with a *small* "n."

CHAPTER TWENTY-ONE

TWO YEARS and nine months after becoming number 19359 in the Atlanta Federal Penitentiary, Marcus Garvey was freed. It was on November 18, 1927, that President Coolidge signed the declaration of commutation of the Jamaican's prison sentence. The relentless campaign waged by U.N.I.A. members and by outraged Afro-Americans and others not connected with the Association had finally paid off.

N.A.A.C.P. official, William Pickens, wrote a strange story of the events leading up to Garvey's release. The Pickens version appeared in the New York *Amsterdam News* for November 30, 1927. Pickens, it will be recalled, had written for Garvey's *Negro World* before his rift with its founder's policies. Pickens' split with Garvey was made public as the former refused to be honored at a U.N.I.A. convention. His story bore the stamp of the former Garvey critic aroused by the gross injustice of so severe a punishment imposed upon the black leader.

Dr. Pickens opened his article by reminding readers how frequently he had publicly expressed disagreement with the Government's treatment of Garvey as compared with its treatment of white offenders. He then declared that an unnamed "friend" had held several conversations on the subject with Justice Department officials. In those sessions Washington was allegedly told that "the plain colored people of the United States were not desirous of seeing merely revengeful punishment put upon Garvey."

The Justice Department responded, according to Pickens, that it was holding on to Garvey "out of concern for Negroes." The Department claimed it had been led to believe their action was protecting the "poor Negroes of the United States against exploitation and robbery." Pickens' friend countered that such a danger could easily be eliminated through the simple traditional expedient of deporting the prison-released alien. Garvey's immediate deportation would also "greatly abate the back-to-Africa nuisance and fraud" according to the Pickens' article.

Having presented that proposal to the Justice Department, Pickens' "friend" hinted that with the approaching presidential election of 1928 the Coolidge Administration stood to gain ground among black voters by turning Garvey loose. Pickens then concluded his story with this:

> We wonder if this had any influence; at least within twenty-four hours after my friend had related to me this last "conversation" with the Department officials, the daily papers announced Garvey's release.

The immigration laws of the nation required Garvey's swift exit as an undesirable alien. Without being allowed to return to New York for a final visit to U.N.I.A. headquarters, he was taken to New Orleans and placed aboard the Panama-bound S.S. *Saramacca* early in December. Hundreds of followers and well wishers braved the downpour to wish him well, and Garvey's farewell message assured them that his greatest work was still ahead.

The *New York World* openly rejoiced at his departure. In its expression of relief that Garvey would no longer be around "separating the colored population from its money," the *World* joined the Justice Department in revealing a hitherto unheard-of concern for the pecuniary well-being of black Americans. The *Crisis, Amsterdam News* and *Chicago Defender* offered more credible farewells. It was apparent in their comments that with all the criticism, just and unjust, they had leveled at Marcus Garvey, the black press recognized that here was an extraordinary human being of far more than average merit. The likes of him would not be seen again in their midst for a long time. Some found that prospect more than a little regrettable.

The *Saramacca*'s brief stopover in Panama was heartwarming indeed. Although Garvey was not allowed ashore, he was greeted aboard ship by a local U.N.I.A. group, who expressed the hope that he would not falter. Their small cash gift must have been a touching reminder to Garvey of their struggle to survive on substandard wages.

A wildly joyful greeting awaited the *Saramacca* as she eased into her berth at Kingston. Marcus Garvey was home. And he was returning as the martyred hero who had succeeded in terrifying Uncle Sam into caging "The Tiger." Then, finding him too hot to hold, the Yankee had to release Garvey and get him off American soil with unusual dispatch.

More than that, Great Britain and France were fearful of letting the *Negro World* circulate in many of their territories of the Americas and Africa. The short, homely, country boy from Saint Ann's Bay had graduated from leading a local printer's strike to upsetting major world powers. That supposedly all-powerful America had locked him safely away for nearly three years proved how much he was feared. Yankees could once again sit back easily and relax over their tranquilizing drinks. But never mind that now. "The Tiger" was being warmly welcomed back into his lair.

Marcus Garvey's insatiable appetite for the glory and the grief of public recognition thrust him immediately into the tremendous task of reorganizing his group. So dependent had the Universal Negro Improvement Association become upon the magic personality of its founder that it seemed to function effectively only when Marcus Garvey was on the scene to direct it.

To many observers Garvey's return to Kingston meant that he had brought the U.N.I.A. back to the place of its birth. The leader now began the job of reviving his still existing but neglected local division. Membership figures rose quickly and it appeared that Garvey was indeed about to carve another spectacular monument to his dedicated and imaginative convictions.

During the spring of 1928 he revisited Central America and other Caribbean areas to achieve that end. Then in May, he and his wife went to England. There in London he set up the European headquarters of the U.N.I.A. Across the channel in Paris he established a branch office. Both moves were the preamble to what he planned as a massive public appearance in London, to take place in one of that city's largest and most well-known auditoriums.

The Royal Albert Hall, with its seating capacity of ten thousand was the behemoth of London's public meeting places. Garvey, accustomed to addressing multitudes, had no doubt that the traditional old Victorian structure would be packed to overflowing. Events in his life over the past few years had convinced him that as a public attraction he need have no qualms about renting the gigantic place for this important debut. But in his anxiety to establish himself as a powerful force in the very capital of British colonial imperialism, Marcus Garvey forgot something. He neglected to heed the persistent little warning vibrations sounding all around him.

To begin with, he and his wife, upon their arrival in London, had not an easy time finding lodgings. There was no unusual shortage of housing—for whites—that is. Nonwhites, Asians, Africans, or whatever met with a problem, however. The British, smoothly adept at the art of holding nonwhites at arm's length, were the master designers of those patterns of color discrimination from which Americans had swiped and fashioned their own cruder versions. Amy Jacques Garvey in *Garvey and Garveyism* makes this terse comment on the British practice of jim crow:

> In England, because of the prejudices against colored people, it was difficult to secure lodgings. After driving around for hours we went to the Hotel Cecil in desperation, and strangely we were accommodated there. "The Cecil" was a swanky London hotel where gaitered flunkeys bowed us in. We could only afford to stay there two days.

The Garveys did finally locate a cheaper place willing to take them until they located a house for rent in West Kensington. Garvey soon opened his office. Meetings with African students and seamen had to be held secretly. Garvey's reputation as a "troublemaker" was spreading among conservatives who had heard him in Hyde Park railing against the evils of European colonialism in Africa and other overseas areas.

Still, the Jamaican did not hesitate to send letters and circulars to those in the British Government he felt were sympathetic to his program. Though response was cool, Garvey had no doubt that his Albert Hall meeting scheduled for June 6, 1928, would be a smashing sellout.

Never in his life had Marcus Garvey been more wrong. In addition to overlooking general British indifference to the indigenous peoples of their colonies, he had imagined Britons would be terribly concerned about what he saw as a mounting threat to their colonial supremacy around the world. But like people everywhere, Londoners at large indulged their particular provincialism. They became involved only when made to *feel* a threat.

Had thousands of them been threatened with a loss of employment because of some massive anti-British maneuver in Africa, Asia, or the West Indies, they would have jammed Albert Hall to hear Garvey. They would have gone if for no reason other than to shout obscenities and threats at the speakers in the effort to relieve the strain of their fears. Such was not the situation, however. Garvey, along with his supporting speaker and musicians, had to address themselves to a house full of empty seats and mocking echoes.

The Garvey speech revealed that he had emerged from an American federal prison unbroken and unwilling to concede anything to the enemy. It was Marcus Garvey's warning that the colonial powers still had him and the questions he raised to deal with.

From London he went to Paris and from there to Geneva where he presented a "Petition of the Negro Race" to the League of Nations. Surely Garvey had no illusions that the League would establish his suggested "free state for Negroes in Africa." Nor did he seriously belive that mandates of former German colonies would be handed over to Africans for self rule.

But the U.N.I.A. leader was determined that the colonial powers and the rest of the world, too, would know that he had warned of the inevitable end of European colonial rule in Africa. His proposal in Geneva that areas of West Africa be united into a commonwealth of Black Nations under the rule of black men, was not as far-fetched as it had seemed when he made it. And it should surprise no one cognizant today of events developing in Africa that Garvey's more realistic concepts of Pan-Africanism, like those of Du Bois, were more than idle dreams.

The return to London and another attempt at gathering a mass meeting, this time at the Century Theatre, was far more successful than the first. Garvey had attracted the attention of British clergyman Charles Garnett, who lent assistance and the prestige of his position by presiding over the meeting. That proved to be a real boost. Subsequent meetings did indeed serve to acquaint staid Britons with the situation of their colored colonials around the globe, though they accomplished little more. Garvey then decided to have a go at audiences in Canada.

The United States presidential election of 1928 was approaching as the Garveys arrived in Montreal during the month of October. Though there were a number of Garvey supporters in that city, the U.N.I.A. leader's sojourn there was brief. Meanwhile Mrs. Garvey, who was allowed to cross the United States border, did so and proceeded on a speaking tour as her husband's deputy. Exactly what transpired with Garvey in Montreal is muddled in conflicting reports.

Garvey's speeches in Canada were aimed at the many people across that border who supported him. In those talks,

Garvey urged black American voters to give their voting support to Alfred E. Smith, "a man of the people," rather than to Herbert Hoover, "a millionaire" who represented the interests of the rich. Garvey's political activity evoked a complaint from the American consul in Montreal to the Canadian authorities. Garvey was then asked to leave the country.

Amy Jacques Garvey makes no mention in *Garvey and Garveyism* of any actual speeches on American politics made by her husband in Montreal. She does say that even though he had been issued a landing pass, Garvey was arrested "after I left" for "illegal entry." According to her account, Garvey was released the day following his arrest with the explanation that "a mistake had been made." It is then that Mrs. Garvey mentions that "rumor had it" that United States Republicans "did not want Garvey to speak for fear his speech would influence the voting Garveyites in the United States."

From Montreal the Garveys set out for Jamaica by way of Bermuda and the Bahamas. Of the two of them only Amy Jacques Garvey was allowed to land at Hamilton. It was a city she found to be "repressive" in its treatment of black residents. She substituted for her husband as official U.N.I.A. speaker in Hamilton. They found Nassau a much more hospitable city where both of them were not only permitted to land but even treated with official courtesy.

Back in Kingston, Marcus Garvey decided he needed another newspaper, and in March 1929 founded *The Black Man,* which continued as a weekly until 1931. Through the columns of *The Black Man* Garvey issued a call for the sixth International Convention of the Negro Peoples of the World. It was to take place in Kingston, and it would be an extravaganza such as the citizens of that island city had never before witnessed. Those who saw it knew that the festive occasion lived up to every promise made in its advance notices.

The forty-five-minute procession of twenty thousand persons moving through Kingston's principal streets during midday on August 1 was appropriate to yet another special occasion. That was the ninety-first anniversary of the abolition of slavery in the British possessions. With the ending of the parade at the open-air stadium of Edelweiss Park, the sixth U.N.I.A. Convention was formally opened.

Convention agenda items stressed the unification of Africans, West Indians, and Negroes of the Americas through programs of education, industry, and trade. It was suggested that the U.N.I.A. establish embassies in the world's capitals to represent and to guard the interests and rights of black peoples. In addition the proposal was made to establish newspapers in the same places and for the same purposes.

Trouble however began to assert itself early in the convention. Garvey was quite blunt in saying what he felt about certain members of the Association in the United States. His accusation that disloyal members there were responsible for ruining the movement during his imprisonment drew instant fire from many American delegates. Bitterness grew especially acute over the question of salary demands made by certain United States Association officials. Garvey was made conscious of that item by George O. Marke, who had sued the American organization for payment of back salary.

A United States court had awarded Marke a judgment against the U.N.I.A. in New York. But that group was no longer solvent and Marke had brought his problem to the court in Kingston. Garvey contended that he was no longer connected with the New York body. He furthermore refused to talk about the assets of the Jamaica U.N.I.A. and flouted a court order to surrender the books of his Jamaica organization for examination. For that he was fined twenty-five pounds by the Jamaica court, a sum which he collected from delegates at the convention a couple of weeks later. Right then and there Marcus Garvey decided it was high time to disassociate himself from any obligatory ties to the U.N.I.A. in America. The chance to do just that came during the Kingston convention.

An argument over where the U.N.I.A. headquarters should be located became another convention issue over which Garvey split with the American delegates. The Jamaican contended that since he had founded the Association its headquarters should be located wherever he was located. His American opposition reminded Garvey that the U.N.I.A. had been incorporated in New York and its home office was still there. Then they played their trump card. The greatest amount of financial support the organization ever received came, they reminded Jamaicans, from the United States. As Garvey angrily and stubbornly stood his ground the Americans picked up their financial marbles and withdrew from the convention.

Marcus Garvey was left to establish a new organization known as the "U.N.I.A., August 1929." Those divisions wishing to remain loyal to Garvey sought and obtained new charters. Many United States divisions, however, continued to function under the old charter granted in 1918. The split was far more serious even than it appeared at the Kingston convention. Indeed, it would return to haunt Garvey as the aforementioned court litigation of the estate of the late

Isaiah E. Morter moved on slowly to its final disposition.

The sixth convention had barely come to an end when Marcus Garvey turned his energies toward local politics. With several others he formed a new political group called the "Peoples Political Party." Garvey had felt that the old system which he saw as keeping the poor unrepresented in the island Legislative Council was due for a change, and he would be the person to bring that change about. Fourteen reforms were drawn up and offered as the planks of the platform of the new party.

The reforms, at first glance, seemed quite reasonable. They sought a larger portion of self-government for Jamaica; land and labor reforms favoring the poor; legal aid for the poor and legal protection against intimidation in voting; and improved urbanization with increases in educational and cultural facilities.

There was yet another reform. It called for a law to impeach and imprison judges who, with disregard for British justice and constitutional rights, dealt unfairly with defendants in the courts. Just who did *not* take kindly to that reform? The Jamaican courts. Moreover, they viewed the proposal as a suggestion by Garvey that he had been "victimized" when fined for contempt in the Marke case, and was challenging the courts' integrity. With self-righteous indignation they again seized Garvey, sentenced him to three months in jail, and fined him one hundred pounds.

Garvey's followers were as loyal as ever. While he was behind bars they elected him to a seat on the Council of the Kingston and St. Andrew Corporation. Garvey promptly applied for a "leave of absence" from jail so he could occupy the elected seat. His application was voted down.

Upon his release he regularly attended meetings of the

Kingston and St. Andrew Corporation only to learn that because of his failure to attend meetings during the three months he resided at the Spanish Town Prison his seat was declared vacant. Still Garvey would not give up. Finally, in a by-election he was returned to his seat on the Council. It was the highest political office Marcus Garvey was ever to attain in Jamaica politics.

Meanwhile, the crash of the American stock market in 1929 was severely felt throughout the hemisphere. And as the United States began to sink into the economic depression of the 1930's, its reverberative waves settled heavily and ominously over the Caribbean area. Jamaica was spared none of the side effects of the holocaust.

CHAPTER TWENTY-TWO

ALTHOUGH JAMAICA in 1926 had been the world's largest single exporter of bananas, first place went to Honduras in 1928. The following year saw Jamaica's crop surge upward. But then came the depression, accompanied by a banana disease that got a head start on most of the island's small growers. Their crops were badly wasted in the areas of Portland and St. Antonio.

In addition to the blight called "Panama Disease" a series of hurricanes in the early 1930's played havoc with the banana supply, causing scores of young people to drift from the crop areas into the cities and towns. There they vainly sought work. Many journeyed to Kingston, as Garvey himself had done earlier. And the port city became the mecca of the island's unemployed.

The year 1930 drove poor Jamaicans out into the streets begging. Children by the hundreds were reduced to one skimpy meal a day, and they could not be expected to walk miles to and from school on that. Older children who were forced to leave the schools with no training turned to becoming loafers and petty thieves. In Kingston the Garveys' first son was born on September 17, 1930, and they named him Marcus. Hard times did not leave the Garvey household untouched, for though they were not literally starving, as were many peasants in both town and country, they were forced to tighten their belts.

Marcus Garvey continued to occupy his seat in the municipality.

There he pushed for such civic improvements as a better water supply, better lighting, and a suitable sewerage system. When asked where the money for such could possibly come from, Garvey reminded his challengers that many Jamaicans acquire fortunes. The rich planters, merchants, and businessmen who made their money from the people, he declared, do nothing to benefit those who helped enrich them.

He suggested, therefore, that such people could be asked "to subscribe to a loan for development, for which they would be paid interest." It was Garvey's feeling that the act would also ease the guilty consciences of the wealthy. Needless to say the Garvey proposals were rejected as reminiscent of socialist planning that lost an election for the Labour party in England.

As the early 1930's marked the beginning of Garvey's decline, he exerted a desperate effort to keep himself and his movement in the public consciousness. *The Black Man* had begun to appear as a monthly magazine late in 1933. But its irregularity, reflecting the financial paucity of the times, also forecast its eventual disappearance four or five years later. Published from London after November 1934, the international character of *The Black Man* exercised the spirit of Duse Mohammed Ali's earlier *African Times and*

Orient Review. As events increasingly wove a mantle of obscurity around Marcus Garvey, an entirely different atmosphere was beginning to permeate the old U.N.I.A. headquarters in New York City.

Members of the Association who had been loyal to its founder during his more triumphant days in the United States had managed to hold together several important splinters of the group. They functioned under the title, "Parent Body Universal Negro Improvement Association, Inc. and African Communities League, Inc." Their address was 233 West 135th Street in Harlem. Twelve officers issued a call for attendance at the International Convention, 1932. The convention committee headed by Lionel A. Francis of Philadelphia, Julia E. R. Clark, Lamar Perkins, Alfred Minus, and Frank Allen of New York were the five official signers of the call.

Others whose familiar names appeared on it were Mrs. Henrietta Vinton Davis of Washington, D.C., Hannah C. Nicholas of New York, Alfonso De Leon, William Ware of Cincinnati, George A. McGuire of New York, Charles A. Petioni, M.D., of New York, A. Hamilton Maloney of Washington, D.C., and Vincent Wattley of New York. The convention was to extend from Sunday, August 7 to Saturday, August 13. Eight items of specific interest to black people made up the agenda; and churches, clubs, lodges, and similar organizations were urged to send delegates versed in the agenda's topics.

At the end of the convention the *New York Age* for August 27, 1932, ran a significant news story on its major developments. Press interest matched that of the delegates in focusing upon two sums of money whose rightful legatees were being decided in Washington, D.C., and Montreal, Canada.

One legacy was that of the late Isaiah Morter, previously mentioned in this narrative.

The other, a reported seventy-three thousand dollars (according to the *New York Age*) had been collected through a Garvey Release Fund by Amy Ashwood Garvey, the U.N.I.A. leader's first wife. That fund had reportedly collected one hundred thousand dollars. Then, in the words of the *Age*:

> In order that the United States Government would not get their money, Garvey instructed his wife to take it to Montreal, Canada, and place it in a British bank.

Mrs. Garvey (wife number one) deposited the money to the account of the U.N.I.A., Inc. Forty thousand dollars of the original amount was expended first, however.

Later, when the Garveys tried to withdraw the remainder, they were told it could be turned over only to an accredited representative of the parent body of the U.N.I.A., Inc. Amy Ashwood Garvey, not even an executive member of that body, was ineligible to receive the money. Garvey himself was completely removed from legal eligibility. As they agonized over their unfortunate position, Lionel Francis, who at the time of that 1932 convention in New York was the duly elected U.N.I.A.'s President-General, prepared to present himself as the legal collector of the monies.

Meanwhile, yet another sum of thirteen thousand dollars belonging to the ill-fated Black Star Line awaited the proper claimant. Lionel Francis, as legal U.N.I.A. representative, backed by the certificate of incorporation of the African Communities League, was also responsible for the Black Star Line. It appeared, therefore, that he would be able to claim that sum, too, for the incorporated New York based Association.

Anguished cries rose from the ranks of those faithful to Garvey. They charged that Dr. Francis, a former physician who reportedly was barred from practicing in Philadelphia, would not use the money properly. The attitude of the *New York Age,* however, was to assume a wait-and-see attitude toward Francis and his officers. And the dignified black weekly concluded its story with a listing of the fifteen convention resolutions which the paper described as "worthwhile and progressive."

The following year the American-based U.N.I.A. broke tradition by unanimously electing a woman, Henrietta Vinton Davis, to the office of President-General of the Association. And in Jamaica Marcus Garvey and his supporters did the best they could with a steadily weakening situation.

Morale was lifted a bit by the laying of a cornerstone for what was proposed as a Liberty Hall building. A report of the event in the *Kingston Daily Gleaner* for March 23, 1933, described a routinely uninspiring ceremony. Speakers included Marcus Garvey, whose subdued remarks reflected little of the fire and drive one normally associated with him.

Actually Garvey, in offering advice to the younger men, was far less than the confident exhorter of huge masses of followers. While congratulating the group for its achievements up to that point, he was cautious in recalling that he had been "bitten" and "burned" in his position of leadership. Garvey hoped this group would give this president its full measure of devotion at least until the proposed building would become their own property.

A year passed. With the advent of 1934 Jamaicans were feeling the raw, cold edge of the economic depression. Black American Garveyites, suffering even more acutely than their white countrymen, were completely unable to lend badly needed financial support to their Jamaican hero. Amy Jacques Garvey in *Garvey and Garveyism* attributes the condition to the aftermath of World War I. She writes this:

> Under a strictly capitalistic system, feeding the machinery of war is good business for industry.

But (and Mrs. Garvey has many supporters in this contention) at war's end production under the capitalist system is slow indeed.

When Roosevelt took over the chieftancy of the nation on March 4, 1933, twenty-two states and the District of Columbia had closed their banks. The entire American banking system was threatened with collapse. On March 5, Roosevelt boldly closed all banks and on March 7 sped a bill to Congress allowing the sound banks to reopen and the Government to supply them with money. His next move was to design a unique relief measure to aid farmers, a plan granting subsidies to farmers, who in turn agreed to reduce their crop production.

Seasoned and orthodox legislators were flabbergasted. Such radical measures had never before been heard of, let alone tried. Roosevelt responded verbally by acknowledging to the Congress he was treading an unprecedented route. But he also reminded them that "an unprecedented condition calls for the trial of new means." The imaginative President, with no formal training or specialized preparations in handling the national economy, had, it seemed, an instinctive revolutionary feel for what had to be done in such a giant emergency.

Roosevelt, the experimental reformist, became, within

the first one hundred days of his Administration, the bane of established conformists. Opposition to him and his New Deal stemmed from the austere offices of Wall Street financiers, through the bastions of industrial tycoons, and down to the diehard racists, who accused him and his wife, Eleanor, of "spoiling niggers." Financiers hated his high-handed breaking of the intricate rules of their own special big-money games. Industry hated the Roosevelt liberal pro-labor stance. Old guard Southern politicos hated Roosevelt's wooing (and winning) of the black vote. And since Afro-Americans were deeply concerned about working and voting, the events of the 1930's had great meaning to them.

The Depression had hit black America especially hard. Existing, as most blacks did, in the tradition of being the last hired and the first fired, the late 1920's and early 1930's found them diffident at the polls in 1932. Traditional Republicanism among black voters, a form of loyalty to the party of Lincoln, fell under the skeptical scrutiny of a few dissidents. The Republicanism of Herbert Hoover, they noted, had done little to help the black race.

Four years of Roosevelt changed all that. In 1934 the poverty-ridden black voters of Illinois retired Oscar De Priest, a token black Republican Congressman, lukewarm to Roosevelt's New Deal. Two years later they sent the first black *Democrat* ever to sit in the national Government, to Washington. He was Arthur Mitchell, who has been followed ever since by black representatives from his state.

Black labor, so traditionally down at the heels, began to look up during the era of the New Deal. Since 1925 Asa Philip Randolph had sought to organize Pullman porters. Randolph, previously mentioned as a Socialist writer for *The Messenger*, was well known to the white establishment.

As early as 1918 he had been hauled down from a speaker's platform in Cleveland, Ohio, and hustled off to jail by agents of the Justice Department. His crime was that of publicly decrying the hypocrisy of the war slogan, "making the world safe for democracy," and refusing to serve in the war on the grounds of being a pacifist.

So when the small group of railroad porters sought an honest and courageous leader, they turned to Randolph, who readily accepted the responsibility. Less "radical" then than in 1918, Randolph was still regarded by Pullman officials as an unsavory menace. Their contention was based not so much on Randolph's behavior as on their own iron-bound and aggressive antilabor policy. During the postwar recession of 1926–27 that ate into Pullman profits, the market for unemployed porters favored the company. The latter did not hesitate when it so desired to replace black porters with Mexicans and Filipinos.

As Randolph proceeded with the formation of The Brotherhood of Sleeping Car Porters, Pullman attacked his past record as a "slacker" during the war. They also called him a "Communist" because in 1920 he had sought the post of secretary of state of New York on the Socialist ticket.

Letters attacking Randolph began to appear in both the white and black press. Still the union grew to a membership of 7,300, and Randolph decided to test its strength by calling, not for a strike, but for a strike *vote*. A gratifying 6,053 supported the idea. Their leader thought the Pullman officials would get the message and recognize the Brotherhood. But entrenched industry motivated to keep itself entrenched by fat profits does not give in easily to workers.

Union members grew indifferent and frightened to the point where half of them pulled away within six months.

Pullman then intimated it would "probably look with more favor" on the union if Randolph were dropped. Brotherhood officials said "No." A check for ten thousand dollars arrived in the mail with a note addressed to Randolph, advising that he was beaten and to "take a trip to Europe." With an empty treasury and *The Messenger,* the Brotherhood's official organ, defunct because of lack of funds, the temptation was excruciatingly great. Randolph returned the check.

The National Urban League favored unions, but its more or less autonomous local branches had to be careful. Pullman, for instance, contributed heavily to the Chicago branch. The N.A.A.C.P. officially favored Randolph but its middle-class black bourgeois membership cared not to associate its activities with the black laboring class. But the great enemy of the union was the black church, and Randolph, son of a minister, knew how to deal with its leaders.

He had now acquired another official organ, the *Black Worker,* and was ready to woo his union's most difficult and most desperately needed support. Randolph studded the columns of the *Black Worker* with biblical phrases as he exhorted the righteous (working masses loyal to God and church) to stand fast against the heartless imperialists who oppressed them in this modern industrial society.

Realizing also how the white church, though completely separate from the black, still served as a model for the latter, Randolph sought and gained its support. After all, white Pullman riders far outnumbered black ones. His appeal to whites through the Social Service Bulletin of the Methodist Federation for Social Science, was essential to victory.

In 1929 a study of the status of porters was made and published by the Federal Council of Churches of Christ in America. Influential white Catholic, Lutheran, and Congregational groups threw their support to the Brotherhood. And by 1932 there were few black churches in the nation that would not follow suit. With this strength behind him, A. Philip Randolph openly declared that the black worker was ready to take the offensive. No minority group subjected to discrimination and exploitation can win any rights, declared the union leader, as long as it remains on the defensive.

When in 1934 the Railway Labor Act was amended to guarantee collective bargaining and to outlaw company unions, the Brotherhood at last had its chance. During the following year black porters and maids, eight thousand strong, were dues-paying members of the Brotherhood. In 1937, twelve years after he had begun his fight, Pullman officials sat down with Randolph and the Mediation Board to negotiate a contract.

Such were the struggles through which black American voters and workers had to come during the days of the Depression. That is why there was little financial support for Marcus Garvey even among his staunchest American supporters. Morale in the black communities had sunk to a low level, what with the need for jobs so desperately acute. Drives for jobs were initiated on Chicago's South Side by a black weekly, *The Whip*. In Detroit, Snow Grigsby wrote and circulated an attack upon the antiblack hiring policy of the city. He called it "The X-Ray Picture of Detroit," and it roused the black citizens of the Motor City to organize the "Detroit Civil Rights Committee." That group in 1933 opened the doors of employment to blacks in the Detroit Edison Company and the Michigan Bell Telephone Company.

Blacks in Cleveland, Ohio, organized their "Future Outlook League" in 1933, and then established branches throughout the state. In Washington, Baltimore, and Los Angeles, black citizens launched drives for job representation where they had been heretofore denied. And in New York's Harlem, where Marcus Garvey had fifteen years earlier established the largest of his U.N.I.A. divisions, there was a similar drive.

A common sight in the early to mid-thirties was the parade of black pickets led by a handsome man in clerical garb, marching and chanting defiantly before the shops of white merchants along West 125th Street. The young clergyman leading that noisy demonstration was Adam Clayton Powell, Jr., a recent graduate of the Colgate University Divinity School. Neither he nor his followers ceased their badgering, marching chant and boycott until the merchants relented and staffed their shops with unemployed black workers.

That is what black America was doing for itself as Marcus Garvey in Jamaica contemplated a change of U.N.I.A. strategy. The Garveys' second son, Julius Winston, born following a torrential and devastating storm, was a year old when his father opened the seventh International Convention in August 1934. The *New York Age* for August 11 reported the event in a brief news story headlined:

> Garvey Opens Convention in Jamaica, B.W.I.

Delegates from Canada, Central and South America, and the United States joined the local membership in seeking to recapture what they could of the spirit of former and more auspicious gatherings. An examination of the condition of the Association convinced the delegates of the wisdom of moving headquarters from Kingston to London.

CHAPTER TWENTY-THREE

DURING THE early part of 1935 Marcus Garvey left Kingston again for London. There, leasing a portion of a house in West Kensington, he continued publishing his magazine, the *Black Man*, and speaking wherever he could gather an audience. During the spring and summer, when the weather permitted, he spoke outdoors in London's Hyde Park. Sunday was a favorite day for speakers there, since spectators, with no routine weekday obligations, had time to listen to them. As the autumn season drew near Garvey began addressing audiences indoors. He had much to say to them in view of what was taking place in a famed country of Africa.

As far back as 1934 a former school teacher and journalist of Italy, turned dictator, had planned a territorial expansion in northeastern Africa. His name was Benito Mussolini and he was the founder of the Italian Facist party. On the third of October, 1935, Mussolini threw the weight of his military might against Africa's oldest independent territory, the Kingdom of Abyssinia. Pictures and stories of Abyssinian village defenders armed with spears, trying valiantly to fend off the well-organized and heavily equipped Italian invaders, began to circulate around the globe.

The entire black world recoiled in shock and anger. Here was a situation made to order for the black American press and for the stormy denunciations of Marcus Garvey. The Jamaican lost no time whatsoever in mounting the rostrums of London to deny the brutal assault upon a defenseless African country. In his typically bombastic fashion, Garvey excoriated Il Duce in terms ecstatically received and applauded by black partisans all over the world.

When the Abyssinian Emperor, Haile Selassie, fled to London in search of diplomatic aid, Garvey was certain the diminutive monarch would be happy to confer with him. Again Marcus Garvey had miscalculated. Selassie's "cold shoulder" treatment of the Jamaican black nationalist so bruised Garvey's pride as to send him off into a raging torrent of vilification of the Emperor.

He accused Selassie of, first, abusing his black countrymen and then of deserting them in their hour of need. Later Amy Jacques Garvey accused Selassie of being unfair to both himself and his country. She cited the truth that the Emperor had kept his people and his land unprepared to meet the demands of the aggressive modern world around them. Neither Garvey nor his wife directly charged Selassie with being antiblack in the sense that many nonblacks so often are. With Garvey's particular viewpoint, such would have been an impossibility inasmuch as he regarded Ethiopians (or Abyssinians) as black.

Visitors to present-day Ethiopia are often surprised to find how "Negroid" Ethiopians are—how closely the masses of them resemble the black peoples of the Americas. Though he was never there, Marcus Garvey always referred to Ethiopia as the "Canaan" of black people. He certainly regarded Haile Selassie as being a black man, contrary pronouncements of "scientists" notwithstanding. Indeed Garvey openly disputed white "experts on race" who decreed otherwise. One such expert was Professor George A. Kersnor, who in the early 1920's had headed a Harvard-Boston expedition to the Egyptian Sudan.

Upon returning home in 1923, Professor Kersnor brought words of high praise for the culture of ancient Ethiopians, whom he declared to be "dark colored races" not related to Negroes. That infuriated Marcus Garvey. To him Kersnor's "findings" were but yet further evidence of the white man's studied determination to conceal and deny the abilities and achievements of black peoples. Writing on that theme in *The Philosophy and Opinions of Marcus Garvey,* the Jamaican snorted:

> Imagine a dark colored man in middle Africa being anything else but a Negro. Some white men, whether they be professors or not, have a wide stretch of imagination.

Garvey's memory quite probably harked back to his meeting with Duse Mohamed Ali, a black man of Egyptian nationality. So when informed that Haile Selassie, the "Conquering Lion of Judah," allegedly claimed to be a descendant of Solomon, Garvey snorted again as he wrote this in *The Black Man* for July-August 1936:

> . . . The new Negro doesn't give two pence about the line of Solomon. Solomon has been long dead. Solomon was a Jew. The Negro is no Jew. The Negro has a racial origin running from Sheba to the present, of which he is proud. He is proud of Sheba but he is not proud of Solomon.

Garvey's pique with Jews, and with Selassie's failure to take serious notice of him during Selassie's hurried visit to London, exposed a corner of his personal human frailty. At the same time it overlooked the strong possibility that the beleaguered Emperor was far more occupied between 1934 and 1936 with preserving his monarchy than with helping plan the redemption of the rest of Africa. He certainly was of no disposition to spend any significant time disclaiming his black ancestry.

While Selassie was trying to get his business straight, Garvey called and presided over a regional U.N.I.A. conference in Toronto, Canada. It was August 1936, and the delegates took Father Divine, a popular black American religious cult leader, severely to task for blasphemy. Divine's followers were fanatically devoted to the stubby ex-handyman once known as George Baker. They went so far as to insist he was God. Their idol seized upon the chance to confirm that belief early in his career as religious leader.

Divine had acquired a shabby four-room house in Sayville, Long Island, which he used as a mission. Sunday evening prayer meetings were joyous occasions, attracting publicity and alarming the white middle-class area residents. As the whites gloomily envisioned their neighborhood "turning black," they tried to buy back the property. Divine's astronomical asking price sent them scurrying to town officials and Divine was arrested, tried, and found guilty of "maintaining a public nuisance."

As Judge Lewis J. Smith sentenced the dynamic preacher to one year in jail, Divine is reported to have intoned:

> Pity the poor judge. He can't live long. He's offended Almighty God!

Four days later when Judge Smith died suddenly of a heart attack, Divine, in his jail cell, remarked, "I hated to do it." His disciples were convinced beyond all doubt, and Father Divine never bothered to change their minds. Marcus Garvey's Roman Catholic upbringing doubtless gagged over such sacrilegious carryings-on. And while he strongly advocated a black deity for black people, Divine was hardly his choice. Garvey's censure of the cult leader, therefore, was swift and severe.

At the same conference Garvey condemned the showing of several popular dramas and films. *The Emperor Jones* was one. *The Green Pastures* and *Imitation of Life* were others. Garvey regarded them as conspiratorial devices designed to relegate and keep the black man in a subservient position in the white man's world.

During that same period the Kingston *Gleaner* for August 26, 1936, had a few gentle editorial words for Garvey. Noting that he was forty-nine years old and carrying on his work in Canada, *The Gleaner* stated that "Garveyism is today a very different thing from what it was ten years ago." Obviously satisfied that Marcus Garvey was no longer a menace, *The Gleaner* then ventured the opinion that the fiery Jamaican never really sought to stir up any serious trouble and strife on the island. The writer even refused to call Garvey a failure, preferring instead to do "justice" to him by calling him a "personality."

One year later, in 1937, Garvey held a second regional conference in Toronto and followed that by founding a school to train interested blacks for leadership roles in the U.N.I.A. He called it the School of African Philosophy. The first eight graduates became U.N.I.A. commissioners for the areas of their residency. Then Garvey moved ahead with plans for a correspondence course offering three academic degrees in African philosophy to any black students who successfully completed his courses of study.

Garvey's feeling regarding the attitude of black people toward themselves seemed especially strong during the late 1930's. He had always been an advocate of racial solidarity, but his zeal in that area seemed to increase with the rapid passage of his allotted time. In an essay titled "A Racial Weakness" written for the August 1937 issue of the *Black Man*, Garvey revealed as much of his love for his people as of his cognizance of their human failings.

Here the U.N.I.A. founder laid bare the weaknesses of sloth, misplaced charity, extravagance, and general lack of vision common to all human beings. That they existed among black people too was not a foregone conclusion that Garvey could accept with philosophic grace.

So conscious was he of the barriers erected against the advancement of black men all over the world that he expected them to eschew ordinary human frailty in their struggle to overcome. Garvey had clearly written the white man off as far as hoping to involve him in the acquisition of black men's rights was concerned. As Garvey saw it, black men, *and black men alone*, held the key to the gateway leading to their freedom.

Toronto, Canada, was the setting for the eighth International Convention of the Negro Peoples of the World. And in what seemed to be a desperate effort to breath new life into a steadily weakening old body, Garvey made a bid to capture youth. For twenty-five dollars each, he called for one thousand students to enroll in his correspondence course in the School of African Philosophy. There is no record that anything like that number responded.

Meanwhile, turbulent developments in Jamaica indicated the wisdom of Garvey's decision to move the center of his activities elsewhere. The Garveys left just as Jamaica fell prey to the plague of hunger. A Committee on Nutrition in the Colonial Empire, after a visit to Jamaica in 1935, reported that unemployment, low wages, the overlarge family, and illegitimacy were the causes. Malnutrition raised the infant mortality rate so that in 1935, out of every 1,000 children born in Jamaica, 137 died.

Conditions became so acute that on September 17, 1937, Jamaica Welfare was founded. Its purpose was not to hand out charity to the needy but to activate programs that trained people to do things for themselves. Peasants, laborers, and farmers were the organization's chief targets, and its first community center at Guys Hill was soon in full operation. Demonstrations in cooking, building fireplaces, improving water tanks, and garden layout were supplemented by the operation of two mobile educational film units for adults and children. Still trouble stalked the island.

In 1937 and 1938 serious riots exploded in Barbados, Trinidad, and Jamaica. The Jamaica outbreak of May 1938 marked the beginning of the end of the Crown Colony regime and the opening of a new social and political era. And ironically enough, the Jamaica riot, sparked by unemployed cane-sugar workers, began with the creation of employment at the Frome sugar estate.

Word that the West Indies Sugar Company was hiring at Frome drew thousands of anxious, hungry, field hands to the site. When the multitude discovered there were jobs for just a few, it directed its frustrated rage against the estate itself. Brutal police action failed to halt rioters as the fighting spread along the countryside and into the city of

Kingston. There laborers working on a housing development were driven off by the unemployed, who demanded jobs for everyone. Strangely enough the rioters seemed to be leaderless. It was as if the acuteness of conditions alone had made riot leadership unnecessary.

Strikes followed the riots. Inaction started by the longshoremen in Kingston soon gathered momentum. Again without leaders to agitate the masses, the billowing cloak of worker resistance quickly enveloped the city into the folds of a general stoppage. Only months before, efforts at organizing some workers had met with rebuffs, even as a move in 1936 to give strength to the Jamaica Workers' and Tradesmen's Union had gone unrewarded.

Alexander Bustamante had tried to organize the sugar workers but they had not responded. Meanwhile in 1936 Jamaican expatriates in the United States had formed the Jamaica Progressive League. Now the League was calling for self-government on a universal suffrage. Back in Jamaica a group of intellectuals welcomed the idea and gave voice to it in its weekly magazine, *Public Opinion.*

But neither *Public Opinion* nor its intellectual founders could take credit for the riots or the strike. Unlike Bustamante or Garvey before him, Jamaican intellectuals were way out of touch with the masses of their poor peasant fellow islanders.

No sooner had the dock workers of Kingston walked out, however, than Bustamante assumed leadership of their protest. A strikingly handsome man of ability and charm, he was assisted by his cousin, Norman W. Manley, founder of Jamaica Welfare. Bustamante had the confidence of the workers and that alarmed the British Government, who quickly seized and jailed him.

Then dock employers agreed to raise wages. But the workers refused to return unless their leader, Bustamante, was freed. With the able intervention of Norman Manley came the release of Bustamante. The strike in Kingston was over. While the next few years saw rifts and other strikes and threats of strikes in Jamaica, the strength of Bustamante and his organized workers grew, as did that of the movement toward Jamaica's independence.

Meanwhile Kingston had seen the last of the big U.N.I.A. functions to take place during the lifetime of Marcus Garvey. Celebrating the twentieth anniversary of its founding there in Kingston, the memorable occasion was not attended by its creator. But Garvey was not forgotten as the news story in *The Gleaner* for September 4, 1935, attested.

The Gleaner reported President C. D. Johnson as recalling that the organization was the brainchild of a Jamaican, and though it had not achieved its full aims, had created a new spirit of pride among black peoples. Moreover Mr. Johnson reminded the gathering that the rumor of Garvey's advocating moving his people "bag and baggage back to Africa," was a distortion of the founder's intention. Garvey wanted his people to become "Africa-minded" and "back to Africa" meant back to culture along racial lines—a senseless mass exodus would be to nobody's advantage and Marcus Garvey knew that, Johnson declared.

A different atmosphere pervaded the Kingston U.N.I.A. four years later. Word from British Honduras and New York was that Isaiah Morter's estate had been awarded to the New York U.N.I.A. headed by Dr. Lionel A. Francis. The stunning blow to the Jamaica unit was a windfall of good fortune to the American unit. Francis, who never claimed a large membership, had been affiliated since 1920 with the

U.N.I.A. He had headed the Philadelphia division in the days when Marcus Garvey had claimed a total U.N.I.A. membership of between four and six million from 1920 to 1924. Estimates by Garvey's critics ranged far lower, and there is as yet no established figure that can be certain.

But Dr. Francis's concern was not with numbers. He made it plain that as far as he, and the members of the group he headed were concerned, they sought only a solution to the black man's *economic problems.* If they could achieve that without being bothered with or by white men, they would be perfectly content to do so. A *New York Post* story dated Monday, November 20, 1939, under the byline of Ted Poston, concluded its account of the reported three-hundred-thousand-dollar settlement with this paragraph:

> Dr. Francis revealed today that the estate will be liquidated as soon as possible and that the money will be used by the organization to sponsor co-operative enterprizes and profit-sharing plans among Negroes in America.

Twice during 1939 Marcus Garvey fell ill in London with pneumonia. Miss Daisy Whyte, his private secretary for ten years, writing in *The Voice of Freedom* for August 1945, recalled the period. Miss Whyte reported that Garvey paid no attention to his health and defied medical advice to "take a rest." She spoke also of the Garvey offices in Beaumont Crescent, West Kensington, London, and of "the staff of English, Irish, and people of African descent" employed by Garvey.

Miss Whyte's mention of the regular summer trips to Canada on which she accompanied her employer, while not suggesting wealth, does suggest that Garvey's last days were not days of destitution. He had access to good medical care as, according to Miss Whyte, Garvey's physician was "an eminent Indian specialist." Of the Garvey acute illness of January 1940, Daisy Whyte wrote:

> His English housemaid came over to the office one day and asked me to rush home, as she did not know what to do for him. A male clerk and I went immediately and saw him trembling as if he had taken a chill, and was unable to speak.

Garvey's physician diagnosed a stroke that had paralyzed the right side, and a weakening of the heart. Again the advice was to ease up, and still Garvey ignored it. He read all his mail, dictated letters, and held bedside interviews. Garvey also insisted on going riding in Hyde Park, where he was greeted by people who never knew, seeing him ride by, that he was crippled.

Miss Whyte reported that in May 1940 a London reporter "wickedly sent out a news release that he had died." Since Garvey would let no one else open his mail and cables, he found himself reading his own black-bordered obituary notices. Wrote Daisy Whyte:

> After the second day of this pile of shocking correspondence, he collapsed in his chair and could hardly be understood after that.

On June 10, 1940, Marcus Mosiah Garvey died. He had lived for fifty-seven years.

CHAPTER TWENTY-FOUR

When you imprison and even kill men you don't, as a matter of course, destroy their ideas. The adage is as true as it is old. Garveyism, therefore, is not dead. Indeed the ideas Garvey held were not exclusively his—did not originate with him—as is evident in the fierce and bloody history of his Maroon ancestors. Even beyond that, Garveyism, literally taken, still exists. There are still active U.N.I.A. members to be found in Harlem, where the Association reached the zenith of its strength under Marcus Garvey's electrifying leadership.

Exactly twenty days after Garvey died in London, Harlem paid tribute to him in a public meeting sponsored by several local civic groups. Five years later Garvey's birthday (August 17) was the occasion for another U.N.I.A.-sponsored International Conference, lasting three days, in New York City. Liberty Hall in Harlem provided the platform for speakers from Nigeria, Liberia, the West Indies, and the United States. The welcome address to the delegates was delivered by Benjamin Gibbons, president of the Garvey Club, who served as chairman of the Conference.

When Jamaica became independent in 1962, the new government did not forget Marcus Garvey. At the independence ceremonies he was named one of the island's national heroes. Two years later his mortal remains were transferred from the catacombs of St. Mary's Catholic Church in London to Jamaica. There the Government had erected a permanent shrine to house the bones of its "first national hero" in King George VI Memorial Park.

The throng of thirty thousand perspiring black souls, gathered at the rites to hear dignitaries of church and state declaim their pride in this honored son, would have pleased Garvey no end. The star-shaped tomb of black marble they had chosen for the reinterment was a creative touch straight out of the flamboyant imagination of Marcus Garvey himself.

Back in the United States, *The New York Times* took the occasion of Mrs. Amy Ashwood Garvey's return to America, after an absence of twenty-seven years, to present a feature story on her and her late ex-husband. The *Times* appropriately chose August 17, 1968, as the day on which to run the story of the lady who, with Marcus Garvey, founded the U.N.I.A. fifty-four years earlier in Jamaica. It was secretary Amy Ashwood who had rushed the gunman, spoiling his aim as he fired at Garvey in the Harlem U.N.I.A. headquarters in 1919. Doubtless her instinctive action altered the course of history in the life of the man and all those later affected and influenced by him. Now she was reviewing a scene she had known a half century earlier.

Pointing to August afternoon crowds on Lenox Avenue between 115th and 116th streets, Mrs. Garvey (wife number one) remarked to *Times* reporter C. Gerald Fraser:

It was people like these, and right here on Lenox Avenue, that gave my husband his greatest success. I couldn't write about him without returning to Harlem.

Amy Ashwood Garvey took note of the filth in Harlem's streets, the decaying slums, and the dope addicts nodding in doorways. She also took note of "The African Nationalist Pioneer Movement in Harlem," a group determined to keep Garveyism alive. She saw the Afro hair styles and heard the term "black" being used with pride, and she knew her husband's teachings had managed to survive the strangulating forces of degradation and rot.

But Garveyism as referred to here signifies something even bigger and more encompassing. And many of Garvey's statements promoting those ideas that refuse to remain imprisoned or to die are reincarnated in the statements and ideas of his successors. One of those most popularly linked to the Garveyan philosophy is Malcolm X. And why not? Do we not find, as we examine Malcolm's life as revealed in one of the most remarkable autobiographies of modern literature, that the seed of Garveyism entered his fertile consciousness during early childhood? Let Malcolm himself tell it.

My father, the Reverend Earl Little, was a Baptist minister, a dedicated organizer for Marcus Aurelius Garvey's U.N.I.A. (Universal Negro Improvement Association). With the help of such disciples as my father, Garvey from his headquarters in New York City's Harlem was raising the banner of black race purity and exhorting the Negro masses to return to their ancestral African homeland—a cause which had made Garvey the most controversial black man on earth.

Malcolm was still cradled in his mother's womb. But four years later he recalls that in Lansing, Michigan, his father was still devoting evening hours of the week to espousing the Garvey philosophy. On Sundays Earl Little looked toward whatever freelance preaching engagements he could obtain in local Baptist pulpits. Little Malcolm sat and listened during those weekly sessions as his father crusaded and recruited for the U.N.I.A. Moreover, he vividly recalled the thrill of looking at the photographs of the spectacular convention parades. Again Malcolm speaks for himself:

> I remember seeing the big shiny photographs of Marcus Garvey that were passed from hand to hand. My father had a big envelope of them that he always took to these meetings.

Malcolm describes the elation he as a child felt when he looked at what to him appeared to be "millions of Negroes thronged in parade behind Garvey" as the latter, bedecked in colors and plumes, rode by in majestic style. And Malcolm never forgot how his father always adjourned meetings by chanting with his listeners the Garvey rallying cry, "Up you mighty race, you can accomplish what you will!" Nor did Malcolm ever cease to suspect that his father's violent and mysterious death shortly thereafter was effected by local whites hostile to his activity in the Garvey movement.

Toward the end of his short life Malcolm had developed an even more profound understanding of his position as a black nationalist leader. He began to know that the black American struggled for his dignity in a world of other men struggling for theirs. Many of the latter were not black. That other black nationalist, Marcus Garvey, knew it also and voiced what he knew. Here are direct quotes from both men. First, Garvey, writing in Volume Two of his *Philosophy and Opinions of Marcus Garvey*:

Gandhi in prison; a George V in his castle; a Congo native massacred; an Albert of Belgium drinking his wine; a Senegalese Negro kicked on the plantation of his master; a Poincare driving in his landau in the Champs d'Élysees; a Negro lynched in Georgia; a Wilson, Harding, or Coolidge, talking about a world court or league; a Chinaman shot down at Kia Chow and the Emperor of Japan drinking tea in his palace at Tokyo; a Jew murdered on the borders of Eastern Europe; and His Holiness, the Pope, seeing no further than the Vatican, will not save the human race. But that lonely man or woman of whatsoever race, who cries out for justice to all humanity, including Europe with its whites, Asia with its brown and yellows, Africa with its blacks, and America and the rest of the world with their mixed populations will, even though there be persecution and injustice done to him, bring succor and aid, late though it be, to the rest of us mortals, that we may see everlasting life.

That quote may (though it certainly should not) come as a complete surprise to those who consider themselves thoroughly familiar with the Garveyan philosophy. That too, with its broad internationalist base, is a part of the creed we have come to know as Garveyism.

Forty years after Garvey wrote it, Malcolm X was interviewed in New York City by Jack Barnes and Barry Sheppard. Both young men were editorial board members of the publication, *Young Socialist*. They asked Malcolm the following question: "How do you define black nationalism, with which you have been identified?" Malcolm's candid reply was typical of him:

I used to define black nationalism as the idea that the black man should control the economy of his community, the politics of his community, and so forth. But when I was in Africa in May, in Ghana, I was speaking with the Algerian ambassador who is extremely militant and is a revolutionary in the true sense of the word (and has his credentials as such for having carried on a successful revolution against oppression in his country). When I told him that my political, social and economic philosophy was black nationalism, he asked me very frankly, well, where did that leave him? Because he was white.

He was an African, but he was Algerian, and to all appearances, he was a white man. And he said if I define my objective as the victory of black nationalism, where does that leave him? Where does that leave revolutionaries in Morrocco, Egypt, Iraq, Mauritania? So he showed me where I was alienating people who were true revolutionaries dedicated to overthrowing the system of exploitation that exists on this earth by any means necessary.

So I had to do a lot of thinking and re-appraising of my definition of black nationalism. Can we sum up the solution to the problems confronting our people as black nationalism?

Marcus Garvey and Malcolm X shared much in common as regards their views of a meaningful black nationalism. But Malcolm has not been the lone black modern spokesman to paraphrase the spoken and written thoughts and opinions of Marcus Garvey.

Paul Robeson gave his own expression to it as he wrote these lines in 1957—lines quoted from his book, *Here I Stand*:

It was in Britain—among the English, Scottish, Welsh, and Irish people of that land—that I learned that the essential character of a nation is determined not by the upper classes, but by the common people, and that the common people of all nations are truly brothers in the great family of mankind. If in Britain there were those who lived by plundering the colonial peoples, there were also the many millions who earned their bread by honest toil. And even as I grew to feel more Negro in spirit, or African as I put it then, I also came to feel a sense of oneness with the white working people whom I came to know and love.

Malcolm's and Robeson's viewpoints parallel that facet of the Garveyan philosophy advocating cooperation with other races and nationals who share a common human experience. Yet another facet of Garvey's teachings stresses the need of peoples of all groups to do certain things for themselves and quite *by* themselves. Such an approach, not necessarily a contradiction of that of cooperation with others, has been voiced by black spokesmen since the arrival and passing of Marcus Garvey.

The novelist Richard Wright, for example, shared that Garveyan view. Take the question of African redemption. Wright joined with A. Philip Randolph and W. E. B. Du Bois in the belief that blacks of the Americas should not presume to take the initiative in redeeming Africa for Africans, but should leave that to Africans themselves. In that regard they differed with Garvey. Wright did, however, concur completely with the Jamaican on the question of Africans maintaining their independence of European control on the African continent. In his book *Black Power*, written before Stokely Carmichael ever thought of using the phrase, Wright said this is an open letter to Kwame Nkrumah of Ghana:

> Kwame, let me put it bluntly: Western lay and academic circles utter many a hard saying against Africa. In defending their subjugation of Africa, they contend that Africa has no culture, no history, no background, etc. I'm not impressed by these gentlemen, lay or academic. In matters of history they have been more often wrong than right, and even when they have been right, it has been more by accident than design, or

they have been right only after facts have already been so clearly established that not even a fool could go wrong.

Garvey wrote this:

> For many years white propagandists have been printing tons of literature to impress scattered Ethiopia, especially that portion within their civilization, with the idea that Africa is a despised place, inhabited by savages, and cannibals, where no civilized human being should go especially black civilized human beings. This propaganda is promulgated for the cause that is being realized today. That cause is Colonial expansion for the white nations of the world.

Then Garvey, again commenting on the same theme, issued a warning to Africa and her friends among the black peoples of the world.

> Africa invites capital to develop its resources. Let not that capital, whether it be financial or man-power, be supplied by white men, but let us as Negroes make our contribution.

Wright's warning Nkrumah thirty years later was equally blunt.

> Beware of a Volta Project built by foreign money. Build your own Volta, and build it out of the sheer lives and bodies of your people! With but limited outside aid, your people can rebuild your society with their bare hands . . . Africa needs this hardness, *but only from Africans.*

The italicized end of Wright's thought is of course more specifically related to Du Bois' concept of Pan-Africanism than to the Garveyan concept. Still, as has been shown by their works, all three men cared about Africa and each made his own contribution to the creation of a fuller understanding of the aspirations of that complex continent.

With their concentration focused directly upon the domestic scene, current black scholars frequently voice Garveyisms. While in considering statesmen, the critical observer shies away from the traditional politician, the thoughts and expressions of at least one black American currently prominent in the domestic political scene command respect and attention.

On the evening of February 22, 1969, the Honorable Richard Gordon Hatcher, eloquent black mayor of Gary, Indiana, paid verbal tribute to W. E. B. Du Bois. The occasion was the closing of the Du Bois centennial-year program sponsored by *Freedomways* magazine. The place was New York City's Town Hall. There Hatcher declared that as mayor of Gary he was chief executive of *all* of the city's peoples. Said he:

> What I cannot do for black brothers I cannot do for white people either, try as I might. The black communities' needs are infinitely greater but the white community in our city is not without problems. For the same reasons which prevent me from solving many of the black problems, I cannot solve many of the white ones either. Neither could my white predecessors.

Then speaking of how the black American is a stranger in his own village, Hatcher, delivering the principal address, paraphrased Franz Fanon in offering this "Garveyism":

> To stop being strangers, we have to find the road to power ourselves. Whether or not one fully accepts other aspects of the thought of Franz Fanon, it is clear that rising black consciousness requires that we be led by our own, determine our own destiny, recognize our own needs, and that white Americans have quite another task to perform—perhaps an impossible one—which is to work to cure the sickness of racism among their own people.

How fitting, in view of the scores of attempts by others to divorce the aims of the two great leaders, Du Bois and Garvey, that Hatcher would voice a sentiment common to the beliefs and strivings of each!

Recently there have been several eloquent expressions from younger black writers whose view of the world parallels Garvey's. Marcus Garvey, as has been shown, was not at odds with *all* black leaders. In fact one of the first things he did in strengthening the U.N.I.A. was to enlist the aid and good will of black clergymen. It was from their membership ranks that Garvey was able to establish his own following.

Every clergyman exerts the influence of leadership, no matter how seemingly minor, among the people he serves. Garvey knew that. And doubtless, because of his own strict Catholic background, the Jamaica leader was critical of those religious leaders and leaders elsewhere who, in his opinion, were not dealing sincerely with the people. Here is what he wrote about them in *Philosophy and Opinions.*

> There is many a leader of our race who tells us that everything is well, and that all things will work out themselves and that a better day is coming. Yes, all of us know that a better day is coming; we all know that one day we will go home to Paradise, but whilst we are hoping by our Christian virtues to have an entry into Paradise we also realize we are living on earth, and that the things that are practiced in Paradise are not practiced here.

Poet Margaret Walker, writing in the late 1930's, had this to say in her most famous work, "For My People."

> For my people blundering and groping and floundering in the dark of churches and schools and clubs and societies, associations and councils and committees, and conventions, distressed and disturbed and deceived and devoured by money-

hungry, glory-craving leeches, preyed on by facile force of state and fad and novelty by false prophet and holy believer; . . . Let a new earth rise. Let another world be born. Let a bloody peace be written in the sky. . . .

Eldridge Cleaver has made this observation on the subject, as this excerpt from "On Becoming" in *Soul on Ice* attests:

> I had come to believe that there is no God; if there is, men do not know anything about him. Therefore all religions were phony—which made all preachers and priests, in our eyes, fakers, including the ones scurrying around the prison who, curiously, could put in a good word for you with the Almighty Creator of the universe but could not get anything down with the warden or the parole board—they could usher you through the Pearly Gates *after you were dead,* but not through the prison gate *while you were still alive and kicking.*

Cleaver's point is well taken here. Death is indeed an inevitable cycle in the earthly experience of man and all living things around him. Marcus Garvey knew and accepted that biological truth. He also knew that those who expose themselves in certain ways were likely to meet death sooner than they might if they did not leave themselves so vulnerable. Said Garvey:

> Any sane man, race, or nation, that desires freedom must first of all think in terms of blood. Why, even the Heavenly Father tells us that without the shedding of blood there can be no remission of sins! Then how in the name of God, with history before us, do we expect to redeem Africa without preparing ourselves—some of us to die?

Malcolm X recognized the truth of it as he wrote:

> Anything I do today, I regard as urgent. . . . I am only facing facts when I know that any moment of any day, or any

> night, could bring me death. . . . To speculate about dying does not disturb me as it might some people. I never have felt that I would live to become an old man. Even before I was a Muslim—when I was a hustler in the ghetto jungle, and then a criminal in prison, it always stayed on my mind that I would die a violent death.

Still another modern day black firebrand, H. Rap Brown, wrote as recently as 1969 in *Die Nigger Die!* these sentiments.

> Only people who've never lived fear death. If you've lived, you know that death is part of the process. A lot of people say that it's regrettable that Malcolm got killed. But Malcolm was not an individual. His life didn't belong to him. No revolutionary can claim his life for himself. The life of the revolutionary belongs to the struggle. Malcolm, like Che, is not dead, because he was totally committed to the struggle. The only people who should make any kind of statement of regret over Malcolm's death are Malcolm's family. Death is the price of revolution.

Rap Brown, himself, has been missing now for more than a year. Many wonder if he, too, has not joined Malcolm and Martin Luther King, Medgar Evers, James Chaney, Michael Schwerner, Andrew Goodman, Viola Liuzzo, Fred Hampton, and victims of the guns at Kent State, Orangeburg, Jackson State, San Quentin (George Jackson), and Attica. Rap Brown is right is declaring that Malcolm and Che still live. That their names and the principles for which they stood are still recalled is testimony to their presence among us. And so it is also with Garvey and those ideas that he voiced and promoted and which we know as "Garveyism."

Marcus Garvey simply will not die. Indeed, he cannot die as long as the inequities and injustices that make his existence so real and so necessary persist. We have Garvey's own word for that as it appeared in the *Negro World* dated February 14, 1925. Writing under the caption, "If I Die in Atlanta," Garvey, more certain of his physical passing that of just where he would be when it happened, said these words:

> Look for me in the whirlwind or the storm, look for me all around you, for with God's grace, I shall come and bring with me the countless millions of black slaves who have died in America and the West Indies and the millions in Africa to aid you in the fight for liberty, freedom, and life.

BIBLIOGRAPHY

BOOKS

Abrahams, Peter. *Jamaica, An Island Mosaic.* London: H. M. Stationery Office, Corona Library, 1957.

Ahuma, Attoh. *The Gold Coast Nations and National Consciousness.* Liverpool: D. Marples and Co., 1911.

Allen, Robert L. *Black Awakening in Capitalist America.* New York: Doubleday & Co., 1969.

Anderson, Bradley, Council, Croteau, Hanks, Johnson, Negus, Ryan. *Area Handbook for Nicaragua.* Washington, D.C.: American University Press, 1970.

Ayearst, Morley. *The British West Indies.* New York: New York University Press, 1960.

Bennett, Lerone, Jr. *Confrontation: Black and White.* Chicago, Ill.: Johnson Publishing Company, 1965.

Bowles, Chester. *Africa's Challenge to America.* Westport, Connecticut: Greenwood Press, Inc., 1956.

Brisbane, Robert H. *The Black Vanguard.* Valley Forge, Pennsylvania: Judson Press, 1970.

Brown, H. Rap. *Die Nigger Die!* New York: The Dial Press, 1969.

Chambers, Bradford. *Chronicles of Negro Protest.* New York: Parents Magazine Press, 1968.

Clark, Kenneth B. *Dark Ghetto.* New York: Harper & Row, 1965.

Cleaver, Eldridge. *Soul on Ice.* New York: Dell Publishing Company, 1968.

Cronon, Edmund D. *Black Moses.* Madison, Wisconsin: University of Wisconsin Press, 1955.

Cruse, Harold. *The Crisis of the Negro Intellectual.* New York: William Morrow and Co., 1967.

Dallas, R. C. *The History of the Maroons.* London: A. Strachan, 1803.

Dean, Vera M. *Builders of Emerging Nations.* New York: Holt, Reinhart, and Winston, 1961.

Delany, Martin R. *The Condition, Education, Emigration, and Destiny of the Colored People of the United States.* New York: Arno Press and *The New York Times,* 1969.

De Lisser, Herbert. *Twentieth Century Jamaica.* Kingston: *The Jamaica Times, Ltd.,* 1913.

Drake, St. Clair, and Cayton, Horace. *Black Metropolis,* 2 Vols. New York: Harper & Row, 1962.

Draper, Theodore. *The Re-discovery of Black Nationalism.* New York: The Viking Press, Inc., 1969.

Du Bois, W. E. B. *The Souls of Black Folk.* Chicago: A. C. McClurg and Company, 1922.

——*The World and Africa.* New York: International Publishers, 1946.

Fage, J. D. *An Introduction to the History of West Africa.* Cambridge: Cambridge University Press, 1962.

——*Ghana.* Madison, Wisconsin: University of Wisconsin Press, 1962.

Foster, William Z. *The Negro People in American History.* New York: International Publishers, 1954.

Franklin, John Hope. *From Slavery to Freedom.* New York: Alfred A. Knopf, Inc., 1956.

Frazier, E. Franklin. *Black Bourgeoise.* New York: Collier Books, 1962.

Freyre, Gilberto. *The Masters and the Slaves.* New York: Alfred A. Knopf, Inc., 1956.

Froude, James A. *The English in the West Indies.* New York: Charles Scribner's Sons, 1888.

Furnas, J. C. *Goodbye to Uncle Tom.* New York: William Sloane Associates, 1956.

Gardner, W. J. *History of Jamaica.* London: T. Fisher Unwin, 1909.

Gatti, Attilio. *New Africa.* New York: Charles Scribner's Sons, 1960.

Garvey, Amy Jacques. *Garvey and Garveyism.* New York: Collier Books, 1970.

——*Philosophy and Opinions of Marcus Garvey,* 2 Vols. Arno Press and *The New York Times,* 1968.

Ginsburg, Ralph. *One Hundred Years of Lynchings.* New York: Lancer Books, Inc., 1969.

Gittings, Joshua R. *The Exiles of Florida.* Columbus, Ohio: Follett, Foster, and Company, 1858.

Harris, Janet and Hobson, Julius. *Black Pride.* New York: McGraw-Hill, Inc., 1969.

Hayford, Joseph Casley. *Gold Coast Native Institutions.* London: Sweet and Maxwell, Ltd., 1903.
Hendriques, Fernando. *Jamaica, Land of Wood and Water.* London: MacGibbon and Kee, 1957.
Herskovits, Melville J. *The Myth of the Negro Past.* New York: Harper & Brothers, 1941.
Higginson, Thomas W. *The Black Rebellion.* New York: Arno Press and *The New York Times,* 1969.
Hughes, Langston. *Fight for Freedom.* New York: Berkley Publishing Corp., 1962.
Isaacs, Edith J. R. *The Negro in the American Theatre.* New York: Theatre Arts, Inc., 1947.
Isaacs, Harold. *The New World of Negro Americans.* New York: The Viking Press, Inc., 1964.
Johnson, James Weldon. *Black Manhattan.* New York: Atheneum Press, 1930–1969.
Kalijarvi, Thorsten V. *Central America: Land of Lords and Lizards.* Princeton, New Jersey: D. Van Nostrand Company, 1962.
La Farge, John. *The Race Question and the Negro.* New York: Longmans, Green and Co., 1944.
Logan, Rayford. *The Betrayal of the Negro.* New York: Collier Books, 1954.
The Autobiography of Malcom X (Assisted by Alex Haley). New York: Grove Press, 1964.
Martz, John D. *Central America, the Crisis and Challenge.* Chapel Hill, North Carolina: University of North Carolina Press, 1959.
McKay, Claude. *Harlem, Negro Metropolis.* New York: E. P. Dutton & Co., Inc., 1940.
Melady, Thomas P. *Profiles of African Leaders.* New York: The Macmillan Company, 1961.
Moore, Richard B. "Africa Conscious Harlem" (from *Harlem, U.S.A.*). Berlin: Seven Seas Press, 1964.
Morrison, Allan. "One Hundred Years of Negro Entertainment" (from *Anthology of the American Negro in the Theatre*). New York: Publishers Co., Inc., 1967.
Myrdal, Gunnar. *An American Dilemma,* 2 Vols. New York: Harper & Brothers, 1944.
Nkrumah, Kwame. *Ghana.* Camden, New Jersey: Thomas Nelson & Sons, 1957.
Nordholt, W. J. S. *The People That Walk in Darkness.* New York: Ballantine Books, 1960.
Osofsky, Gilbert. Harlem: *The Making of a Ghetto.* New York: Harper & Row, 1963.
Ottley, Roi. *New World A-Coming.* Boston: Houghton Mifflin Company, 1943.

Padmore, George. *Pan Africanism or Communism?* London: Dennis Dobson, 1956.

Patterson, William. *The Man Who Cried Genocide.* New York: International Publishers, 1971.

Peck, Anne M. *The Pageant of Middle American History.* New York: Longmans, Green and Co., 1947.

Redding, E. Saunders. *The Lonesome Road.* New York: Doubleday & Co., 1958.

——*On Being Negro in America.* New York: The Bobbs-Merrill Co., 1951.

Robeson, Paul. *Here I Stand.* New York: Othello Associates, 1958.

Rogers, J. A. *Great Men of Color,* 2 Vols. New York: J. A. Rogers, 1947.

Schoener, Allen. *Harlem on My Mind 1900–1968.* New York: Random House, 1968.

Scott, Emmett J. *Negro Migration During the War.* New York: Arno Press and *The New York Times,* 1969.

Segal, Ronald. *The Race War.* New York: The Viking Press, Inc., 1966.

Sherlock, Phillip M. *West Indies.* London: Andre Deutsch, 1964.

Sherman, Richard B. *The Negro and the City.* Englewood Cliffs, New Jersey: Prentice-Hall, Inc., 1970.

Silberman, Charles E. *Crisis in Black and White.* New York: Vintage Books, 1964.

Tannenbaum, Frank. *Slave and Citizen.* New York: Alfred A. Knopf, Inc., 1947.

Van Deusen, John G. *The Black Man in White America.* London: Thames and Hudson, Ltd., 1966.

Walker, Margaret. *For My People.* New York: Arno Press and *The New York Times,* 1969.

Webb, Constance. *Richard Wright.* New York: G. P. Putnam's Sons, 1968.

Williams, Eric. *Capitalism and Slavery.* London: Andre Deutsch, 1964.

Wilson, James Q. *Negro Politics (The Search for Leardership).* New York: The Free Press, 1960.

Woodson, Carter G. *The Negro in American History.* Washington, D.C.: Associated Publishers, Inc., 1945.

Wright, Richard. *Black Power.* New York: Harper & Brothers, 1954.

UNPUBLISHED MANUSCRIPTS

Chalk, Frank. *Du Bois and Garvey Confront Liberia (Two Incidents of the Coolidge Years).* Montreal, Canada: 1967, courtesy Schomburg Collection, New York City.

McKay, Claude. *My Green Hills of Jamaica.* New York: 1948, courtesy Schomburg Collection, New York City.

MAGAZINES AND PAMPHLETS

Agyeman, Nana Yaw. *West Africa on the March.* New York: William Fredericks Press, 1952.

Budu, Acquah, K. *Ghana, the Morning After.* London: Godwin Press, Ltd., circa 1961.

Du Bois, W. E. B. "Marcus Garvey." New York: *The Crisis,* December 1920, courtesy Schomburg Collection, New York City.

——"Marcus Garvey." New York: *The Crisis,* January 1921, courtesy Schomburg Collection, New York City.

Frazier, E. Franklin. "The Garvey Movement." New York: *Opportunity,* November 1926, courtesy Schomburg Collection, New York City.

Garvey, Marcus. "A Racial Weakness." London: *The Black Man,* August 1937.

——"Letter to William Pickens." New York: *The Messenger,* August 1922, courtesy Schomburg Collection, New York City.

Hall, Douglass. "The Colonial Legacy in Jamaica." Kingston: *New World Quarterly,* Vol. 4, No. 3, 1968.

Hall, Gwendolyn. "Negro Slaves in the Americas." New York: *Freedomways,* Summer 1964.

Hayford, Joseph Casley. "Gold Coast Land Tenure and the Forest Bill." London: *African Times and Orient Review,* August 1912, courtesy Schomburg Collection, New York City.

Lowenthal, David. "Race and Color in the West Indies." Boston: *Daedalus* (Journal of the American Academy of Arts and Sciences), 1967.

Malcolm X Talks to Young People. New York: Young Socialist Alliance, December 1969.

Miller, Kelly. "After Marcus Garvey—What of the Negro?" New York: *The Contemporary Review,* April 1927, courtesy Schomburg Collection, New York City.

Mohamed, Duse. Editorials in *African Times and Orient Review.* London: July and August 1912, courtesy Schomburg Collection, New York City.

Moore, Richard B. "Caribbean Unity and Freedom." New York: *Freedomways,* Summer 1964, courtesy Schomburg Collection, New York City.

O'Neal, James. "The Next Emancipation." New York: *The Messenger,* September 1922, courtesy Schomburg Collection, New York City.

Owen, Chandler. "Should Marcus Garvey Be Deported?" New York: *The Messenger,* September 1922, courtesy Schomburg Collection, New York City.

Pickens, William J. "Letter to Marcus Garvey." New York: *The Messenger,* August 1922, courtesy Schomburg Collection, New York City.

Randolph, A. Philip. "Garveyism." New York: *The Messenger,* September 1921, courtesy Schomburg Collection, New York City.

——"Reply to Marcus Garvey." *The Messenger,* August 1922, courtesy Schomburg Collection, New York City.

——"The Only Way to Redeem Africa." New York: *The Messenger,* November 1922, courtesy Schomburg Collection, New York City.

Talley, Truman. "Marcus Garvey–The Negro Moses?" New York: *World's Work,* December 1920 and January 1921, courtesy Schomburg Collection, New York City.

Washington, Booker T. "Tuskegee Institute." London: *African Times and Orient Review,* August 1912.

Westerman, George W. *The West Indian Worker on the Canal Zone.* Panama: National Civic League of Panama, 1951.

——*Fifty Years (1903–1953) of Treaty Negotiations Between the United States and the Republic of Panama.* Panama: 1953.

——*Some Spots in U.S.-Panama Relations.* Panama: 1952.

NEWSPAPERS

The New York Times; The *New York Post;* The *New York Amsterdam News;* The *Negro World;* The *New York Age;* The *Voice of Freedom* (New York); The *Black Man* (London); The *Baltimore Afro-American;* The *Norfolk Journal and Guide;* The *Chicago Defender;* The *Kingston Gleaner;* The *Boston Chronicle.* (All newspaper references with the exception of those from *The New York Times* are from the Schomburg Collection of The New York Public Library. Those of *The New York Times* are from the library of that newspaper.

INDEX

Abbott, Robert S., 75-77, 104, 160, 172, 202, 219
Abrahams, Peter, 16, 20
Abyssinia, 266-267
Addams, Jane, 55
African Communities League, Inc., 257, 258
African Nationalist Pioneer Movement in Harlem, 279
African Orthodox Church, 153
African Times and Orient Review, 44, 46, 48, 50, 256-257
Afro-American Council, 52
Afro-American Realty Company, 64
Afros (hair style), xv, 279
Ahuma, Attoh, 39, 40, 42-44
Albany, Georgia, 69
All God's Chillun Got Wings (O'-Neill), 222-224
Allen, Frank, 257
American Colonization Society, 122
Amos, James E., 188
Amsterdam News, 168, 169, 182, 190, 232, 234, 238, 240, 243, 245
Anarchy, 165
Anderson, Charles W., 78-79
Anthology of the American Negro in the Theatre (Patterson), 69
Antonio Maceo (boat), 118, 157
Arawaks, 4, 5
Ashwood, Amy (Garveys' first wife), 106, 108-111, 160, 181, 183, 258, 278-279
Association for the Study of Negro Life and History, 210

Bagnall, Robert W., 172
Bahamas, 250
Baker, George, *see* Divine, Father
Baker, Newton D., 86
Baltimore, Maryland, 265
Baltimore Afro-American, 90
Banana trade, 17-18, 255
Barbados, 272
Barclay, Arthur, 212
Barclay, Edwin, 122, 209
Barnes, Jack, 281
Beal, J. J., 69
Beit, Alfred, 132
Benjamin, P. A., Company, 20, 23
Berlin Conference, 15-16
Bermuda, 250
Birth of a Nation, The, 68-69
Black Cross Navigation and Trading Company, 207, 224
"Black is Beautiful," xviii
Black Man, The, 250, 256, 266, 268, 271
Black Manhattan (Johnson), 66, 79, 84
Black Moses (Cronon), 44, 83, 100, 103, 104, 105, 112, 113, 137, 146, 199
Black Power (Wright), 283
Black Rebellion (Higginson), 8
Black Star Steamship Company of New Jersey, 129, 139
Black Star Steamship Line, 100-104, 109, 111-115, 116-121, 127, 128-129, 131, 135, 136-140, 142, 146, 157-159, 176, 180, 181, 183-190, 195-197, 207, 208, 227, 228, 258
Black Vanguard, The (Brisbane), 51, 57, 68, 92, 97
Black Worker, 263

Blair, Mary, 223
Bocas del Toro, Panama, 30, 138
Booker T. Washington (ship), 119, 208, 224
Brazil, 218-221
Briggs, Cyril, 157-158, 159, 164
Brisbane, Robert H., 51, 56, 57, 68, 80, 92, 97
Brooklyn Eagle, 125
Brotherhood of Sleeping Car Porters, 77, 262-264
Broun, Heywood, 223
Brown, H. Rap, 288
Brown, James A., 234
Bruce, John E., 91, 92
Buffalo Evening Times, 230
Bundy, LeRoy, 164
Burrowes, Godfather, 15, 19
Bustamante, Alexander, 273-274
Byrnes, James F., 77

Calder, John V., 22
Canada, Garvey and, 249-250, 269, 270-271, 275
Capitalism, Garvey quoted on, 148-149
Capitalism and Slavery (Williams), 10
Carmichael, Stokely, 283
Carter, G. Emonei, 224
Castle, William, 213
Castro, Cipriano, 33-34
Caswell Motor Company, 241
Central America, Garvey and, 26, 28, 137-138, 246
Century Magazine, 133, 162
Certain, Jeremiah, 120
Chalk, Frank, 210-211
Chaney, James, 288
Charleston, South Carolina, 95
Chicago, Illinois, 73, 75, 96, 104, 264
Chicago Defender, 4, 69, 71, 75, 76-77, 90, 96, 104, 142, 155, 157, 159, 163, 169, 190, 219, 220, 221, 240, 241-242, 245
Christian Century, 127
Clansman, The (Dixon), 68
Clark, Edward Young, 227
Clark, Julia E. R., 257
Cleaver, Eldridge, 287
Cleveland, Ohio, 264
Cockbourne, Joshua, 103, 112, 113, 114, 183
Cockpits, the, 5, 6
Cohen, Walter L., 221-222
Coleman, Julia P., 172
Colombia, 33, 34
Columbus, Christopher, 4, 28
Columbus, Diego, 5
Commentary Review, The, 237, 238
Committee of Eight, 170-172, 179, 202
Communism, 148-150, 213
Convention People's Party, 151-152
Coolidge, Calvin, 210, 211, 221, 228, 236, 241, 242, 243, 244
Coromantyns, 8, 9
Costa Rica, 28-29, 137
Crisis, The, 56, 60, 74, 76, 133, 136, 144, 210, 212, 245
Cromwell, Oliver, 5
Cronon, Edmund D., 44-45, 83, 100, 103, 104, 105, 112, 128, 137, 146, 157, 199
Crusader, The, 157-158, 159
Cuba, 137, 138
Cuffee, Paul, 122
Current History Magazine, 13
Curtis, Mrs. Helen, 212

Dancy, Benny, 196-198
Davis, C. P., 95-96
Davis, Henrietta Vinton, 125, 163, 175, 178, 257, 258
De Bourg, Sidney, 175, 189
Debs, Eugene V., 69, 239
"Declaration of the Rights of the Negro Peoples of the World," 124
De Leon, Alfonso, 257
Denby, Navy Secretary, 156
Denison, Texas, 154-155
Depression (1930's), 259-261, 264
De Priest, Oscar, 261
Detroit, Michigan, 264
"Detroit Civil Rights Committee," 264

Detroit Edison Company, 264
De Valera, Eamon, 3, 141
Dewey, John, 55
Die Nigger Die (Brown), 288
Distinguished Service Order of Ethiopia, 124
Divine, Father, 269-270
Dixon, Alexander, 21-22
Dixon, Thomas, 68
Dougherty, Harry M., 170
Douglass, Frederick, 64, 239
Du Bois, W. E. B., 51, 52-56, 60, 74-75, 77, 87, 114, 133-136, 143-146, 150-152, 162, 165, 166, 210-213, 215, 227, 249, 283, 284-286
Dunbar, Paul Lawrence, 64
Dyer, Frederick, 169
Dyer, Bill, 156-157

Eason, James W. H., 163, 164, 189
  assassination of, 168-169
East Saint Louis, Illinois, 83-84
Ellegor, F. Wilcom, 163
Emperor Jones, The (O'Neill), 222, 270
Esquivel, Don Juan de, 5
Ethiopia, 267-268
Europe, James Reese, 141
Evers, Medgar, 288
Eyre, Edward John, 16, 20

Fanon, Franz, 285
Federal Bureau of Investigation, 142, 148
Federal Council of Churches of Christ in America, 263
Ferris, William H., 91
Fife, Duke of, 132
Firestone, Harvey, 211
Firestone Tire and Rubber Company, 213, 236
Forbes, George, 51, 52
Fortune, T. Thomas, 52, 91
Francis, Lionel A., 257, 258, 259, 274-275
Franklin, John Hope, 74
Fraser, C. Gerald, 278
Frazier, E. Franklin, 234-238
Freedomways magazine, 285
Friends of Negro Freedom, 166
From Slavery to Freedom (Franklin), 74
Furnas, J. C., xvii
"Future Outlook League," 264

Garcia, Elie, 120, 121, 123, 158, 163, 179, 190, 208-210, 212, 213-215
Gardner, W. J., 6, 7, 8, 9
Garnett, Charles, 249
Garrison, William Lloyd, 239
Garvey, Amy Ashwood (first wife), *see* Ashwood, Amy
Garvey, Amy Jacques (second wife), 21, 35, 58, 82, 99, 100, 105, 106, 108-110, 117, 143-144, 158, 163-164, 169-170, 185, 187-188, 193, 225-226, 246, 247, 249, 250, 260, 267
  marriage, 160-161
Garvey, Indiana (sister), 12
Garvey, Julius Winston (son), 265
Garvey, Marcus (son), 256
Garvey, Marcus, Jr.
  arrest of, 157-158, 250, 253
  assassination attempt, 105-107, 278
  birth, 12
  Canada and, 249-250, 269, 270-271, 275
  Central America and, 26, 28, 137-138, 246
  childhood, 13-14
  Costa Rica and, 28-30
  critical of flaws in UNIA, 173-178
  critics of, 97-98, 104, 121, 125-126, 130-136, 143-150, 157-178, 229, 230
  death, 276
  deportation, 244-245
  divorce, 160
  films and plays condemned by, 270
  founding of the Universal Negro Improvement Association, 58-59

government printing office job, 24
ideas of, compared with those of Booker T. Washington, 57-58
illness, 275-276
imprisonment, 205, 225-230, 234
influence of Robert Love on, 20-22, 24, 25
London and, 38, 39, 50, 246-248, 249, 265, 266-269, 275-276
marriage to Amy Ashwood, 110, 134
marriage to Amy Jacques, 160-161
oratory, 27, 77, 78, 79, 108, 119
Panama and, 30-33
pardon granted to, 242, 243
Paris and, 246, 248
physical description of, 62-63, 133
printer, 18-20, 23-24
printer's apprentice, 15, 17
religion and, 152-153, 216-217, 270
resignation as UNIA President-General, 163
steamship company, *see* Black Star Steamship Line
trial of, 179-203
U.S. and, 1-4, 62

Garvey, Marcus, Sr. (father), 10-12, 13, 14, 15, 18, 19, 63
Garvey, Sarah (mother), 11-12, 13, 14, 18-19, 106
Garvey and Garveyism (A. J. Garvey), 35, 58, 106, 108, 109, 143, 158, 164, 225, 247, 250, 260
Garvey Club, 278
Garvey's Watchman, 24
Gary, Indiana, 73, 285
Ghandi, M., 141, 239
Gibbons, Benjamin, 277-278
Gilpin, Charles, 222
Gold Coast, 42, 151-152
Gold Coast Leader, The, 42
Gold Coast Nation and National Consciousness, The (Ahuma), 42
Gold Coast Native Institutions (Hayford), 40
Goodbye to Uncle Tom (Furnas), xvii
Goodman, Andrew, 288
Gordon, George William, 16, 20
Grant, Sir John Peter, 16
Gray, Edgar M., 180-181
Great Men of Color (Rogers), 198
Green Pastures, The, 270
Green River Distilling Company, 183
Griffith, David Wark, 68
Grigsby, Snow, 264
Guardian, The, 51-52
Guatemala, 137
Guinn, Frank, 69

Haile Selassie, 267-269
Hairy Ape, The (O'Neill), 223
Hampton, Fred, 288
Harding, Warren G., 155, 239
Harlem, 1-2, 62-68, 70, 77-80, 101, 105, 110, 143, 241, 257, 265, 277, 278-279
Harlem: The Making of a Ghetto (Osofsky), 64
Harlem Property Owners' Improvement Corporation, 65
"Harlem School of Social Science," 78
Harper, Frank, 48
Harris, Charles, 137, 138
Harris, George W., 172
Harris, William, 241
Harrison, Hubert H., 78-79, 91
Harriss, W. L., 103-104, 184
Hatcher, Richard Gordon, 285-286
Hawkins, W. Ashby, 164
Hayford, Archie Casley, 152
Hayford, Joseph Casley, 39-41, 42, 46, 152
Hayward, William, 88
Haywood, District Attorney, 189
Healy, Leo H., 184-185
Heflin, Tom, 221
Hendriques, Fernando, 25, 35-36
Here I Stand (Robeson), 282
Higginson, Thomas W., 8
Hiorth, Jacob R., 208, 224, 227
History of Jamaica, The (Gardner), 6, 7

Holder, Wesley McDonald, 233
Hollis, Mack, 76
Home News (Harlem), 65
Honduras, 34
Hong Kheng, S.S., 139-140
Hoover, Herbert, 250, 261
Houston, Texas, 85, 156
Howard, Daniel Edward, 212
Howells, William Dean, 55
Hughes, Charles Evans, 137, 211

Imitation of Life, 270
Indentured servants, xvii
Independent (magazine), 55
Ireland, 3
Ivory Coast, 213

Jackson, Andrew, 222
Jackson, George, 288
Jacques, Amy, *see* Garvey, Amy Jacques
Jamaica, xvi-xvii, 4-26, 34-37, 137, 138, 245-246, 250-254, 255-256, 265, 272-274
  banana trade, 17-18
  independence, 278
  rebellious slaves in, 5-10
Jamaica, an Island Mosaic (Abrahams), 16, 20
Jamaica, Land of Wood and Water (Hendriques), 25, 35
Jamaica Advocate, The, 21
Jamaica Progressive League, 273
Jamaica Welfare, 272, 273
Jamaica Workers' and Tradesmen's Union, 273
James, Major, 6
Jesus of Nazareth, 98, 99
Jews, 198-199, 268, 269
Johnson, C. D., 274
Johnson, Gabriel, 123, 209
Johnson, Henry, 89
Johnson, Henry Lincoln, 156
Johnson, James Weldon, 66, 79, 84, 94
Jones, Samuel, 96
Justice Department, U.S., 93, 241-242, 244, 245, 262

Kanawah (boat), 117-119, 137, 138, 157, 159, 185
Kersnor, George A., 268
Kilroe, Edwin P., 100, 102, 146-147, 180, 181, 184
King, Charles D. B., 121, 123, 209, 210, 212
King, Martin Luther, Jr., 288
Kingston, Jamaica, 18-19, 23, 245, 246, 250-254, 255-256, 265, 273-274
Kingston Daily Gleaner, 259, 270, 274
Knights of the Nile, 124
Knoxville, Tennessee, 96
Kohn, Armin, 182, 204
Ku Klux Klan, 68, 70, 143, 154-155, 161, 162, 163, 166, 172-173, 198, 216, 221, 227-228

La Follette, Robert, 221
Langston, John M., 64
Lansing, Michigan, 279
Latham, Charles L., 138
League of Nations, 151, 188, 248
Lee, Prince, 154-155
Lenin, Nikolai, 149
Leopold II (Belgium), 15
Lesseps, Ferdinand Marie de, 30
Lewis, William Henry, 210
Liberia, xix, 121-123, 208-216, 236
Liberia (ship), 71-72
Liberian News, 213
Liberty Hall (Harlem), 101, 118, 124, 130, 141, 150, 163, 206, 277
Lincoln League, 221
Linous, Charles, 189
Little, Earl, 729-280
Liuzzo, Viola, 288
London, England, Garvey and, 38, 39, 50, 246-248, 249, 265, 266-269, 275-276
Lonesome Road (Redding), 11, 75, 84
Longview, Texas, 95-96
Love, Robert, 20-22, 24, 25
Lowell Courier-Citizen, 126
Lusk Committee (New York), 93

Luther, Martin, 98, 99
Lynchings, 96, 97, 144, 156, 240
Lyon, Ernest, 213

MacGregor, Sir William, 41
Mack, Julian W., 179-180, 182, 183, 187, 189, 190, 191, 194-195, 198, 199, 204-205
Magill, Charles T., 155-156
Malcolm X, xviii, 279-283, 287-288
Maloney, A. Hamilton, 257
Manley, Norman W., 273-274
Manoedi, Mokete, 143
Marke, George O., 188, 233, 251, 253
Maroons, 5-8, 10, 277
Massachusetts Bonding Company, 158
Mattuck, Maxwell S., 179, 180, 185, 188, 189, 196-199, 204, 227, 228
McCormick, Senator, 221
McDougald, Cornelius W., 179, 181-182
McGuire, George A., 125, 153, 175, 178, 216, 257
McKay, Claude, 90
Menocal, President (Cuba), 137
Messenger, The, 131-133, 148, 161-162, 164-167, 237, 239, 261, 263
Methodist Federation for Social Science, 263
Michigan Bell Telephone Company, 264
Minstrel shows, 200-201
Miller, G., 125
Miller, Kelly, 86, 229, 237-240, 242
Minus, Alfred, 257
Mitchell, Arthur, 261
Mitchell, Dave, 154-155
Mohamed Ali, Duse, 39, 44-46, 48, 50, 82, 89, 256, 268
Morant Bay, Jamaica, 16
Moravians, 10
Morgan, Henry, 5
Morris, Charles S., 130-131
Morter, Isaiah, 231, 253, 258, 274
Moss, Carlton, 69
Mulzac, Hugh, 189
Mussolini, Benito, 266, 267

Nacionale, La, 30
Nail, John E., 172
Nantes, Lauro de, 218-220
National Association for the Advancement of Colored People, 55-56, 60, 81, 84, 94, 97, 145, 150, 179, 180, 212, 227, 235, 236, 238, 263
National City Bank of New York, 132
National Club, The, 24
National Urban League, *see* Urban League
Nationalism, black, xv, 281-282
Nautical Gazette, 128-129
Negro Business League, 52
Negro Factories Corporation, 107, 127, 131
Negro in our History, The (Woodson), 122
Negro Times, 228
Negro World, The, 4, 89-93, 99, 100, 104, 107, 109, 114, 139, 146, 147, 159, 180, 198, 228, 243, 245, 289
New Deal, 261
New Orleans, Louisiana, 168-170
New York Age, 4, 57, 130, 257, 258, 259, 265
New York Evening Bulletin, 229
New York Globe, 125
New York Post, 275
New York Sun, 78
New York Times, 4, 126, 169, 170, 182, 190, 278
New York World, 157, 223, 229, 245
Niagara Movement, 55
Nicaragua, 34
Nichols, Hannah C., 257
Nkrumah, Kwame, 151-152, 283-284
Norfolk Journal and Guide, 125
Norris, J. Austin, 164
North American Steamship Corporation, 103

Omaha, Nebraska, 96
O'Neill, Eugene, 222-224
Operation Crossroads Africa, 127
Opportunity magazine, 234
Orion (ship), 139-140, 142, 157, 158
Orr, Edward, 159
Osofsky, Gilbert, 64
Our Own, 24
Ovington, Mary White, 55
Owen, Chandler, 131, 132, 164

Pace, Harry, 172
Padmore, George, 145, 149, 152
Pan Union Company, 113
Pan-African Congress, 143-145, 150-151, 211
Pan-Africanism, 144-146, 150, 152, 249, 284
Pan-Africanism or Communism (Padmore), 149, 152
Panama, 30-33, 137, 138, 240, 245
Panama Canal, 30-33
Panama Railroad Company, 208
Pankin, Jacob, 160
Paris, France, Garvey and, 246, 248
Patterson, Lindsay, 69
Payton, Philip A., Jr., 63-64
Penn, William, 5
"Peoples Political Party" (Jamaica), 253
Peters, J. J., 234
Petioni, Charles A., 257
Phillips, Wendell, 239
Phillips County, Arkansas, 96-97
Philosophy and Opinions of Marcus Garvey, The, xviii, 35, 58, 85, 98, 147, 148, 153, 173, 193, 268, 280, 286
Phyllis Wheatley (ship), 119, 141, 157
Pickens, William, 91, 125, 162, 172, 243-244
Pine Bluff, Arkansas, 76
Planet, 207
Port Maria, Jamaica, 8
Portland, Oregon, 154
Poston, Ted, 275
Potts, Sheriff (Albany, Ga.), 69
Pounds, Winston, 240
Powell, A. Clayton, Jr., 265
Powell, A. Clayton, Sr., 129-130
Prensa, La, 33
Press, black, xix, xx, 52, 55, 65, 71, 74, 75, 76, 77-78, 86, 89-93, 157, 245, 262, 267
Preston, R. L., 163
Provincetown Players, 222-223
Public Opinion, 273
Pullman Company, 70, 77, 262-264

Racism, xvi-xvii, 3, 13, 68, 87, 93, 94, 172, 192, 199, 200, 202, 217, 218, 242
  arts and, 222-224
Railway Labor Act, 264
Randolph, A. Philip, 77, 131, 132, 161, 162, 166, 261-264, 283
Reading, Lord, 188
"Red Summer of 1919," 93, 94-97, 143
Redding, Saunders, 11, 75, 84
Rees, Mrs. James H., 70
Religion, Garvey and, 152-153, 216-217, 270
Republican Party, 155-156
Reynolds, Mrs. Elise, 154
Richardson, Adrian, 118, 137, 138, 185
Riots, race, 94, 95-97
Robeson, Paul, 222, 282-283
Robinson, James H., 127
Robinson, Joe, 221
Rogers, Henry H., 117
Rogers, Joel A., 198, 199, 236
Roosevelt, Eleanor, 261
Roosevelt, Franklin D., 260-261
Roosevelt, Theodore, 48, 50, 60, 78
Ryan's Weekly, 162

Sacco, Nicola, 239
Salomon, President (Haiti), 20
Sam, Alfred C., 70-72, 104
Saramacca, S.S., 244, 245
Sarbah, John Mensah, 39, 40, 41
Sargent, John G., 241
Sayville, Long Island, 269

School of African Philosophy, 270, 271
Schuyler, George S., 131
Schwerner, Michael, 288
Scott, Emmett J., 86-88, 89, 125
Selective Service Act, 73
Selective Service System, 87
Shadyside, S.S., 116-118, 119, 159
Shakespeare, William, 169
Sheppard, Barry, 281
Shipstead, Henrik, 221, 222
Sierra Leone, 213
"Silent Protest Parade," 84-85
Silverstone, Anthony R., 139-140, 142, 158
Simmons, Roscoe Conklin, 221
Sissle, Noble, 88, 89
Slave trade, opposition of Catholic Church to, 9
Smith, Alfred E., 250
Smith, Lewis J., 269-270
Smith, Rudolph, 163
Solomon, 268
Soul on Ice (Cleaver), 287
Souls of Black Folk, The (Du Bois), 53, 54
Spanish Slave Code (1789), 9
Spartanburg, South Carolina, 88
Spingarn, Joel A., 55, 81
Stock market crash (1929), 254
Story, Morefield, 55
Susquehanna (ship), 208
Sutton estate, 8
Swift, Leon R., 116, 117, 118

Taft, William Howard, 60, 210
Taki, 8
Talley, Truman Hughes, 133
Taylor, John G., 65
Tennyson, S.S., 136-137
Texas Rangers, 96
Thompson, Noah, 141-142, 164
Thompson, Orland M., 120, 129, 136, 138-140, 142, 158, 179, 188, 190
Tobias, George, 119, 120, 158, 179, 190
Todakyn, H. H., 164
Toote, Frederick Augustus, 188
Trans-Isthmian Railroad, 30
Trinidad, 272
Trotter, William Monroe, 51, 52, 53, 54, 56
Tuskegee Institute, 48-49, 61
  Negro Conference at, 46-48
Tyler, George, 105-106

United Fruit Company, 18, 28, 34
United States Shipping Board, 140, 142, 157, 158, 208
Universal African Legion, 2
Universal Black Cross Nurses, 2
Universal Negro Alliance, 168
Universial Negro Improvement Association (UNIA), xviii, xix, 1, 35, 38, 82, 89, 92, 98, 99, 100, 101, 104, 105-110, 114, 115, 121-125, 128, 132-133, 139, 140, 142-143, 145-150, 153, 159, 167, 168-171, 173-178, 180, 186, 187, 205, 208-210, 212, 213, 215, 231, 243, 246, 274
  Chicago division, 104
  finances, 107-110, 232, 252, 257
  formation of, 58, 278
  International Conventions
    First, 1-4, 48, 123-126, 127, 130, 209
    Second, 140, 141-150, 152
    Third, 161-164
    Fourth, 213, 216
    Fifth, 232
    Sixth, 250-253
    Seventh, 265
  New York Chapter, 80, 82-83, 234
  salaries of officers, 173-178
University College of the West Indies (Jamaica), 36
Up From Slavery (Washington), 48, 50
Urban League, 65, 235, 263

Vanzetti, Bartolomeo, 239
Venables, Robert, 5
Venezuela, 33
Villard, Oswald Garrison, 60, 69
Voice of Freedom, The, 275

Volstead, Andrew T., 112
Volstead Act, 112-113

Walker, Margaret, 286
Walling, William E., 55
Walrond, Eric, 91
Walsh, Thomas J., 221
Walters, Oscar, 125
Ware, William, 257
Warner, Richard E., 181
Washington, Booker T., 48-49, 50-58, 60, 61, 64, 78, 86, 87
Washington, D. C., 96, 265
Watson, James, 146
Watson, Tom, 156
Wattley, Vincent, 257
Weeks, John W., 156
West African National Congress, 40, 152
West Indian Worker on the Canal Zone, The (Westerman), 31
West Indies Sugar Company, 272
Westerman, George, 31-32
Weston, George A., 110, 128, 226, 233, 234
Whip, The, 264
Whyte, Daisy, 275-276
Williams, Eric, 10
Williams, Vernal, 179
Willis, W. W., 155
Wilmont, Arkansas, 240
Wilson, Woodrow, 60, 69, 73, 155, 165
Wise, Jacob, 117
Wise, Stephen, 69
Wolheim, Louis, 223
Wood, Leonard, 81
Woodson, Carter G., 122, 166
World and Africa, The (Du Bois), 146
World War I, 72, 73, 77, 80-81, 85-86, 87-89, 94
World's Work, 133
Wright, Richard, 283-284

Yarmouth, S.S., 102-104, 111-115, 119, 128, 183-184, 187, 198
Young, Charles, 74
Young Socialist, 281

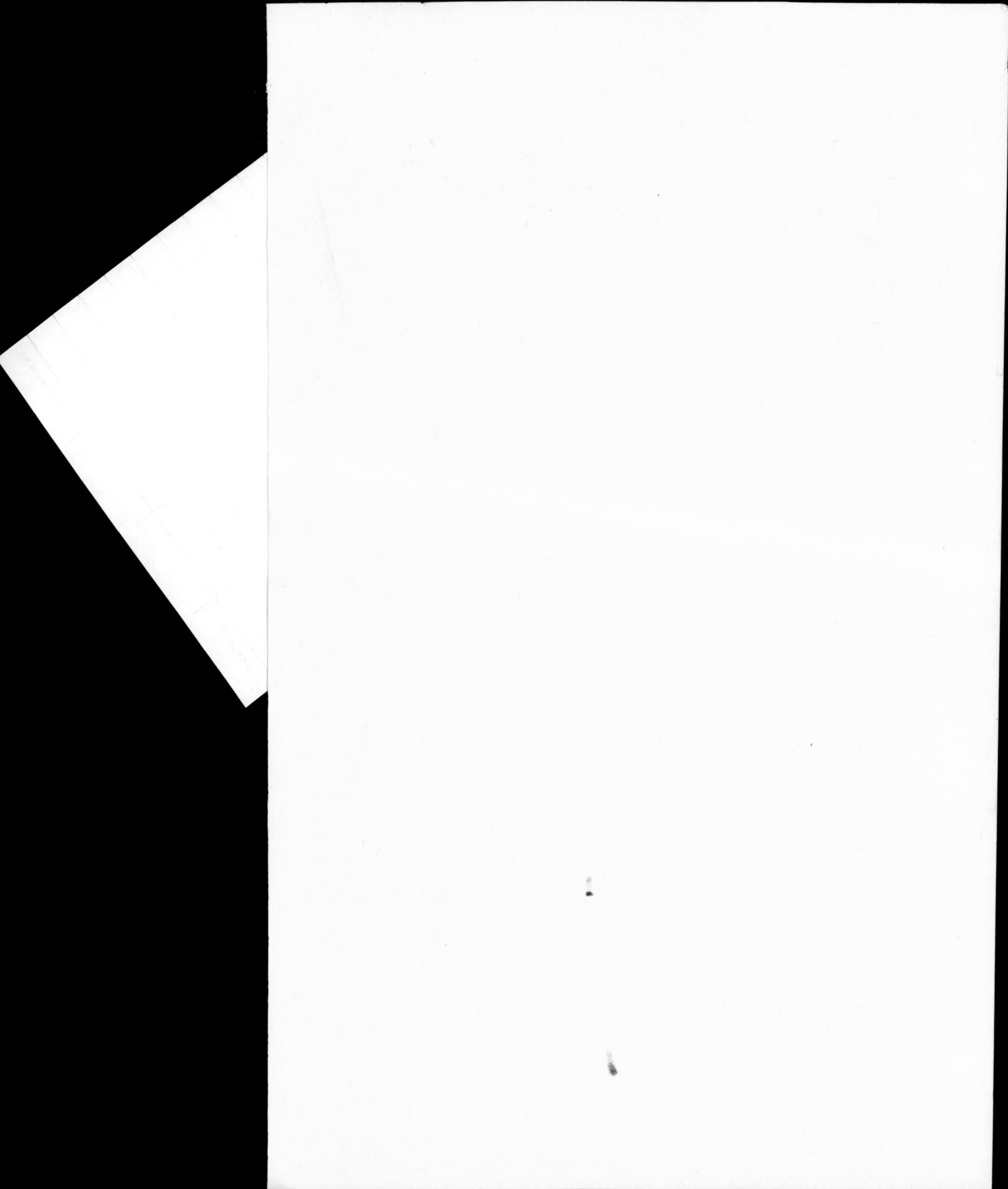